Towards a Theory of Morphopragmatics
of Korean Connectives

Towards a Theory of Morphopragmatics
of Korean Connectives

Chong-Hoon Chun

도서출판 박이정

This book was printed by Jesam and bound by Jesam.
Printed in South Korea.

Chong-Hoon Chun
Towards a Theory of Morphopragmatics
of Korean Connectives
ISBN 978-89-7878-960-8 (93710)

Chong-Hoon Chun
Born in Seoul, South Korea, in 1966. Ph.D. in
Linguistics, the University of New South Wales.

한국어 연결어미의 형태 - 화용론 이론을 향하여

발행일 2007년 12월 20일
지은이 전종훈
펴낸이 박찬익
펴낸곳 도서출판 **박이정**
주 소 130-070 대한민국 서울시 동대문구 용두동 129-162
등 록 1991년 3월 12일 제1-1182호

ISBN 978-89-7878-960-8 (93710)

For So-Young and Tae-Hyun

Contents

Foreword

This Ph.D. thesis was submitted in 2007 to the University of New South Wales. I sincerely acknowledge President Chan-Ik Park at Pagijong Press for all his assistance in the publication of this book

Thesis Abstract

The main aim of this thesis is to gain a deep understanding of the meanings of Korean conjunctive verbal suffixes from a pragmatic viewpoint, using real, not constructed data. In order to attain the purpose, this thesis conducts an in-depth analysis of the nature of the meanings, and the use, of six Korean conjunctive verbal suffixes: *-ko, -nuntey, -nikka, -se, -ciman,* and *-to*. The term **the use** refers to the truth-functionality of suffixes, i.e., whether they conjoin or disjoin the two propositions, which are recovered from two segments, truth-functionally. The data are obtained from 360 minutes of audio-taped Korean natural conversations. It adopts as its reasoning tool four major pragmatic theories - Gricean theory, neo-Gricean theory, Relevance Theory, and Default Semantics. However, it does not use the data to compare the four theories. This thesis emphasises how to elucidate the meanings of Korean conjunctive verbal suffixes that modern pragmatic theories cannot neatly explain.

In Chapter 1 previous approaches on the six suffixes are analysed. It is pointed out that while these studies correctly equate the meanings of a given suffix with propositional relations that obtain between the two segments (linked by the suffix), they fail to see the importance of **the use** of the suffix. Chapter 2 provides an overview of the four pragmatic theories. The focus is on strengths and weaknesses of the four theories. In Chapter 3, we introduce propositional relations and the notions of encoding and inferred. What is meant by conjoining and disjoining truth-functionally is also explained. Chapter 4 specifies the data. In Chapter 5, propositional relations between two propositions which are recovered from two conjoined segments are characterised. Chapter 6 applies the scope test to meanings of the six suffixes and distinguishes encoded and inferred meanings. It discusses encoded meanings of the six suffixes, which conjoin the two propositions truth-functionally, and discusses inferred meanings of only four of the six suffixes, which disjoin the two propositions truth-functionally. In Chapter 7, we discuss the nature of the meanings of the six suffixes from two theoretical angles, Relevance Theory and Default Semantics, and in particular we argue against a unitary procedure hypothesis. Chapter 8 concludes the thesis and also includes suggestions for future studies.

Thesis Acknowledgements

I could not complete this thesis without the support and encouragement of many people.

First, I am deeply grateful to Dr. Gi-Hyun Shin, my supervisor. Without his encouragement I wouldn't have started this thesis. He gave me insight and guidance. His detailed and critical comments facilitated vast improvements to this thesis. Without his support, my work would not exist.

I am also grateful to Dr. Mengistu Amberber for good comments and encouragement.

My thanks go, also, to Dr. Duck-Young Lee at the Australian National University who first introduced me to pragmatics and whose help and encouragement were crucial in my making the move to Australia.

I also acknowledge many people for providing their conversations for my data collection.

I also would like to thank my friends Eileen Savage, Mitt Haney, Jennifer Hughes, Margaret Krizan, Kiu Kian Wun, Kato Akiko, Yoshinobu Torao, Yuka Kanehira, Masahiro Toma, Angela Kim, Naomi Ogi, and Djasaman Saragih, with whom I could always share my good days and bad days in Australia.

I would like to thank John Shelton for proofreading this thesis.

As always, I thank my son, Tae-Hyun and my wife, So-Young, whom I do not know how to thank enough. My wife, especially, sacrificed herself for my work. I should also like to express my sincere gratitude not only to my parents but also to my parents-in-law for their eternal love.

List of Tables

List of Symbols

***sentence**	Ungrammatical sentence
+>	Implicates
[ ]	Overlapping talks
→	Drawing attention to location of phenomenon of direct interest to discussion.
( )	Uncertainty on the transcriber's part except ( ) of *-y(e)se* and *-y(e)to*

List of Abbreviations

Grammatical glosses

AC	Accusative particle
AD	Adverbialiser suffix
AH	Addressee honorific suffix
DC	Declarative sentence-type suffix
FML	Familiar speech suffix
GN	Genitive suffix
HT	Honorific title
IM	Imperative sentence-type suffix
IN	Indicative mood suffix
INF	Infinitive suffix
MD	Pre-nominal modifier suffix
NM	Nominative particle
NOM	Nominaliser suffix
PL	Plural suffix
POL	Polite speech level suffix
PR	Propositive sentence-type suffix
PRS	Prospective suffix
PST	Past tense suffix
Q	Interrogative sentence-type suffix
QT	Quotative particle
RT	Retrospective mood suffix
SH	Subject honorific suffix
SUP	Suppositive mood suffix
TC	Topic-contrast particle
X.Y	(X and Y are fused)
X-Y	(X and Y are not fused)

Yale Romanisation System

(2) Vowels

(1) Consonants

ㄱ	k
ㄲ	kk
ㄴ	n
ㄷ	t
ㄸ	tt
ㄹ	l
ㅁ	m
ㅂ	p
ㅃ	pp
ㅅ	s
ㅆ	ss
ㅇ	ø (syllable-initial)
ㅇ	ng (syllable-final)
ㅈ	c
ㅉ	cc
ㅊ	ch
ㅋ	kh
ㅌ	th
ㅍ	ph
ㅎ	h

ㅏ	a
ㅐ	ay
ㅑ	ya
ㅒ	yay
ㅓ	e
ㅔ	ey
ㅕ	ye
ㅖ	yey
ㅗ	o
ㅘ	wa
ㅙ	way
ㅚ	oy
ㅛ	yo
ㅜ	wu
ㅝ	we
ㅞ	wey
ㅟ	wi
ㅠ	yu
ㅡ	u
ㅢ	uy
ㅣ	i

1
Introduction

1.1 The Study

This is a study of the pragmatics of Korean connectives.

In Korean, connectives are verbal suffixes, more specifically 'conjunctive verbal suffixes' (Sohn 1994: 355; Suh 2006: 1114, 1159-1161). Consider the following examples.

(1) a. Today is Friday, **and** tomorrow is Saturday.

      b. onul-un   kumyoil-i-**ko**

          *Today-TC Friday-be-**KO[and]***

          nayil-un   thoyoil-i-ta

          tomorrow-TC Saturday-be-DC

          'Today is Friday, and tomorrow is Saturday.'

Unlike the English connective **and**, which is a separate part of speech, the Korean conjunctive verb suffix **-ko** must be attached to the stem of the preceding verb.

Conjunctive verbal suffixes are one of the most important grammatical categories in Korean language. They link clauses (hereafter segments) in structural terms. There are 210 conjunctive verbal suffixes in Korean, but the number does not seem to be fixed (Chang 1999: 26). To spell out the meanings of each conjunctive suffix is not a straightforward task. Some suffixes appear to have more than nine different 'meanings'.

Reflecting their importance, there is a body of literature on Korean conjunctive verbal suffixes. Previous studies generally focused on their syntactic and semantic aspects, and studies on the pragmatics of the suffixes are relatively small in number (Kwon 1994: 353-357, 360-364). Because of their syntactic and semantic orientation, previous research has been generally based on 'articulated' data, rather than those collected from naturally occurring utterances.

The purpose of this book is to use real, not constructed, data on Korean conjunctive verbal suffixes and to gain a deep understanding of their meanings from a pragmatic standpoint. This study will adopt as its reasoning tool four leading pragmatic theories: Gricean theory, neo-Gricean theory, Relevance Theory, and Default Semantics. Here, it should be noted that we will not make a contrastive study of these four theories. On the contrary, we will put emphasis on how to elucidate meanings of these suffixes that modern pragmatic theories cannot neatly explain.

In order to achieve the purpose, we will conduct an in-depth analysis of the nature of the meanings, and the use, of six Korean conjunctive verbal suffixes: *-ko, -nuntey, -nikka, -se, -ciman*, and *-to*. In particular, we look at the tokens of the six suffixes in the data obtained in naturally occurring conversation pieces among Korean native speakers. The rationale for choosing the six suffixes as the subjects of this study is that they are the most frequent suffixes, having not only truth-conditional meanings (that is, semantic in nature) but also non-truth-conditional meanings (that is, pragmatic in nature) among those in the data. This study adopts the following definition for pragmatics.

"Pragmatics = Meaning minus Truth Conditions." (Gazdar 1979: 12)

On the basis of this definition, we take those meanings of connectives that conjoin the two propositions truth-functionally as their semantic meanings, and accordingly those meanings that do not conjoin the two propositions truth-functionally and their pragmatic meanings. Furthermore, we call *truth-functionally conjoining* and *truth-functionally disjoining* **the use** of connectives (see Chapter 3 for more details). In this book, we employ the term 'disjoin' as an antonym of the term 'conjoin'.

To see what we mean by 'truth-functionally conjoining', consider the following example.

(2) Tom took off his clothes **and** had a bath.

Two propositions can be recovered from segments coupled by *and* in (2) as follows.

(3) a. Tom took off his clothes at t.
     b. Tom had a bath at t+n.

In (3), Tom's taking off in clause (a) precedes his having a bath in clause (b).

The propositional relation between (3)a-b is a forward sequential relation. That relation is inferred. That is to say, the connective *and* in (2) has one encoded meaning, i.e., a logical operator &. Here, the logical operator & of *and* in (2) yields a single conjoined proposition as follows:

(4)   [Tom took off his clothes at t] & [Tom had a bath at t+n].

So, the truth-value of (4) relies on the truth-value of (3)a and that of (3)b, and the truth-table for & (see Table 3.1 in Chapter 3).

To see what we mean by 'truth-functionally disjoining', consider another example.

(5)   Bill is a philosopher and he is, therefore, brave. (Grice 1989: 21)

Two propositions can be recovered from segments coupled by *therefore* in (5) as follows.

(6)   a. Bill is a philosopher.
      b. Bill is brave.

If it is assumed that philosophers are brave, in (6) 'Bill's being a philosopher' in clause (a) provides evidence for the belief in clause (b), i.e., that Bill is brave. In (6) clauses (a-b) are identified as a premise and an implicated conclusion respectively. This relation is encoded by *therefore* in (5). In other words, the encoded meaning of *therefore* in (5) does not conjoin two propositions (6)a-b truth-functionally, but rather signals that (6)b is an inferential conclusion of (6)a. So, this meaning does not contribute to the truth conditions of two propositions (6)a-b.

In this book, we seek to answer the following questions:

(1) With respect to the nature of the meanings communicated by the six Korean conjunctive verbal suffixes, are they decoded or inferred?
(2) In terms of **the use** of these suffixes, that is, their truth-functionality, do they conjoin or disjoin two propositions truth-conditionally?

In order to answer these two questions, this study will apply the scope test of the connective *but* (Rouchota 1990) in judging whether meanings of the six conjunctive suffixes are encoded or inferred. This test refers to deciding whether or not meanings of connectives fall within the scope of the truth-conditional connective *if ... then*. Furthermore, this study will selectively borrow concepts that are related to meanings of connectives from the four pragmatic theories, Gricean theory, neo-Gricean theory, Relevance Theory, and Default Semantics, and expound each meaning of the six suffixes with chosen concepts. This is based on the following two rationales. First, these four theories share the view that two propositions, which are recovered from segments linked by connectives, are *truth-functionally conjoined* or *disjoined* according to the meanings of connectives. Second, the four theories respectively show analytic strengths and weaknesses when applied to the data that this study collected. (See Chapter 3 for more details.)

In this book, less attention will be paid to the following two issues: the morphopragmatic status of sentence-final suffixes and acceptability of the conjunctive verbal suffixes *-ko* and *-se* with certain predicates. Let us touch upon the first issue. As we demonstrate in Chapter 4, there are instances where the segment after a given suffix is omitted. In this case there is an issue as to the morpho-syntactic nature of the suffix, i.e., whether the suffix is a conjunctive verbal suffix or a sentence-final suffix. In this book, we will not deal with those instances because this issue has a different scope.

Let us turn into the second issue. Consider (7).

(7) a. cip-ey   ka-*se* pap-ul   mek-ess-ta
     *house-to go-**SE** meal-AC eat-PST-DC*
     'After I went home, I ate a meal.'
  b. * cip-ey   ka-***ko*** pap-ul   mek-ess-ta
     *house-to go-**KO** meal-AC eat-PST-DC*

Note that the propositional relation that obtains between segments coupled by *-se* and *-ko* is a forward sequential relation. This is because going home precedes eating a meal. However, (7)a is grammatically correct, but (7)b is not. The question is why this is so. The answer is that the acceptability of a given suffix depends on the meaning of the predicate of the segments before the suffix (cf. K-D. Lee 1993: 454-455, 459-460). That is to say, this is related to semantics of the predicate of the segment before the suffix. In this sense, we will not take up this issue, either.

Before going further, we provide a literature review of studies on the conjunctive verbal suffixes *-ko*, *-nuntey*, *-nikka*, *-se*, *-ciman*, and *-to*. Discussions on the four pragmatic theories will be offered in Chapter 2.

1.2 Previous Research on the Six Suffixes

Previous studies on the six suffixes, such as those conducted by Yang (1972), K-D. Lee (1979, 1980, 1993), Tsai (1985), Jeong (1986), Choi (1989, 1991), Jeon (1989), Yoon (1989, 2005), Yi (1996, 2000), H-J. Lee. and C-H. Lee (1999, 2001), and Suh (2006) share the view that propositional relations, which obtain between the two segments linked by these suffixes, constitute the meanings of suffixes. They postulate that the suffixes involve the following propositional relations. First, *-ko* involves four relations: (1) enumeration, (2) simultaneity, (3) sequence, and (4) cause. Second, *-se* involves two relations: (1) sequence and (2) cause. Third, *-nikka* involves two relations: (1) reason and (2) explanation. Fourth, *-ciman* involves two relations: (1) opposition and (2) contrast. Fifth, *-to* involves three relations: (1) condition, (2) opposition, and (3) contrast. Sixth, *-nuntey* involves seven relations: (1) time, (2) reason, (3) opposition, (4) contrast, (5) introduction, (6) background, and (7) explanation.

Notice that many of the relations are shared by more than one suffix, as shown in the table below.

Table 1.1: Propositional Relations Based on Previous Studies

Propositional Relations	Suffixes
Time	*-nuntey*
Condition	*-to*
Enumeration	*-ko*
Simultaneity	*-ko*

Sequence, Succession, Temporal Precedence	*-ko, -se*
Cause, Reason	*-ko, -se, -nikka, -nuntey*
Opposition, Contrast, Counter-Act/Event	*-ciman, -to, -nuntey*
Introduction	*-nuntey*
Background	*-nuntey*
Explanation	*-nikka, -nuntey*

Let us consider these propositional relations one by one.

Time

The time relation (Korean *sikan*) obtains between X and Y in the [X-*nuntey* Y] sequence, in which X refers to a segment whose predicate is a non-finite form and Y stands for a segment whose predicate is non-finite or finite. Previous studies (e.g. Tsai 1985: 163) define the time relation as that where X represents the temporal situation in which an event depicted by Y occurs or did or will occur. Previous studies postulate that the time relation is encoded by *-nuntey*.

Consider the following example.

    (8) nay-ka Kim-kwun-eykey mwuesinka selmyeng-ul

          I-NM   -Mr.-to   something explanation-AC

          ha.y   cwu-ko iss-**nuntey**   Pak-kwun-i takaw-ass-ta

          *do.INF give-KO ISSTA-**NUNTEY**   -Mr.-NM approach-PST-DC*

          'When I was explaining something to Mr. Kim, Mr. Park came to me.' (Tsai

          1985: 163)

Two propositions, such as (9)a-b, can be recovered from (8).

    (9) a. The speaker was explaining something to Mr. Kim.

          b. Mr. Park came to the speaker.

In Tsai's account, Mr. Park's coming occurred at the time in which the speaker's explaining happened; clauses (a) and (b) have a time relation. She argues that -*nuntey* in (8) encodes a time meaning.

Condition

The condition relation (Korean *coken*) obtains between X and Y in the [X-*to* Y] sequence. Previous studies (e.g. Jeon 1989: 92) define the condition relation as that where X represents a condition or a supposition or a protasis and Y depicts a consequent or an apodosis. Previous studies postulate that the condition relation is encoded by -*to*.

Consider the following example.

    (10) cinachikey chincelha-**y(e)to** ohay-lul   pat-nun-ta

             too   *kind-**TO***   *misunderstanding-AC receive-IN-DC*

             'If you are too kind, you will be misunderstood.' (Jeon 1989: 95)

Two propositions, such as (11)a-b, can be recovered from (10).

    (11) a. The hearer excessively shows people kindness.

          b. The hearer will be misunderstood by people.

In Jeon's terms, the conclusion (11)b results from the supposition (11)a; (11)a-b establish a condition relation. She argues that -*to* in (10) encodes a condition meaning.

Enumeration

The enumeration relation (Korean *yelke*) obtains between X and Y in the [X-*ko* Y] sequence. Previous studies (e.g. Tsai 1985: 28; Jeong 1986: 27; Choi 1989: 39, 1991: 47; Jeon 1989: 34; Yoon 1989: 8, 2005: 14-45; Yi 1996: 199, 2000: 254; H-J. Lee and C-H. Lee 1999: 17, 2001: 54) define the enumeration relation as that where facts or events conveyed by X and Y are separately mentioned. Furthermore, previous studies consider the [X-*ko* Y] sequence as a Korean counterpart of *and*-conjunction. Here, it is notable that K-D. Lee (1993: 473) and Suh (2006: 1124) treat an enumeration relation as a logical relation & on the ground that -*ko* encodes a logical operator &.

Consider the following example.

(12)   Chelswu-ka hakkyo-ey ka-**ko** Yenghuy-ka cip-ey   ka-n-ta
       *-NM school-to go-**KO**   -NM house-to go-IN-DC*
    'Chelswu goes to school and Yenghuy goes home.' (Jeon 1989: 34)

Two propositions, such as (13)a-b, can be recovered from (12).

(13)   a. Chelswu goes to school.
      b. Yenghuy goes home.

According to Jeon, (13)a and (13)b hold an enumeration relation in that two events, i.e., going to school and going home, are separately mentioned. In Suh's (2006: 1105, 1124) sense, a single conjoined proposition, such as (14), can be recovered from the [X-*ko* Y] sequence in (12).

(14)   [Chelswu goes to school] & [Yenghuy goes home].

This is because the truth-value of (14) is identical to the truth-value of (15) where the positions of the proposition before & in (14) and the proposition after & in (14) are reversed.

(15)   [Yenghuy goes home] & [Chelswu goes to school].

Thus, clauses (13)a-b establish a logical relation &.

<u>Simultaneity</u>

The simultaneity relation (Korean *tongsi*) obtains between X and Y in the [X-*ko* Y] sequence. Previous studies (e.g. Tsai 1985: 35) define the simultaneity relation as that where events conveyed by X and Y occur at the same time.

Consider the following example.

(16)   haksayng-tul-i swulcip-eyse swul-ul   masi-**ko** nolay-lul
       *student-PL-NM bar-at   liquor-AC drink-**KO** sing-AC*
       ha-p-ni-ta
       do-AH-IN-DC
       'Students are singing while drinking in a bar.' (Tsai 1985: 38)

Two propositions, such as (17)a-b, can be recovered from (16).

    (17) a. Students are drinking in a bar.

            b. Students are singing in the bar.

Tsai says that (17)a and (17)b establish a simultaneity relation on the ground that drinking temporally overlaps with singing. Further, she argues that this relation is not encoded by *-ko* in (16) but pragmatically inferred. This is supported by K-D. Lee (1993: 469-470). He points out that *-ko* encodes the meaning of the logical operator &; a simultaneity relation that obtains between X and Y in the [X-*ko* Y] sequence is drawn by inference.

Sequence, Succession, and Temporal Precedence

The sequence, succession, and temporal precedence (Korean *swuncha*, *kyeyki*, and *senhayng* respectively) obtain between X and Y in two types of sequences: the [X-*ko* Y] sequence and the [X-*se* Y] sequence. Previous studies share the view that the three relations refer to those where the event conveyed by X precedes the event conveyed by Y.[1] For the sake of

---

[1] Previous studies are as follows.

    (i)   *Swuncha* 'Sequence' (e.g. *-ko* and *-se*)
        (e.g. Yang 1972: 5; Choi 1989: 156, 1991: 164; K-D. Lee 1993: 453, 473; H-J. Lee and C-H. Lee 1999: 343, 2001: 655; Suh 2006: 1126)
    (ii) *Kyeyki* 'Succession' (e.g. *-ko* and *-se*)
        (e.g. Tsai 1985: 40; Jeon 1989: 53; Yoon 2005: 203)
    (iii) *Swuncha* 'Sequence' (e.g. *-ko*) and *Kyeyki* 'Succession' (e.g. *-se*)
        (e.g. Suh 2006: 1177)
    (iv) *Senhayng* 'Temporal Precedence' (e.g. *-se*)

exposition, we adopt sequence as a representative label. According to previous studies (e.g. Suh 2006: 1126-1127, 1179-1180), the sequential reading of the [X-*ko* Y] sequence is inferred, but the sequential reading of the [X-*se* Y] sequence is decoded. This is because -*ko* encodes the logical operator & and -*se* encodes a sequence meaning.

Previous studies raise two points as to the difference between the [X-*ko* Y] sequence and the [X-*se* Y] sequence that involve a sequence relation. One is whether or not the event conveyed by X is a prerequisite preliminary stage for the event conveyed by Y. The other is whether or not the predicate word of X is identified as *itong tongsa* 'locomotion verb' and *casey tongsa* 'verb of posture'.

Previous studies (e.g. Yang 1972: 6-7; Tsai 1985: 44-46; Jeon 1989: 58-59; Choi 1989: 163-164, 1991: 171-172; H-J. Lee and C-H. Lee 1999: 346, 2001: 659) posit that in the [X-*ko* Y] sequence like (18)a the event depicted by X is not a prerequisite to the occurrence of the event depicted by Y, and that in the [X-*se* Y] sequence like (18)b the event depicted by X must take place in order for the event conveyed by Y to occur.

(18) a. ku-nun seyswuha-**ko**   ppang-ul   mek-ess-ta
          *he-TC wash one's face and hands-**KO** bread-AC eat-PST-DC*
          'He washed his face and then ate bread.' (K-D. Lee 1993: 453)

(e.g. Yi 1996: 177, 2000: 226)

(v) *Senhayng* 'Temporal Precedence' (e.g. -*ko*) and *Swuncha* 'Sequence' (e.g. -*se*)

(e.g. H-J. Lee and C-H. Lee 1999: 17, 2001: 55)

    b. ku-nun swuphemakheyth-ey ka-**se** ppang-ul sa-ss-ta

       he-TC supermarket-to   go-SE bread-AC buy-PST-DC

       'He went to the shop and then bought bread (there).' (K-D. Lee

       1993: 454)

First, in (18)a washing the face is not a necessary condition for eating bread. Second, in (18)b going to the shop is indispensable for buying bread. Examples such as (18)a-b support that whether or not the event conveyed by X is a prerequisite preliminary stage since the event conveyed by Y is the yardstick to discriminate between -*ko* and -*se* that involve sequence.

    However, the above line of reasoning encounters such a counterexample as (19)a-b.

    (19)   a. mwun-ul yel-**ko**   tulew-ala

             *door-AC open-**KO** enter-IM*

             'Open the door and come in.'

        b. * mwun-ul yel-**ese**   tulew-ala

             door-AC open-SE enter-IM (Yang 1972: 7)

In Yang's account, (19)a is acceptable, but not (19)b. He concedes that in (19)a the two segments linked by -*ko* obtain a sequence relation, and that in (19)a opening the door is a prerequisite for entering into the doorway. This means that his approach, i.e., whether or not the event conveyed by X is a prerequisite preliminary stage for the event conveyed by Y, does not work here.

    By contrast, K-D. Lee (1993: 454-455, 459-460) argues that two types of verbs, i.e., *itong tongsa* 'locomotion verb' and *casey tongsa* 'verb of posture', are accepted as a predicate word of segments before -*se* rather than -*ko* if and only if -*ko* and -*se* involve a sequence relation. First, the notion of *itong tongsa* 'locomotion verb' is a verb that indicates movement: e.g. *kata* 'go' and *ota* 'come'. Second, the notion of *casey tongsa* 'verb of posture' is a verb that indicates posture: e.g. *ancta* 'sit', *ephtulita* 'lie on the ground', *nwupta* 'lie down', and *seta* 'stand'.

Consider the following examples.

(20) a. * ku-nun makheyth-ey ka-**ko** ppang-ul sa-ss-ta
        *he-TC   market-to   go-**KO** bread-AC buy-PST-DC*

    b. ku-nun makheyth-ey ka-**se** ppang-ul sa-ss-ta
        *he-TC   market-to   go-**SE** bread-AC buy-PST-DC*
        'He went to the market and then he bought bread.'

(21) a. * ku-nun nwup-**ko**   chayk-ul po-ass-ta
        *he-TC   lie down-**KO** book-AC see-PST-DC*

    b. ku-nun nwuw-**ese**   chayk-ul po-ass-ta
        *he-TC   lie down-**SE** book-AC see-PST-DC*
        'He lay down and then he read a book.' (K-D. Lee 1993: 459)

In (20) and (21), *ka-* 'go' and *nwuw-* 'lie down' before -*ko* and -*se* are a locomotion verb and a verb of posture, respectively. K-D. Lee points out that (20)b and (21)b are acceptable but (20)a and (21)a are not admissible because (20) and (21) have a sequential reading. In (20)b going to market precedes buying bread and in (21)b reading a book follows lying down. It is inferred from K-D. Lee that the exploration of meanings of verbs gives a clue to figure out differences between *-ko* and *-se* that involve a sequence relation. We will not, however, pursue this in this book.

Cause and Reason

There appear to be two views on the cause and reason relation (Korean *wenin* and *iyu* respectively).[2] One group of scholars (e.g. Jeong 1989, Choi 1989, 1991; Yoon 1989; Yi 1996, 2000; H-J. Lee and C-H. Lee 2001) claim that cause and reason are two distinctive propositional relations. Cause refers to those where an event or a fact or a state depicted by X is a cause of the state depicted by Y, and this relation obtains between X and Y in two types of sequences: the [X-*ko* Y] sequence and the [X-*se* Y] sequence. Reason designates those where the event or the fact or the state conveyed by X provides the hearer with a reason for the speaker's proposal or order by Y, and this relation obtains between X and Y in two types of sequences: the [X-*nikka* Y] sequence and the [X-*nuntey* Y] sequence. The other group of scholars (e.g. Yang 1972, Tsai 1985, Jeon 1989) treat cause and reason as two subtypes of a propositional relation. They call this relation 'reason', and

---

[2] Previous studies are as follows.

    (i)   *Wenin* 'Cause' (e.g. *-se*) and *Iyu* 'Reason' (e.g. *-nikka*)
         (e.g. Jeong 1986: 76, 85; Choi 1989: 93-94; 1991: 107-110; Yoon 1989: 118-120, 2005: 175-178; Yi 1996: 186-188, 2000: 237-239)

    (ii) *Wenin* 'Cause' (e.g. *-ko* and *-se*) and *Iyu* 'Reason' (e.g. *-nikka*)
         (e.g. H-J. Lee and C-H. Lee 2001: 55, 659)

    (iii) *Iyu* 'Reason' (e.g. *-se* and *-nikka*)
         (e.g. Yang 1972: 2)

    (iv) *Iyu* 'Reason' (e.g. *-ko*, *-se*, *-nikka*, and *-nuntey*)
         (e.g. Tsai 1985: 69; Jeon 1989: 102-103)

thus cause and reason used by the first group of scholars are represented as reason₁ and reason₂ respectively. However, they share with the first group of scholars the view that the reading of [X-*ko* Y] sequence is inferred and the reading of the other sequences is decoded.

(22)a-b involve the cause relation.

(22) a. Hahongi-nun kokwuma-lul   mek-**ko** paythal-i
          *Hahongi-TC sweet potato-AC eat-**KO** stomach trouble-NM*
          na-ss-ta
          occur-PST-DC
          'Because Hahongi ate a sweet potato, she suffered from stomach trouble.'

       b. Hahongi-nun kokwuma-lul   mek-**ese** paythal-i
          *Hahongi-TC sweet potato-AC eat-**SE**   stomach trouble-NM*
          na-ss-ta
          occur-PST-DC
          'Because Hahongi ate a sweet potato, she suffered from stomach trouble.' (Jeon 1989: 114)

Two propositions, such as (23)a-b, can be recovered not only from (22)a but also from (22)b.

(23) a. Hahongi ate a sweet potato.
       b. Hahongi suffered from stomach trouble.

In Jeon's account, eating a sweet potato caused suffering from stomach trouble; clauses (a) and (b) establish a cause relation. Jeon points out that the causal reading of (22)a is drawn by inference and that of (22)b is encoded by -*se*. This is supported by K-D. Lee (1993: 458-459, 474) and Suh (2006: 1127-1128, 1190-1192). K-D. Lee and Suh posit that -*ko* encodes the logical operator & and -*se* encodes a cause meaning.

Let us turn into the reason relation. Jeon argues that in (24)a-b segments before -*nikka* and -*nuntey* are identified as reasons for segments after the two suffixes.

(24) a. pi-ka   o-**nikka**   ppalli ka-ca
         rain-NM come-NIKKA quickly go-PR
         'Because it's raining, let's go quickly.' (Jeon 1989: 112)
      b. sikan-i   nuc-ess-**nuntey**   ppalli ttwieka-ca
         time-NM late-PST-NUNTEY quickly run-PR
         'Because it was late, let's run quickly.' (Jeon 1989: 111)

In (24)a raining gives the hearer a reason for the speaker's proposal that the speaker and the hearer should go quickly. She says that in (24)b the fact that it was late also gives the hearer a reason for the speaker's proposal that the speaker and the hearer should run quickly. Further, she points out that -*nikka* and -*nuntey* encode only a reason (in her terms reason$_2$) meaning.

However, this encounters a drawback because -*nikka* encodes a cause meaning. Consider (25)a-b.

(25) a. nwun-i   manhi w-**ase**   kil-i   makhy-ess-ta
         snow-NM much come-SE road-NM be blocked-PST-DC
         'Because it snowed heavily, the road was blocked.'

b. nwun-i manhi o-**nikka** kil-i makhy-ess-ta

*snow-NM much come-**NIKKA** road-NM be blocked-PST-DC*

'Because it snowed heavily, the road was blocked.' (Yoon 1989: 118)

Yoon concedes that the fact that it snowed heavily caused the road's being blocked. Nevertheless, he argues that *-se* in (25)a encodes a cause meaning but *-nikka* in (25)b encodes a reason meaning. According to Yoon, in (25)a the fact that it snowed heavily provides the hearer with a reason for the speaker's asserting that the road was blocked in the sense that the implicated conclusion such as (26)b is inferred from the premise such as (26)a.

(26) a. It snows heavily.
      b. The road is blocked.

However, (26)b is not an implicated conclusion but the effect of a heavy fall of snow such as (27).

(27) [As a result of its snowing heavily] [The road is blocked].

This is supported by Suh (2006: 1187). Suh posits that *-nikka* encodes a cause meaning. Furthermore, a unitary account of *-nuntey*, i.e., that *-nuntey* encodes only a reason meaning, encounters counterexamples such as (28).

(28) ku salam-iya wuntong senswu-i-**ntey**

      *the person-as only for athlete-be-**NUNTEY***

      kukes-ccum-iya tul-keyss-ci-yo

that-approximately-as only for lift-will-SUP-PL

'Because he is an athlete, he will probably lift up that much.' (Tsai 1985: 98)

Tsai, who sticks to the unitary account, argues that in (28) the fact that he is an athlete is a reason of for the speaker's guessing the athlete's ability of lifting. However, her analysis is not the case. This is because a guess conveyed by the segment after *-nuntey* in (28) does not indicate an event or a fact, which occurs in the real world, and the fact conveyed by the segment before *-nuntey* in (28) is not identified as a reason for speech acts such as orders and proposals. Here, it is notable that the fact he is an athlete is a premise for deriving the athlete's ability of lifting.

Opposition, Contrast, and Counter-act/event

There appears to be two views on the opposition and contrast, and counter-act/event relation (Korean *taylip, tayco, pantay-hayngwi/sathay* respectively).[3] One group of scholars (e.g. Choi 1989, 1991) argue that

---

[3] Previous studies are as follows.

(i)   *Pantay-hayngwi/sathay* 'Counter-act/event' (e.g. *-ciman, -to,* and *-nuntey*)
       (e.g. Yang 1972: 8-11)
(ii)   *Tayco* 'Contrast' (e.g. *-ciman*)
       (e.g. Jeong 1986: 24-25)
(iii) *Tayco* 'Contrast' (e.g. *-ciman*)
       (e.g. Yi 1996: 201, 2000: 256-257)
(iv) *Taylip* 'Opposition' (e.g. *-ciman, -to,* and *-nuntey*)
       (e.g. Tsai 1985: 111-120)
(v)   *Taylip* 'Contrast' (e.g. *-ciman, -to,* and *-nuntey*)
       (e.g. Jeon 1989: 64, 66-67)

opposition and contrast are two different propositional relations. Opposition refers to those where the predicates of the proposition recovered from X is the opposite of those from Y (e.g. 'be short' vs. 'be tall'). Contrast refers to those cases where an expectation, which is a proposition **derived from** X, is denied by another proposition recovered from Y. The other group of scholars (e.g. Yang 1972, Jeong 1986, Yi 1996, 2000; Tsai 1985; Jeon 1989; Yoon 1989; Suh 2006) combine the two different propositional relations into one relation and name it opposition or contrast or counter-act/event. They regard the opposition relation and the contrast relation, which the first group of scholars suggest, as opposition$_1$ and opposition$_2$ or contrast$_1$ and contrast$_2$ or counter-act/event$_1$ and counter-act/event$_2$ respectively.

Tsai (1985: 112) postulates that the [X-*ciman* Y] sequence, the [X-*to* Y] sequence, and the [X-*nuntey* Y] sequence have the contrast (in her terms opposition$_2$) reading as well as the opposition (in her terms opposition$_1$) reading. Further, she (1985: 113) posits that opposition and contrast readings of the three sequences are decoded.

Let us consider (29), where an opposition relation obtains.

> (29) a. apeci-nun khi-ka   cak-**ciman**   atul-un khi-ka   khuta
>   *father-TC height-NM short-**CIMAN** son-TC height-NM tall*

> (vi)   *Taylip* 'Contrast' (e.g. -*ciman* and -*to*)
>   (e.g. Yoon 1989: 59, 61, 2005: 74, 76)
> (vii) *Tayco* 'Contrast' (e.g. -ciman)
>   (e.g. Suh 2006: 1147, 1149)
> (viii) *Taylip* 'Opposition' (e.g. -*ciman* and -*nuntey*) and *Tayco* 'Contrast' (e.g. -*ciman*)
>   (e.g. Choi 1989: 69, 138, 1991: 75, 145)

'The father is short, but his son is tall.'

b. apeci-nun khi-ka   cak-**ato**   atul-un khi-ka   khuta

*father-TC height-NM short-**TO** son-TC height-NM tall*

'The father is short, but his son is tall.'

c. apeci-nun khi-ka   cak-**untey**   atul-un khi-ka   khuta

*father-TC height-NM short-**NUNTEY** son-TC height-NM tall*

'The father is short, but his son is tall.' (Tsai 1985: 112)

The propositions of X and Y in the [X-*ciman/to/nuntey* Y] sequence in (29)a-c can be recovered as follows.

(30) a. The father is short.

b. His son is tall.

On Tsai's accounts, *is short* in (30)a presents a contrast to *is tall* in (30)b; in (30) clause (a) and clause (b) have an opposition relation.

Let us turn to the contrast relation. Consider the following examples.

(31) a. wuli-nun cec   mek-te-n   him-kkaci   ta

we-TC   mother's milk eat-RT-MD strength-even all

nay-e   mil-ess-**ciman**

*call forth-INF push-PST-**CIMAN***

pawi-nun cokumto wumciki-ci an.h.ass-ta

rock-TC at all   move-MOM not.do.PST-DC

'We pushed the rock with all our strength, but we couldn't move it at all.'

b. wuli-nun cec   mek-te-n   him-kkaci   ta

we-TC   mother's milk eat-RT-MD strength-even all

nay-e   mil-ess-**eto**

*call forth-INF push-PST-**TO***

pawi-nun cokumto wumciki-ci an.h.ass-ta

rock-TC at all   move-MOM not.do.PST-DC

'We pushed the rock with all our strength, but we couldn't move it at all.'

c. wuli-nun cec   mek-te-n   him-kkaci   ta

we-TC   mother's milk eat-RT-MD strength-even all

nay-e   mil-ess-**nuntey**

*call forth-INF push-PST-**NUNTEY***

pawi-nun cokumto wumciki-ci an.h.ass-ta

rock-TC at all   move-MOM not.do.PST-DC

'We pushed the rock with all our strength, but we couldn't move it at all.'

(Tsai 1985: 113)

Two propositions, such as (32)a-b, can be recovered respectively from X and Y the [X-*ciman/to/nuntey* Y] sequence in (31)a-c.

(32) a. We pushed the rock with all our strength.

  b. We could not move the rock.

Furthermore, the expectation, such as (33), can be drawn from (32)a.

(33) We could move the rock.

According to Tsai, the expectation (33) is denied by the proposition (32)b; a contrast relation obtains between clauses (32)a and (32)b.

Introduction

The introduction relation (Korean *toip*) obtains between X and Y in the [X-*nuntey* Y] sequence. Previous studies (e.g. K-D. Lee 1979: 123-125, 1980: 121-123, 1993: 520-522; Yi 1996: 206, 2000: 263) define the introduction relation as those where X introduces a certain object or an event on which the speaker focuses in Y. K-D. Lee (1980: 113, 1993: 519) postulates that the introduction relation is encoded by -*nuntey*.

Consider the following example.

(34)   [Context: The speaker wants to talk about Germany after he said
        something about France.]
        ku taum tokil-ey   ka-ss-**nuntey**,   motwu   maywu
        that next Germany-to go-PST-NUNTEY everyone very
        chincelhay-ss-ta
        kind-PST-DC
        'Then I went to Germany and the people there were all very kind and nice.'
        (K-D. Lee 1980: 123)

Two propositions, such as (35)a-b, can be recovered from (34).

(35)   a. The speaker went to Germany after he/she visited France.
        b. All people in Germany are very kind and nice.

In K-D. Lee's terms, (35)a introduces *Germany* on which the speaker focuses in (35)b; (35)a-b hold an introduction relation. He argues that -*nuntey* in (34) encodes an introduction meaning.

Background

The background relation (Korean *paykyeng*) obtains between X and Y in the [X-*nuntey* Y] sequence. Previous studies (e.g. K-D. Lee 1979: 125-127, 1980: 123-133, 1993: 522-529) define the background relation as those where what is conveyed by X is a background that backs up representatives (in their terms 'assertion', 'representative' and 'relatedness'), directives (in their terms 'directives' and 'questions') and commissives conveyed by Y.[4] K-D. Lee (1980: 133, 1993: 519) posits that the background relation is encoded by -*nuntey*.

Consider the following example.

(36) iltung-ul   hay-ss-**nuntey**,   nayil   ohwu-ey   sikyey hana
     the first rank-AC do-PST-NUNTEY tomorrow afternoon-at watch one
     sa   cwu-ma
     buy.INF give-IM
     'You won the first prize. So, I will buy a watch for you tomorrow afternoon.' (K-D. Lee 1980: 129)

Two propositions, such as (37)a-b, can be recovered from (36).

---

[4] Searle (1976) defines representatives, directives and commissives as sub-types of utterance. Levinson (1983: 240) summarises these three notions as follows.

(i) **representatives**, which commit the speaker to the truth of the expressed proposition (paradigm cases: asserting, concluding, etc.)
(ii) **directives**, which are attempts by the speaker to get the addressee to do something (paradigm cases: requesting, questioning)
(iii) **commissives**, which commit the speaker to some future course of action (paradigm cases: promising, threatening, offering)

(37) a. The hearer won the first prize.

b. The speaker will buy a watch for the hearer tomorrow afternoon.

K-D. Lee argues that in (36) the event, i.e., winning the first prize, depicted by X guarantees commissives, i.e., promising to buy a watch, depicted by Y. According to him, (37)a is a background for the hearer's inferring the following premises:

(38) a. Brilliant students deserve some prizes.

b. You have proved yourself to be brilliant.

c. You deserve a prize. (K-D. Lee 1980: 130)

However, (38)a-c show that (37)a is not a background but rather is a premise itself. That is to say, (37)a and (38)a-c are identified as premises for deriving the implicated conclusion like (37)b. So, (37)a-b involve a propositional relation such as premise-conclusion.

Explanation

The explanation relation (Korean *selmyeng*) obtains between X and Y in two types of sequences: the [X-*nikka* Y] sequence and the [X-*nuntey* Y] sequence. Previous studies (e.g. Jeon 1989: 127-128) define the explanation relation as one where what is conveyed by X is a situation and what is conveyed by Y is an explanation for this situation. Jeon (1989: 128) postulates that -*nikka* and -*nuntey* encode an explanation meaning. Here, it is notable that from the viewpoint of other scholars (e.g. Martin et al. 1967,

Martin 1992, and K-D. Lee 1979, 1980, 1993) the explanation relation is identified as a time relation or an introduction relation.

Consider the following example.

(39) sikol-ey   ka-**nikka**   kongki-ka coh-te-la
      *country-to go-**NIKKA** air-NM   good-RT-DC*
      'When I went to the country, I breathed fresh air.' (Jeon 1989: 129)

Two propositions, such as (40)a-b, can be recovered from (39).

(40) a. The speaker went to the country.
      b. The speaker breathed fresh air in the country.

Jeon argues that (40)a-b have an explanation relation in that (40)a represents a temporal situation and (40)b gives an explanation for this situation. However, the reading of the [X-*nikka* Y] sequence is a time relation rather than an explanation relation in that a temporal situation itself stands for a temporal relation. This is supported by Martin et al. (1967: 1281) and Martin (1992: 903). They point out that -*nikka* in examples such as (39) encodes a time meaning "*when* (in the past)". In this sense, a single conjoined proposition, such as (41), can be recovered from (39).

(41) [When the speaker went to the country], [the speaker breathed fresh air in the country].

Consider another example.

    (42) wuli cip   seythakki-nun   Kumseng ceyphwum-i-**ntey**

           our   house washing machine-TC   *product-be-**NUNTEY***

           cham thunthunha.y

           really strong.INF

           'My washing machine is the product of *Kumseng* and it's really good.'

           (Jeon 1989: 128)

From (42) two propositions, such as (43)a-b, can be recovered.

    (43) a. The speaker's washing machine was manufactured by *Kumseng*.

          b. The washing machine has a good quality.

In Jeon's account, in (43) clauses (a) and (b) hold an explanation relation on the ground that (43)a represents a situation and (43)b gives an explanation for this situation. In K-D. Lee's (1979, 1980, 1993) sense, two propositions (43)a-b, however, have an introduction relation. This is because X in (42) introduces *wuli cip seythakki* 'my washing machine' on which the speaker focuses in Y in (42).

As shown above, the two readings, i.e., the time reading of the [X-*nikka* Y] sequence in (39) and the introduction reading of the [X-*nuntey* Y] sequence in (42), support the view that the explanation relation is not a possible propositional relation that obtains between X and Y in these two types of sequences.

So far, we have discussed previous research on six conjunctive verbal suffixes *-ko*, *-nuntey*, *-nikka*, *-se*, *-ciman*, and *-to*. We note that previous studies on the six suffixes depended heavily on the constructed data. This has natural shortcomings, namely, one cannot see clearly inferential aspects of meanings of the four suffixes *-ko*, *-nuntey*, *-nikka*, and *-se* that are shown in the data that we collected.

The remainder of this book is organised in the following manner. Chapter 2 will describe briefly how four pragmatic theories, Gricean theory, neo-Gricean theory, Relevance Theory, and Default Semantics, explain the recovery of propositions. This is because the description is a prerequisite to understanding concepts will be utilised in explaining meanings of connectives. Expecially, it will focus on the strengths and weakness of the four theories. Chapter 3 will develop our theoretical framework. It will expound four notions that are essential to the framework: propositional relation, the scope test, the difference between encoded and inferred meanings, and the use of connectives. Further, it will give theoretical rationales for the selective adoption of concepts, held by the four pragmatics theories. Chapter 4 will offer expositions on the data. First, this chapter provides the methodology for the data acquisition. Second, this chapter illustrates the data transcriptions. Third, this chapter shows the frequencies of Korean conjunctive verbal suffixes *-ko*, *-nuntey*, *-nikka*, *-se*, *-ciman*, and *-to*. Fourth, this chapter also touches upon difficulties of recovering Y in the [X-target suffix (Y)] sequence, in particular the unsaid segment after the suffix. Chapter 5 will characterise propositional relations that obtain between X and Y in the [X-target suffix Y] sequence. Chapter 6 will apply the scope test in judging whether or not the propositional relations that will be shown in Chapter 5 are encoded meanings of the target suffixes. Further, it will show that encoded and inferred meanings of the target suffixes involve a single conjoined truth-conditional proposition and two truth-functionally disjoined propositions respectively. Chapter 7 will discuss two issues of the nature of encoded and inferred meanings of the six conjunctive verbal suffixes, from the two theoretical viewpoints, Relevance Theory and Default Semantics. The one is the distinction of concepts and procedures of encoded meanings of the six suffixes, advocated by Relevance Theorists; the other is the scale of encoded and inferred meanings of these suffixes, suggested by Default Semanticists. Chapter 8 will conclude this book, by suggesting two questions for further studies. The first question is - What is the acceptability of Korean conjunctive verbal suffixes? The second one is - What is the role played by these suffixes is when they play in inferred propositional relations that obtain between two segments linked by them?

2
Four Pragmatic Theories

The purpose of this chapter is to provide brief descriptions of how four pragmatic theories, Gricean theory, neo-Gricean theory, Relevance Theory, and Default Semantics, explain the recovery of propositions. This is fundamental in the study of the use of connectives. By **use**, we mean whether a given connective conjoins or disjoins two propositions truth-conditionally. In particular, we focus on strengths and weaknesses of the four theories. Our point of departure is thus to figure out how we can identify propositions.

Why do we selectively borrow concepts that are related to meanings of connectives from four theories, not, for instance, any one of them, in the study of Korean conjunctive verbal suffixes: *-ko*, *- nuntey*, *-nikka*, *-se*, *-ciman*, and *-to*? While these concepts help us to specify the use of these conjunctive endings, in particular, whether or not the meanings of a given suffix conjoin, or disjoin, the two propositions truth-conditionally, they have their own strengths and weaknesses according to theory that advocates them. That is to say, the four theories have difficulty in taking up all meanings of the six suffixes, but they respectively provide a strong explanatory power of explanations for the following meanings. First, Relevance Theory can explain our term 'truth-conditional encoded meaning'. Second, Gricean and neo-Gricean theories can make clear our term 'non-truth-conditional encoded meaning'. Finally, Default Semantics enables us to find out that there are more than two propositional relations, which involve our term 'non-truth-conditional inferred meaning', and these propositional relations are posited on a single scale on the basis of the quantity of the hearer's inference. (See Chapters 3, 6 and 7 for more details.) Thus, from the four theories we are forced to adopt selectively concepts essential to analysing meanings of these conjunctive endings from the four theories.

In Chapter 1, we discussed previous approaches on the six suffixes, such as those conducted by Yang (1972), K-D. Lee (1979, 1980, 1993), Tsai (1985), Jeong (1986), Choi (1989, 1991), Jeon (1989), Yoon (1989, 2005), Yi (1996, 2000), H-J. Lee and C-H. Lee (1999, 2001), and Suh (2006). Two points emerged here. First, propositional relations that obtain between the two segments connected by a suffix constitute meanings of the suffix. Second, the focus was on the taxonomy of the meanings of these suffixes; the issue of whether or not the meanings contribute to the truth conditions of the linked segments is largely ignored. Studies on English connectives, *and*, *but*, *therefore*, *so*, *because*, and *moreover*, teach us, apart from many other things, that the meanings conjoin or disjoin the two propositions truth-functionally. This is significant because the truth-functionality of a suffix is closely connected to whether meanings of the suffix are encoded or inferred. That is, encoded meanings of suffixes conjoin two propositions truth-functionally but inferred meanings of suffixes disjoin two propositions truth-functionally. (One can say that the connective *and* has truth-conditional inferred meanings, i.e., N-GCIs (e.g. simultaneity meaning), taken by neo-Gricean theory. However, these meanings bring a problem to neo-Gricean theory. See Chapter 3 for more details.)

Our contribution to the study of Korean conjunctive verb endings lies in the emphasis on the use of the six suffixes, particularly on the distinction between conjoining and disjoining truth-functionally and on being encoded and inferred. This is not to contradict the previous approaches but to complement them. Further specification of the lexical meanings of each of the conjunctive suffixes is thus beyond the scope of our discussions in this book.

Let us consider what is meant by a proposition. According to Lyons (1977:141-142), a proposition is "what is expressed by a declarative sentence when that sentence is uttered to make a statement." He also mentions that "[it] is sufficient to say that propositions are expressed by sentences (and contained in utterances) and may be either true or false" (Lyons 1977:38). From these it follows that propositions are conveyed by the speaker's utterances, and that propositions take the form of a declarative sentence which has a truth-value.

The four theories share the view that a proposition is recovered from the meaning of a word or words, which make up an utterance.[5] However, the theories differ from one another in labelling propositions. First, Gricean theory labels propositions as 'what is said'. The notion of what is said refers to a proposition, which non-cancellable meanings of a word or words form. Second, neo-Gricean theory labels propositions as 'sentences'. The notion of sentence designates a proposition, which consists of two levels of meanings

---

[5] Utterances are composed of a single word or a single phrase or a single sentence, i.e., a string of words (Hurford and Heasley 1983: 15).

of a word or words: coded compositional semantic and inferred presemantic pragmatic. Third, Relevance Theory labels propositions as 'explicatures'. The notion of explicature stands for a proposition, which is composed of two levels of meanings of a word or words: encoded linguistic semantic and inferred pragmatic. Fourth, Default Semantics labels as 'semantic representation' a proposition, which comprises Default-Semantic meanings of a word or words. So, it is essential to be clear about the notion of proposition proffered by each of the theories.

This chapter reviews how four theories, Gricean theory (e.g. Grice 1975), neo-Gricean theory (e.g. Levinson 1983, 1995, 2000), Relevance Theory (e.g. Sperber and Wilson 1986/1995; Wilson 2004), and Default Semantics (e.g. Jaszczolt 1999; H-K. Lee 2001), account for identification of propositions. The four theories share the view that there is a gap between the meaning of a word or words, which make up an utterance, and the proposition, which the speaker intends to communicate, but their accounts of how to bridge the gap are not identical with one another.

2.1 Gricean Theory

Grice (1975) postulates levels of meanings as follow.

Table 2.1: Levels of Meanings Based on Gricean Theory

Truth-Conditional Semantics		Pragmatics		
Sentence Meanings	Speaker's	Meanings		
	What is said	What is implicated		
		Conversational Implicatures		Conventioanl Implicatures
		Generalised Conversational Implicatures	Particularised Conversational Implicatures	

He considers the meaning of words or a sentence, which constitute an utterance, and the proposition, which the speaker intends to convey through the utterance, as 'sentence meaning' and 'speaker's meaning', respectively. He divides 'speaker's meaning' into 'what is said' and 'what is implicated'. 'What is implicated' is further divided into 'conversational implicautre' and 'conventional implicature'. In this section, we focus on 'what is said' and 'conversational implicature', and we will take up 'conventional implicaure' in Chapter 3.[6]

According to Grice (1975), a gap between sentence meaning and what is said is bridged by reference assignment and disambiguation. He (1975: 44) postulates that it is essential to identify the following three types of entities, which in order for the hearer to recover what the speaker intends to convey by way of an utterance. The first type is "the identity of" a certain particular

---

[6] A notion of conventional implicature refers to a non-cancellable meaning that connectives such as *but*, *therefore*, *so*, and *moreover* have (Grice 1968, 1975, 1989).

individual. The second type is "the time of utterance". The third type is "the meaning, on the particular occasion of utterance, of" a certain "phrase".

Consider the following examples.

(1)　　a. He is in the grip of a vice.

　　　　b. *x* was unable to rid himself of a certain kind of bad character trait

　　　　c. some part of *x*'s person was caught in a certain kind of tool or instrument

　　　　(Grice 1975: 44)

On Grice's accounts, the hearer would have to conduct three tasks, in order to recover what is said from (1)a. The first task is to assign the referent *he* in (1)a to a certain particular male person or animal *x*. The second task is to assign the indexical value to the time uttering in (1)a. The third task is to disambiguate the phrase *in the grip of a vice* on the occasion of uttering (1)a, i.e., to select one between (1)b-c.

In Grice's terms, what is said determines what is conversationally implicated. He points out that there is a correlation between that *p*, i.e., what is said, and that *q*, i.e., a conversational implicature. In other words, that *q* is a conversational implicature inferred from that *p* if and only if communicators think or know that that *q* is necessary in order to render that *p* consistent with the presumption that the speaker observes the cooperative principle.

According to Grice, the speaker and the hearer have to cooperate to some extent as a minimum if they intend to communicate successfully. He calls this 'the cooperative principle', formulated as follows.

(2)   The Cooperative Principle

Make your conversational contribution such as is required, at the state at which it occurs, by the accepted purpose or direction of the talk exchange in which you are engaged. (Grice 1975: 45)

Grice breaks down the cooperative principle into four maxims: 'Quantity', 'Quality', 'Relation', and 'Manner'. The four maxims are as follows.

(3)   a. The Maxim of 'Quantity'

      i. Make your contribution as informative as is required
      (for the current purpose of the exchange).

      ii. Do not make your contribution more informative than is required.
      (Grice 1975: 45)

b. The Maxim of 'Quality'

Try to make your contribution one that is true.

      i. Do not say what you believe to be false.

      ii. Do not say what for which you lack adequate evidence.
      (Grice 1975: 46)

c. The Maxim of 'Relation'

Be relevant. (Grice 1975: 46)

d. The Maxim of 'Manner'

Be perspicuous.

      i. Avoid obscurity of expression.

      ii. Avoid ambiguity.

      iii. Be brief (avoid unnecessary prolixity).

      iv. Be orderly. (Grice 1975: 46)

Grice (1975) subdivides conversational implicatures into generalised conversational implicatures (hereafter GCIs) and particularised conversational implicatures (hereafter PCIs).

A GCI refers to a meaning that is triggered by a certain form of an utterance without any special context.

Consider the following examples.

(4) a. X is meeting a woman this evening.

b. The person to be met was someone other than X's wife, mother, sister, or perhaps even close platonic friend. (Grice 1975: 56)

According to Grice, (4)b is a GCI of *a woman* in (4)a. He points out that in order to fulfil the first maxim of Quantity in (3)ai the [indefinite article + noun] form such as *a woman* in (4)a triggers a GCI that a person is not closely related to a certain identifiable person such as *X*. Here, it is notable that the GCI (4)b determines what is said such as (5) because the GCI causes the hearer to assign the referent to *one woman who is not closely related to X* in (5).

(5)   X is meeting **one woman who is not closely related to X** this evening.

A PCI stands for a meaning that is inferred from what is said in a special context.

Consider other examples.

(6)   [Context: A is writing a testimonial about a pupil who is a candidate for a philosophy job, and his letter reads as follows]
Dear Sir, Mr. X's command of English is excellent, and his attendance at tutorials has been regular. (Grice 1975: 52)

In Grice's sense, what is said such as (7) is recovered from (6).

(7)   [Mr. X speaks excellent English] & [he has regularly attended tutorials].

In Grice's account, PCI such as (8) is inferred from (7) in a particular context that Mr. X is A's pupil, in order to fulfil the first maxim of Quantity in (3)ai.

(8)   Mr. X is no good at philosophy. (Grice 1975: 52)

Notice that Grice considers what is said and conversational implicatures as the level of semantics, i.e., truth-conditional contents, and the level of pragmatics, i.e., communicative uses, respectively. A conversational implicature is determined by what is said, as we saw in (6) above. On the other hand, a conversational implicature also determines what is said on the ground that the cooperative principle plays an important role in conducting reference assignment (see (4) above). This is supported by neo-Gricean theorists (e.g. Levinson: 2000: 186-198) and Relevance Theorists (e.g. Carston 2002: 96-101). Levinson (2000: 186) and Carston (2002: 103) call the circular relation between what is said and what is conversationally implicated as "Grice's circle" and "semantic/pragmatic circles"

respectively.

The circular relation provides other theoretical approaches with a question of elucidating the semantics/pragmatics interface. In order to settle this question, the three approaches, i.e., neo-Gricean theory, Relevance Theory, and Default Semantics, each present distinct revisions of Gricean theory. In Sections 2.2. to 2.4., we will briefly review these three theories, respectively.

2.2 Neo-Gricean Theory

To Levinson (1995, 2000), levels of meanings are as follows.

Table 2.2: Levels of Meanings Based on Neo-Gricean Theory

Compositional Semantics	Presemantic Pragmatics	Sentence Semantics	Postsemantic Pragmatics	
Fragmentary Semantic Representations	Utterance-Type Meanings	Sentence Meanings	Speaker's Meanings	
	Q-Implicatures, I-Implicatures, M-Implicatures		Particularised Conversational Implicatures	Conventioanl Implicatures

Fragmentary semantic representations (sentence meanings in Grice's terms) stand for meanings of words or a sentence, which make up an utterance. Utterance-type meanings refer to generalised conversational implicatures that particular linguistic forms trigger (hereafter N-GCIs; N stands for neo-Gricean). Further, utterance-type meanings designate default inferences (or presumptive meanings) that capture the communicators' intuitions about preferred interpretations. However, default inferences are cancellable if they are inconsistent with the context. Sentence meaning (in Grice's terms what is said) designate proposition-bearing representations, each of which holds the truth-value: truth or false. Sentence meanings (hereafter neo-Gricean sentence meanings) are recovered from fragmentary semantic representations by default inferences. Lastly, speaker's meanings consist of PCIs and conventional implicatures. PCIs refer to meanings derived from neo-Gricean sentence meanings by the cooperative principle, whereas conventional implicatures stand for coded meanings of connectives *but*, *therefore*, *so*, and *moreover*.

In this section, we consider three levels of meanings, i.e., fragmentary semantic representations, utterance-type meanings, and neo-Gricean sentence meanings. We will not be concerned with speaker's meanings as we already reviewed PCIs in Section 2.1. We will take up conventional implicatures in Chapter 3.

In Levinson's (2000) sense, a gap between fragmentary semantic representations and neo-Gricean sentence meanings is bridged by processes such as reference assignment, disambiguation and completion of subsentential utterances (in Levinson's terms ellipsis unpacking), and N-GCIs (or default inferences) determine neo-Gricean sentence meanings in order to fulfil default heuristics. Levinson (1995, 2000) postulates that default heuristics consist of three types, Q, I and M, which originate from Gricean maxims.

(9)   Three Default Heuristics

    a. Q: What isn't said, isn't

          (cf. the first maxim of Quantity)

          e.g. "Some of the boys came" +> 'not all'

    b. I: What is expressed simply is stereotypically exemplified

          (cf. the second maxim of Quantity)

          e.g. "John's book is good" +> the one he

             read, wrote, borrowed, as appropriate

    c. M: What's said in an abnormal way isn't normal

          (cf. the first and fourth maxims of Manner)

          e.g. "Bill caused the car to stop" +>

             'indirectly, not in the normal way, for example, by use of the

             emergency brake' (Levinson 2000: 35-39)

To see how these heuristics work, consider the following example.

(10)   "Every old car needs to have the battery checked."

      'Each car needs to have the battery which belongs to that car checked.'

      (I-implicature) (Levinson 2000: 182)

According to Levinson, in (10) the hearer assigns the referent *the battery* to part of a previously conveyed *car* according to the I-inference that each car has one battery.

Consider another example.

(11)   a. "She submitted an uneven article. Some of the paper was excellent."

        (Q, I)

    b. *article*$_1$: 'thing'

        article$_2$: 'short academic treatise'

        paper$_1$: mass noun 'stuff for writing on'

        paper$_2$: count noun 'academic treatise'

        uneven$_1$: 'bumpy'

        uneven$_2$: 'variable quality'

    c. GCIs:

        i. "Some of the paper" Q +> 'not all of the paper'

        ii. the referent of *an article*$_2$ = the referent of *the paper*$_2$

            (I-preference for local coreference)

        iii. *uneven article* should be read 'variable quality academic treatise'

            rather than 'bumpy academic treatise' (attributable to an I-inference

            to the stereotypical interpretation) (Levinson 2000: 176-177)[7]

According to Levinson, in (11) the linguistic form *some, uneven article* and *paper* are disambiguated by Q-inference and I-inference.

Consider another example.

    (12) A: "Who came?"

           B: "John" <came> (I-implicauture) (Levinson 2000: 183)

Levinson says that in (12)B the hearer recovers the elliptical word *came* in terms of I-heuristics that inspires minimal expressions.

In order to resolve the so-called Grice's circle, Levinson (2000) identifies

---

[7] Levinson (2000) does not explain a notion of 'I-preference'. This notion designates 'I-inference that gives a preference' because the referent of *an article*$_2$ equal to the referent of *the paper*$_2$.

PCIs and conventional implicatures as neo-Gricean speaker's meanings and defines N-GCIs, which are inferred not by the cooperative principle but by default heuristics, as presumptive meanings. He argues that neo-Gricean sentence meanings are truth-conditional contents, and that default heuristics and the cooperative principle are involved in presemantic pragmatics and postsemantic pragmatics, respectively. His arguments remind us that PCIs do not determine neo-Gricean sentence meanings, and hence that PCIs are not involved in truth-conditional semantics (in Levinson's terms sentence semantics). However, in certain cases neo-Gricean sentence meanings can be recovered by PCIs (see pages 55 and 56).

2.3 Relevance Theory

Relevance Theorists (e.g. Sperber and Wilson 1986/1995; Wilson 2004) provide levles of meaning as follows.

Table 2.3: Levels of Meaning Based on Relevance Theory

Linguistic Semantics	Pragmatics	
Sentence Meanings	Speaker's Meanings	
	Explicautres	Implicatures

Sentence meanings refer to linguistic structures described by the semantic component of a grammar. Speaker's meanings stand for propositions that the speaker intends to communicate by uttering a sentence or other linguistic form on a particular occasion. Incidentally, in Relevance Theory a proposition is referred to as an "assumption". Sperber and Wilson (1986/1995) and Wilson (2004) postulate that an assumption is a structured set of concepts. According to Sperber and Wilson (1986/1995), linguistic forms, which encode concepts, gain access to three types of conceptual information, i.e., lexical, logical and encyclopaedic, stored at each relevant entry or point in the hearer's memory as follows. First, lexical entries store information about phonological structure, syntactic category membership and syntactic co-occurrence of the related linguistic form. For instance, the linguistic form *drive* corresponds to the phonemic /draiv/, and as the syntactic category verb occurs either with or without an NP immediately following the form. Second, logical entries store a set of deductive rules that describe a set of input and output assumptions, i.e., a set of premises and conclusions. Third, encyclopaedic entries store information about the objects, events and properties that the related linguistic form denotes (or recognises) and/or extends. For example, encyclopaedic entries store the concepts that the linguistic form *dog* denotes and/or extends, i.e., a set of assumptions about *dog*.

Relevance Theorists divide speaker's meanings into two types of propositions, i.e., 'explicatures' and 'implicatures' (hereafter SW-implicatures; SW stands for Sperber and Wilson), as follows.

(13) a. A proposition communicated by an utterance is an **explicature** if and only if it is a development of a logical form encoded by the utterance.

        b. A proposition communicated by an utterance, but not explicitly, is an **implicature**. (Wilson 2004)

They define 'logical form' as follows.

> "A logical form is a well-formed formula, a structural set of constituents, which undergoes formal logical operations determined by its structure." (Sperber and Wilson 1986/1995: 72)

Explicaures are further divided into two: 'basic explicatures' and 'higher-level explicatures'. Basic explicatures designate propositions that have the a truth-value; truth or false. Higher-level explicatures refer to propositions that express the speaker's attitude towards the embedded part of them.

Let us consider the notion of 'relevance'. Sperber and Wilson say provide the following definition of relevance.

(14) Relevance

An assumption is relevant in a context if and only if it has some contextual effects[8] in that context. (Sperber and Wilson 1986/1995: 122)

Sperber and Wilson (1986/1995: 15-16) point out that a context is a subset of the assumptions about the world (e.g. information about the immediate physical environment, the immediately preceding utterances, expectations about the future, scientific hypotheses, religious belief, anecdotal memories, general cultural assumptions, beliefs about the mental state of the speaker).

---

[8] Note that in Relevance Theory the term now used instead of "contextual effects" is "cognitive effects".

There are three types of contextual effects, as follows.

(15) Three Types of Contextual Effects
    a. Contextual implication: It is a conclusion derived from a set of premises that old and new assumptions constitute.
    b. Strengthening: It strengthens a previously held assumption.
    c. Contradiction: It displaces or erases a previously held assumption.

How do Relevance Theorists explain that relevance determines speaker's meanings: basic explicatures, higher-level explicatures, and SW-implicatures?

Basic explicatures, which constitute the truth-conditional contents of utterances, are identified according to the following procedure. First, the hearer gains access to appropriate new and old contextual assumptions stored at encyclopaedic entries in his/her memories. Second, he/she adopts these assumptions as a set of premises and then derives a conclusion. Third, this conclusion causes him/her to conduct disambiguation, reference assignment and completion of subsentential utterances. Fourth, he/she recovers an explicature of the utterance.

Consider the following example.

(16) [Context: Someone walks up and down outside the White House in America with a placard saying.]
George W. Bush is a crook. (Adapted from Katz 1972: 449)

According to Wilson (2004), the hearer viewer assigns the referent *George W. Bush* in (16) to President George W. Bush through three phases. First, the person who read the placard accesses to both new contextual assumptions, such as (17)a, and old contextual assumptions, such as (17)b-c.

(17) a. The placard related to George W. Bush is outside the White House in America.

b. The President of United States of America lives in White House in America.

c. George W. Bush is the present President of United States of America.

Second, he/she adopts these assumptions as premises and hence derives conclusion such as (18).

(18) George W. Bush in the placard is the name of the present President of United States of America.

Third, he/she assigns the target expression to *President George W. Bush*.

According to Wilson (2004), higher-level explicatures, which express the speaker's attitude towards the embedded basic explicatures that the speaker intends to communicate, are identified through two phases. First, the hearer recovers basic explicatures. Second, he/she recovers parts embedding these basic explicatures. Those parts are recovered by linguistic, paralinguistic and contextual information such as syntactic or morphological mood indicators, intonation, and facial expressions.

Consider another example.

(19) John (happily):   I love you.

In Wilson's (2004) sense, the hearer recovers higher-level explicatures from (19) through two steps. First, the hearer recovers basic explicature such as (20) from (19).

    (20)   John loves Susan.

Second, he/she recovers parts embedding basic explicature such as (20) by the speaker's intonation or facial expressions as follows.

    (21)   a. John is telling Susan that he loves her.
             b. John is telling Susan happily that he loves her.
             c. John is admitting to Susan that he loves her.
             d. John believes that he loves her.

An SW-implicature refers to a conclusion derived from a set of premises, i.e., 'an explicature' recovered from utterance and 'contextual assumptions' in the hearer's memory. Here, a set of premises and an SW-implicature are an 'implicated premise' and an 'implicated conclusion', respectively.

Consider the following example.

    (22)   Peter: Can we go out this evening?
              Mary: I have to finish my essay. (Wilson 2004)

For Wilsons, in (22) Peter derives an SW-implicature from Mary's utterance through three stages. First, Peter recovers an explicature such as (23) by assigning the referents *I* and *my* of Mary's utterance in (22) to *she* and *her*,

respectively.

(23) Mary has to finish her essay.

Second, Peter causes the word *essay* of Mary's utterance in (22) to have access to a contextual assumption such as (24) that is stored in his encyclopaedic entries.

(24) Having to finish an essay would prevent Mary from going out.
       (Wilson 2004)

Finally, Peter derives an implicated conclusion, i.e., SW-implicature, such as (25), from two implicated premises, i.e., an explicature, such as (23), and contextual assumption, such as (24).

(25) They can't go out this evening because Mary has to finish her essay.
       (Wilson 2004)

Relevance Theorists argue that the notion of relevance provides us with a solution for Grice's circle. However, relevance does not seem to be immune to the circularity: explicatures determine SW-implicatures and SW-implicatures determine explicatures. On the one hand, the gap between sentence meanings and explicatures is bridged by processes such as reference assignment. We say SW-implicatures determine explicatures because reference assignment is conducted by SW-implicatures, as we saw in (18) above. On the other hand, explicatures are adopted as implicated premises for deriving SW-implicatures (see (22) above); therefore, explicatures determine SW-implicatures.

2.4 Default Semantics

Default Semanticists (e.g. Jaszczolt 1999; H-K. Lee 2001) suggest one established level of meanings, which can be schematised as follows.

Table 2.4: Levels of Meanings Based on Default Semantics

Default Semantics	
Meanings of Word or Words	Semantic Representations

Meanings of a word or words make up an utterance. The 'semantic representation' stands for a full propositional representation. In fact, there are two views within Default Semantics: Jaszczolt (1999) and H-K. Lee (2001). Jaszczolt (1999: 211) advocates the principle of the degrees of intentions. However, H-K. Lee (2001: 35-36) postulates that semantic representations have one scale of Default-Semantic meanings on the basis of the quantity of inference, i.e., the amount of the context, for identifying each propositional form.[9] In the Default-Semantic sense, semantic representations comprise propositional forms such as what is said, explicature, GCI, PCI, and

---

[9] According to H-K. Lee (2001: 9), a notion of 'default' is based on Levinson's (2000) 'default inference'. As has been pointed out in Section 2.2., default inferences are defeasible if they are inconsistent with the context (see page 41).

SW-implicature and each form has the same nature on the ground that these representations are determined by 'the speaker's intentions in communication' or 'context'.

According to Jaszczolt (1999), who has established Default Semantics, a gap between the meaning of a word or words, which constitute an utterance, and the semantic representation is bridged by the speaker's intentions in communication. She (1999: 208-211) suggests the principle of the degrees of intentions.

> (26) The Principle of the Degrees of Intentions
>   Intentions come in various sizes, i.e., they allow for degrees. (Jaszczolt 1999: 211)

Consider the following example.

> (27) The best architect designed this church. (Jaszczolt 1999: 202)

Jaszczolt (1999: 211-212) says that (27) can have three readings such as Cases A, B, and C, according to contexts. The degrees of intentions in these three cases are as follows.

> (28) Case A > Case B > Case C
> (29) a. *Case A*. Suppose contexts in which the speaker provided the hearer with information that helps the hearer to consider Christopher Wren as an eminent architect and he/she is talking about Christopher Wren.

    b. *Case B*. Suppose contexts in which the speaker provided the hearer with information that helps the hearer to consider John Smith as an eminent architect but he/she is talking about Christopher Wren.

    c. *Case C*. Suppose contexts in which the speaker did not provide the hearer with any information about an eminent architect and the speaker is talking about whoever happened to have designed the church.

Case A is a referential use. In this case, the hearer easily assigns the referent *the best architect* in (27) to Christopher Wren. Jaszczolt points out that the speaker's intentions in a referential use are the strongest because this use is a default reading. By contrast, Case B is a referential mistake. In this case, the hearer mistakenly assigns the referent *the best architecture* in (27) not to Christopher Wren but to John Smith. According to her, in a referential mistake the prior utterance of the speaker (in her terms speech act) secures the referent. Case C is an attributive use. In this case, the speaker intends to communicate his/her intentions but he/she fails. She says that the speaker's intentions in an attributive use are the weakest.

Note that Jaszczolt does not account for how the speaker's intentions secure disambiguation and completion of subsentential utterances.

The issue of identification of semantic representations has been taken up by H-K. Lee (2001: 12), who points out that some utterances are interpreted more naturally "without the need for processing the speaker's intentions." She argues that semantic representations are identified by 'contexts' rather than the speaker's intention. She (2001: 6-7) proffers the following two types of contexts: 'the hearer's background knowledge' and 'linguistic contexts'. First, the background knowledge is obtained from the hearer's experience and takes the form of a proposition necessary to deriving an implicated conclusion. Second, linguistic context consists of grammatical (or syntactic) and semantic features. For instance, the topic-contrast particle *un/nun* in Korean is grammatical feature and whether predicates are stative or non-stative is a semantic one. So, processes such as disambiguation, reference assignment and completion of subsentential utterances are conducted by Default-Semantic contexts.

Consider another example.

> (30)　[Context: Mike is the director of a television thriller and is discussing with his assistant Susie how he wants the next scene to go.]
> Mike:　In the next scene, when the police arrive, the criminal makes a bolt for the door. (Wilson 2004)

Here, the expression *makes a bolt for the door* has ambiguities as follows.

> (31)　a.　When the police arrive, the criminal runs for the door.
> b.　When the police arrive, the criminal gets out his tool kit and constructs a door-beltbolt.

Taking H-K. Lee's (2001) point of view, we can say that Susie interprets (30) as (31)a, according to her background knowledge such as (32)a-b.

> (32)　a.　Mike who is the director of a television thriller wants to say how the next scene goes when the police arrive.
> b.　If the police arrive at the scene of offence, the criminal instantly leaves.

Here, it is notable that this background knowledge could equally be called a contextual assumption that Relevance Theorists suggest.

Consider another example. It appeared as (27) but we repeat below.

(27') [Context: The speaker provided the hearer with information that helps the hearer to consider Christopher Wren as an eminent architect. The speaker is talking about Christopher Wren.]
The best architect designed this church. (Jaszczolt 1999: 202)

Here, the hearer assigns the referent *the best architect* in (27') to Christopher Wren by her background knowledge (33), which is gained from the speaker's prior utterance.

(33) Christopher Wren is an eminent architect.

Take yet another example, where we see the case of completing a subsentential utterance.

(34) [Context: A boy has his finger wounded and cries.]
    a. Boy: Mummy, I hurt myself.

       Mother:You are not going to die.

    b. The addressee$_i$ is not going to die from the cut in his$_i$ finger.

    c. The addressee has to stop crying. (Adapted from H-K. Lee 2001: 35-36)

H-K. Lee (2001) would argue that the hearer recovers the Mother's recovery of unsaid utterances in (34)a by the hearer's background knowledge (35), and that the hearer identifies a semantic representation, i.e., what is said, such as (34)b.

(35)   A boy has his finger wounded and cries.

H-K. Lee (2001: 36) postulates that the difference among propositional forms such as what is said and PCI is not the quality of inference but the quantity of inference, and that these propositional forms have the same nature. According to her, propositional forms such as what is said and PCI, which are treated as semantic representations according to Default Semantics, are posited on the scale of Default-Semantic meanings of semantic representations on the basis of the quantity of inference, i.e., the amount of Default-Semantic context, for identifying each form. For example, (34)b-c are identified as 'what is said' of (34)a and 'a PCI' of (34)a respectively. In her terms, the amount of Default-Semantic context for identifying (34)c is bigger than one for identifying (34)b. She further argues that the quantity of inference for identifying PCIs is greater than that of identifying GCIs. GCIs are triggered by particular words, and that PCIs are recovered by particular words plus Default-Semantic contexts of the utterance. So, she says that GCIs and PCIs are posited in the following order, according to the amount of Default-Semantic context essential to the identification of each form.

(36)   GCIs < PCIs (Adapted from H-K. Lee 2001: 36)

In sum, the scale of Default-Semantic meanings can be as follows.

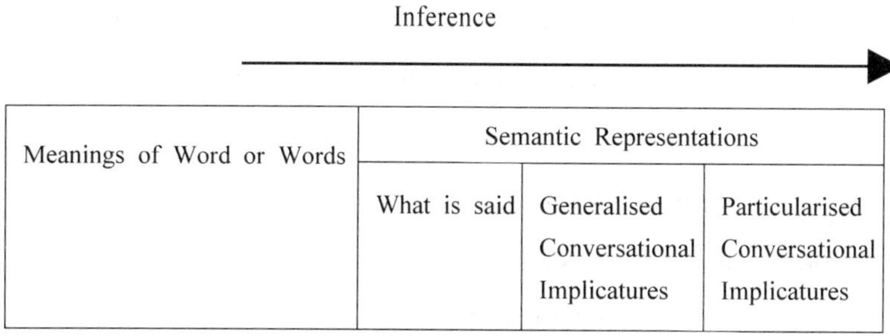

Meanings of Word or Words	Semantic Representations		
	What is said	Generalised Conversational Implicatures	Particularised Conversational Implicatures

Figure 2.1: The Scale of Default-Semantic Meanings

However, the scale in Figure 2.1 above encounters a problem which is this: linguistic contexts, i.e., semantic and syntactic features, which she treats as Default-Semantic contexts, are not inference that participate in identifying Default-Semantic meanings of semantic presentation. According to H-K. Lee (2001: 171-175), whether predicates are stative or non-stative and whether or not subjects of linked two segments are identical to each other designate 'semantic and syntactic constraints' respectively. (H-K. Lee (2001: 171, 173) labels semantic and syntactic features as "semantico-syntactic constraints".) Take the Korean conjunctive suffix *-se* for example. She (2001: 180, 2002: 862) says that *-se* has only 'causal meaning' if and only if the subjects of X and Y in the [X-*se* Y] sequence are not identical to each other. This linguistic context is not inference that plays a part in recovering semantic representation but the semantic constraint on *-se*. (See Chapter 7.)

So far we have described briefly how each of the four theories identifies propositions, and, in doing so, pointed out their theoretical weaknesses. This is to motivate the adoption of the four theoretic concepts in our discussions in this book. As we have seen, the four theories define a proposition differently: for Gricean theorists it is 'what is said', for neo-Gricean theorists 'sentence', for Relevance theorists 'explicature', and for Default Semanticists 'semantic representation'. Briefly, a 'sentence' is 'what is said' plus GCI, an 'explicature' is 'what is said' plus meaning inferred by contextual assumption, and a 'semantic representation' is 'what is said' plus meaning inferred by the hearer's background knowledge and linguistic context. The lesson we have learnt here is that Gricean and neo-Gricean theorists did not emphasise the importance of the role of context in identifying the propositions. In the following chapter we formulate our theoretical framework while stating theoretical rationales as to why four theoretic concepts are selectively borrowed.

3

Theoretical Framework

The purpose of this chapter is to explain reasons for the selective adoption of concepts, given by the four theories, Gricean theory, neo-Gricean theory, Relevance Theory, and Default Semantics, on the use of connectives, i.e., how they truth-functionally conjoin and disjoin propositions, with reference to levels of meanings. This is to set out our theoretical framework for discussions on the use of six Korean conjunctive verbal connectives, *-ko*, *-nuntey*, *-nikka*, *-se*, *-ciman*, and *-to*.

In this chapter, we explain four notions that are fundamental to our theoretical framework: propositional relations, the scope test, differences between encoded and inferred meanings, and the use of connectives.

We also present a range of propositional relations with definitions, which we examine in detail in this book.

3.1 Propositional Relation

The term **propositional relation** refers to the relationship that obtains between two adjacent propositions. This is as defined by Coherence Theorists (Hobbs 1979, 1985; Mann and Thompson 1985, 1986, 1988), who also use the terms such as coherence relation (Hobbs 1979, 1985) or relational propositions

(Mann and Thompson 1985, 1986, 1988). Consider (1).

(1) The huge rod was released at an altitude of about 6 miles. It struck with such force that it buried itself deep into the ground. (Mann and Thompson 1986: 63)

In (1), according to Mann and Thompson, the hearer infers a 'forward sequential relation' from the two (recovered) propositions since the event depicted by the first proposition, i.e., "a huge rod was released at an altitude of about 6 miles", precedes that depicted by the second proposition, i.e., "the rod buried itself deep into the ground with the force involved". Coherence theorists say that the two propositions are coherent if the hearer infers a meaning relation, or meaning relations, from the two propositions.

In Chapter 1 we pointed out that previous studies on Korean conjunctive verbal suffixes generally equate the propositional relations that obtain between the two propositions linked by a connective with the meanings of the connective. We presented there (see pages 7 and 8) a handful of labels for propositional relations that appeared in studies on the six Korean conjunctive verbal suffixes: *-ko, -nuntey, -nikka, -se, -ciman*, and *-to*. They are: (1) time, (2) condition, (3) enumeration, (4) simultaneity, (5) sequence, succession, and temporal precedence, (6) cause and reason, (7) opposition, contrast, and counter-act/event, (8) introduction, (9) background, and (10) explanation. We will challenge and discuss in detail the view that the meanings of a given connective are the propositional relations between the two propositions, but here we make the point that the inventories are not sufficient enough.

Let us elaborate the inventories. First, we will take the relations, time, condition, enumeration, simultaneity, and introduction, as they are in the literature. We will put all the names of propositional relation in capital letters from now on, and hence we will refer to them as TIME, CONDITION, ENUMERATION, SIMULTANEITY, and INTRODUCTION, respectively.

Second, following Blakemore (1987) and Carston (2002), we change the label 'sequence, succession, and temporal precedence'to FORWARD SEQUENTIAL, 'cause and reason' to CAUSAL, and 'opposition, contrast, counter-act/event' to two separate relations: CONTRAST and DENIAL OF EXPECTATION. These changes are to better represent the propositional relations involved.

Third, we discard 'background' and 'explanation'. In our view, examples for these two relation provided in the literature can be re-grouped under relations such as CAUSAL, CONTRAST, DENIAL OF EXPECTATION, TIME, INTRODUCTION, etc. Consider (2), which K-D. Lee (1980) cited as an example for the background relation, which we identify as an example for a CAUSAL.

(2) iltung-ul   hay-ss-**nuntey**,   nayil   ohwu-ey   sikyey hana
     the first rank-AC do-PST-NUNTEY tomorrow afternoon-at watch   one
     sa   cwu-ma
     buy.INF give-IM
     'You won the first prize. So, I will buy a watch for you tomorrow afternoon.' (K-D. Lee 1980: 129)

Further, consider (3), which Jeon (1989) called an example for the explanation relation, which we identify as an example for INTRODUCTION.

> (3)   wuli cip   seythakki-nun   Kumseng ceyphwum-i-**ntey**
>   *our house washing machine-TC   product-be-**NUNTEY***
>   cham thunthunha.y
>   *really strong.INF*
>   'My washing machine is the product of Kumseng and it's really good.'
>   (Jeon 1989: 128)

Fourth, we include five new propositional relations: INFERENTIAL (H-K. Lee 2001), BACKWARD INFERENTIAL (Carston 2002), REPETITION (Blakemore 1993), REFORMULATION (Blakemore 1997), and EXEMPLIFICATION (Carston 1992). The introduction of these propositional relations has been motivated by our analysis of the data, which will be presented in detail in Chapter 5.

Our inventories of propositional relations thus consist of fourteen labels: TIME, CONDITION, ENUMERATION, SIMULTANEITY, INTRODUCTION, FORWARD SEQUENTIAL, CAUSAL, CONTRAST, DENIAL OF EXPECTATION, INFERENTIAL, BACKWARD INFERENTIAL, REPETITION, REFORMULATION, and EXEMPLIFICATION. Below we provide brief descriptions of the fourteen relations with English examples. Citing English examples are to help the reader understand our point; it should not be understood that these relations are motivated by English first and then applied to Korean.

TIME refers to the propositional relation where the event communicated by the first proposition, such as (4)a, represents the temporal situation on which the communicated by the second proposition, such as (4)b, occurs, occurred, or will occur (Tsai 1985: 163).

(4) a. Mr. Kim was saying something to Mr. Kim.
     b. Mr. Choi came to Mr. Kim.

CONDITION refers to the relation where the first proposition, such as (5)a, represents a protasis and the second proposition, such as (5)b, depicts an apodosis (Jeon 1989: 93).

(5) a. It will rain tomorrow.
     b. I will write a letter to John tomorrow.

ENUMERATION is essentially the logical relation &. The truth-values of the two propositions involved are constant, regardless of the ordering of the propositions (Suh 2006: 1124).

(6) a. Tom goes to school.
     b. John goes home.

SIMULTANEITY refers to the propositional relation where events depicted by the two propositions such as (7)a-b occur at the same time (Tsai 1985: 35).

(7)   a. Tom and Bill shook hands.

       b. Tom and Bill smiled.

INTRODUCTION refers to the relation where the first proposition introduces a certain object or an event, such as (8)a, on which the speaker focuses in the second proposition, such as (8)b (K-D. Lee 1979: 123-135).

(8)   a. A person is coming from over there.

       b. He is my friend.

FORWARD SEQUENTIAL involves two sequenced events, where the event conveyed by the first proposition, such as (9)a, precedes that conveyed by the second proposition, such as (9)b (Carston 2002: 231).

(9)   a. Tom ate breakfast at t.

       b. Tom did his homework at t+n.

CAUSAL refers to the propositional relation where the event depicted by the first proposition, such as (10)a, causes the depicted by the second proposition, such as (10)b (Carston 2002: 227).

(10)   a. John hit Mary.

       b. Mary cried.

CONTRAST obtains when the two propositions, such as (11)a-b, contrast with each other (Blakemore 1987: 125-131).

(11) a. Tom is tall.

b. Bill is short.

DENIAL OF EXPECTATION refers to the propositional relation where an expectation derived from the first proposition is denied by the second proposition (Blakemore 1987: 131-141). In the examples below, (13) is the expectation derived from (12)a and denied by (12)b.

(12) a. Tom studied very hard.

b. Tom failed the entrance examination.

(13) Tom passed the entrance examination.

INFERENTIAL refers to the propositional relation where the first proposition, such as (14)a, functions as evidence for the speaker's belief that the second proposition, such as (14)b, is true (H-K. Lee 2001: 195).

(14) a. The box was crushed.

b. The box was badly packed.

BACKWARD INFERENTIAL refers to the propositional relation where the second proposition, such as (15)b, is identified as evidence for the speaker's belief that the first proposition, such as (15)a, is true (Carston 2002: 228).

(15) a. Tom fell to the bottom.

b. Tom slipped on the stairs.

Speakers do repeat themselves in a redundant manner. REPETITION obtains when the second proposition, such as (16)b, is identical with the first proposition, such as (16)a (Blakemore 1993: 116).

(16)   a. Tom read the book.

b. Tom read the book.

REFORMULATION refers to the propositional relation where the two propositions involved resemble each other, in which elaboration, specification, and/or strengthening result (Blakemore 1997: 10). Examples below are from Mann and Thompson (1988:277).

(17)   a. A well-groomed car reflects its owner.

b. The car you drive says a lot about you.

EXEMPLIFICATION refers to the propositional relation where the second proposition, such as (18)b, gives instances of the first proposition, such as (18)a (Carston 1992: 164).

(18)   a. Tom attended many educational institutes.

b. Tom attended a swimming pool and private schools for calligraphy, ice skating, and English conversation.

3.2 The Nature of the Meanings of Connectives

The question we attempt to answer in this section is whether the propositional relation between the two segments is encoded by the conjunctive verbal suffix or drawn by inference (where the conjunctive verbal suffix plays some role).

Three notions are fundamental here: truth-conditional encoding (that is, semantic in nature), non-truth-conditional encoding (that is, pragmatic in nature), and inference (that is, pragmatic in nature). That the meanings of a connective are truth-conditional means that the connective's meanings have truth-value, and the opposite can be said regarding non-truth conditional meanings of a connective. Encoded meanings of a given suffix can be defined as meanings simply carried by the connective. By contrast, inferred meanings of a given suffix can be defined as meanings drawn by the hearer's inductive background knowledge (H-K. Lee 2001, 2002).

What criteria do we use when deciding whether or not the propositional relation between the two segments is encoded by a given conjunctive verbal suffixes? Let us examine three possible answers to this question.

One is the cancellability test, taken by the three theories, Gricean theory, neo-Gricean theory, and Default Semantics. According to them, the propositional relation that obtains between the two segments linked by a given connective is defeasible by contexts if and only if it is identified as an inferred meaning of the connective. This test is mainly adopted to *and*-conjunction. Although they differ in how they explain this recovery of inferred propositional relations that *and*-conjunction involves, these three theories share the view that the three relations are inferred meanings of the connective *and*: FORWARD SEQUENTIAL, CAUSAL, and SIMULTANEITY. However, their explanations on the recovery bring problems to their own theoretical frameworks (see Section 3.2.1. for more details).

The other is the test of whether or not native speakers recognise the propositional relation that obtains between the two segments coupled by a given conjunctive verbal suffix as an encoded meaning of the suffix. This test is based on the assumption that native speakers know what encoded meanings of a give conjunctive verbal suffix mean (although in an unstructured way) and how to use them. However, it also has difficulty in establishing one more criterion for judging which one is chosen from native speakers' different intuitions on the meanings of the suffix.

Another is the scope test, conducted by Rouchota (1990). According to her, this test refers to estimating whether or not the meaning of a given connective falls within the scope of the truth-conditional connective *if ... then*. That is, the meaning of the connective falls within the scope of *if ... then* if and only if it is encoded by the connective. Consider (19).

> (19) If Susan is tall but Mary is short, Peter won't fall in love with either of them.
> (Rouchta 1990: 71)

In Rouchota's account, *but* in (19) has two encoded meanings, & and contrast meaning, i.e. "is tall" vs. "is short", because the two meanings are embedded in the antecedent of (19). In this study, we will adopt this test as a criterion of distinguishing encoded and inferred meanings of Korean conjunctive verbal suffixes on the ground that it does not have any problem differently from other two tests.

Our truth-conditional encoded meaning is identical to the conceptual meaning in Relevance theory (Carston 2002: 243; Wilson 2004). However, our non-truth-conditional encoded meaning is not identical with the procedural meaning in Relevance theory; it is essentially the conventional implicature found in Gricean and neo-Gricean theories, but with some modifications. Our inferred meaning is identical to improved non-truth-conditional inferential meaning of Default Semantics (e.g. H-K. Lee 2001). Below, we elaborate these points.

3.2.1 Truth-conditional encoded meaning

Truth-conditional encoded meanings of connectives refer to meanings of connectives that conjoin two propositions truth-conditionally and yield a single conjoined proposition. Gricean theorists, neo-Gricean theorists, Relevance Theorists, and Default Semanticists regard truth-conditional encoded meanings of connectives as 'sentence meanings', 'compositional semantic meanings', 'conceptual meanings', and 'non-inferential meanings', respectively.

We have explained in Chapter 2 'sentence meanings', 'compositional semantic meanings', and 'conceptual meanings', however only in general terms. We now provide more detailed explanations on conceptual meanings and inferential meanings below.

In their discussions of English connectives, *and*, *or*, *if*, and *before*, Relevance Theorists (e.g. Sperber and Wilson 1986, 1995; Blakemore 1987, 1989, 1992, 2002; Carston 1988, 1990, 1992, 1993, 1996, 1998, 1999, 2002; Rouchota 1990; Wilson 1998, 2004; Wilson and Sperber 1990, 1993a, 1993b, 1998; Blakemore and Carston 1999, 2005; Iten 2000, 2005; Hall 2004) treat them as truth-conditional connectives. According to them (e.g.

Sperber and Wilson 1986/1995; Wilson 2004), there are three types of conceptual meanings: lexical, logical, and encyclopaedic information, and *and* encodes only lexical and logical information. In other words, *and* does not encode encyclopaedic information, which allows the hearer an access to contextual assumptions.

In their analysis of English connectives, *and*, *but*, *therefore*, *so*, *because*, and *moreover*, Default Semanticists (e.g. H-K. Lee 2001, 2002) define inferential meaning of a given connective as a meaning that is inferred by the hearer's inductive background knowledge.

Let us first discuss truth-conditional encoded meanings of a conjunctive verbal suffix. As stated above, we take truth-conditional encoded meanings to be conceptual meanings as discussed in Relevance Theory. Our view is that the notion of conceptual meaning has more explanatory power than the other three notions put forwarded by the other three theories. We demonstrate this below.

Take *and* for example. In the literature, *and*-conjunction is found to involve, apart from the logical relation &, three inferred propositional relations: FORWARD SEQUENTIAL, CAUSAL, and SIMULTANEITY. Gricean-theoretic concept cannot explain any of the three inferred propositional relations. This is simply because GCIs are truth-conditional. Consider (20). The *and*-conjunction involves SIMULTANEITY.

(20) A thief was looking around carefully **and** stole into the house.

From (20) two propositions, such as (21)a-b, can be recovered.

(21) a. A thief looked around carefully at t.

b. A thief stole into the house at t.

The propositional relation that obtains between (21)a and (21)b can be SIMULTANEITY, because looking around carefully and stealing into the house overlaps temporally. From a Gricean theorist's point of view, *and* in (20) has two types of meanings: the 'sentence meaning *&'* and a GCI (a 'simultaneity' meaning). According to Gricean theory, *and* in (20) triggers a GCI, *during this time*, which fulfills the Maxim of Quantity, 'make your contribution as informative as is required (for the current purpose of the exchange)', of the Cooperative Principle, resulting in:

(22) [A thief was looking around carefully at t] & [during this time a thief stole into the house at t].

However, this analysis encounters a problem. It forces us to assume the existence of the truth-functionality of the GCIs. That is, the GCI of *and* in (20) contributes to the truth conditions of *and*-conjunction. This contradicts what they say: GCIs are not truth-conditional. This point has been made by other scholars (e.g. Strawson 1952: 79-82; Cohen 1971; 54-59).

From a neo-Gricean theorist's point of view, *and* in (20) has two meanings. One is a compositional semantic meaning *&*, and the other meaning *during this time*, which defeats an N-GCI, such as *then* or *as a result*. According to neo-Gricean theory, the hearer's knowledge of thievery eliminates an N-GCI, which *and* in (20) triggers, in favour of an inferred meaning *during this time*. However, this analysis raises a problem.

Levinson (1983, 2000) argues that the English connective *and* has two levels of meanings: the compositional semantic meaning & and two presemantic pragmatic meanings, i.e., N-GCIs. (Presemantic pragmatic meanings of *and* are: *then* and *as a result*.) But, the 'simultaneity' meaning of *and* in (20) does not belong to any either of the levels. This is because by definition this 'simultaneity' meaning of *and* defeats its N-GCIs, and hence it has nowhere to go.

From the Default Semanticists' standpoint, *and* in (20) has two types of meaning. One is the logical relation &. The other is the simultaneity meaning, *during this time*, which overrules the 'temporal meaning' or the 'causal meaning'. However, this analysis brings a problem to the scale of Default-Semantic meanings of connectives. According to Default Semantics, meanings of connectives are posited on a single scale according to the 'quantity' of inference, i.e., the hearer's background knowledge. H-K. Lee (2001, 2002) claims that meanings of *and* are arranged in the order of 'logical meaning', 'temporal meaning', 'causal meaning', and 'inferential meaning'on a single scale, as shown in Figure 3.1 below.

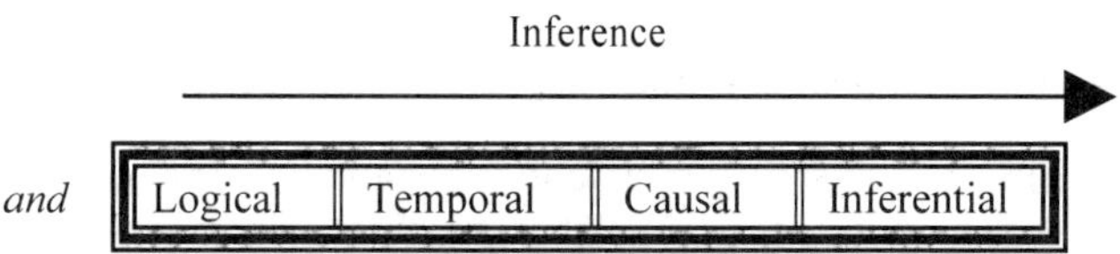

Figure 3.1: The Scale of Default-Semantic Meanings of *and*
Adopted from H-K. Lee (2001: 213)

However, the 'simultaneity' meaning of *and* in (20) cannot be posited on the scale in Figure 3.1 above because by definition this 'simultaneity' meaning discards the Default-Semantic meanings of *and*. Therefore, it is difficult to apply Default-Semantics to (20).

Within the Relevance Theoretic framework, *and* in (20) encodes only one conceptual meaning $\&$. The hearer, by accessing to contextual assumptions, such as (23), recovers time indices, t's, such as in (24), while realising that the two indices refer to the same point in time, and infers SIMULTANEITY.

(23)   Thieves make sure whether people are in the house where they try to steal.

(24)   [A thief looked around carefully at t] $\&$ [a thief stole into the house at t].

Thus, the above discussion on of 'sentence meaning', 'compositional semantic meaning', 'conceptual meaning', and 'non-inferential meaning' forces us to adopt Relevance-Theoretic term 'conceptual meaning' as our truth-conditional encoded meanings. One may say that SIMULTANEITY obtaining in *and*-conjunction is truth-conditional inferred meaning, i.e., the simultaneity meaning of the connective *and*. However, this position cannot be supported for the following two reasons. First, as discussed on pages 71 to 73 in detail, the simultaneity meaning of *and* does not have a place to go within neo-Gricean theory and Default Semantics. Second, as supported by Relevance Theory, the SIMULTANEITY is not related to $\&$ but to two indexical values t and t of the two propositions conjoined by $\&$. It is supported by Relevance Theorists.

3.2.2 Non-truth-conditional encoded meaning

Let us turn to non-truth-conditional encoded meanings of a conjunctive verbal suffix. As far as connectives are concerned, Gricean theory (e.g. Grice 1961, 1968, 1975, 1981, 1989; Gazdar 1979; Posner 1980) recognises three types of meanings: sentence meanings, i.e., truth-conditional non-cancellable, conventional implicatures, i.e., non-truth-conditional non-cancellable, and GCIs, i.e., non-truth-conditional inferred.

Notice that Gricean theory takes the conventional implicature to be an inferred meaning (Levinson 1983:127), a non-cancellable meaning that designates a speech act which comments on what is said (Grice 1975: 44). From his point of view, *so* in (25) has a conventional implicature 'explaining'.

    (25)   Barbara isn't in town. So, David isn't here. (Blakemore 1992: 136)

From (25) two propositions, such as (26)a-b are recovered.

    (26)   a. Barbara is not in town.

           b. David is not at the place of utterance.

In Grice's sense, the conventional implicture of *so* in (25) signals that (26)b is an inferential consequence of (26)a.

Incidentally, Grice does not elaborate what he means by consequence. We label 'consequence' as 'inferential consequence' following Blakemore (1987: 78-85), who divides the notion into two: the consequence based on the cause and effect relation and that based on the premise and conclusion relation. Grice's notion of consequence is defined as the latter. This is because a conventional implicature of connectives does not make any contribution to the truth conditions of segments coupled by them.

We argue that, as far as connectives are concerned, conventional implicatures are encoded. As Blakemore (1987) argues, a connective 'signals' a meaning relation between the premise and the conclusion. It is not a meaning relation that is calculated on the basis of the pragmatic principle; individual connectives carry 'instructions' on how to interpret the relations between the premises and the conclusions. She calls these instructions 'procedural meanings' encoded by connectives such as *so* in (27)B.

(27)   A: You take the first turning on the left.

B: So we don't go past the university (then). (Blakemore 1992: 139)

In her account, the procedural meaning of *so* in (27)B instructs the hearer to identify the contextualisation of the implicit utterance before *so* in (27)B and the explicit utterance after *so* in (27)B as a contextual implication. This procedural meaning is identified through three phases. First, the hearer adopts both contextual assumption, such as (28)a, recovered from A's utterance in (27) and accessible contextual assumption, like (28)b, as implicated premises and hence draws an implicated conclusion, such as (28)c.

(28)   a. A turns the car to the first left corner.

    b. If a driver turns the car to the first left corner, he/she will not pass the university.

    c. A will not pass the university.

Second, the hearer infers explicature such as (29) from the utterance linked by *so* in (27)B.

(29)   A will not pass the university.

Third, the hearer identifies the contextualisation of the utterance connected by *so* in (27)B and the implicit utterance before *so* in (27)B as a contextual implication in that (29) is the implicated conclusion of the elliptical utterance before *so* in (27)B.

It is interesting to note that neo-Gricean theory (e.g. Levinson 1983, 1995, 2000) - where three types of meanings, 'compositional semantic meanings', i.e., truth-conditional coded, 'conventional implicatures', i.e., non-truth-conditional coded, and 'N-GCIs', i.e., truth-conditional inferred, are also recognised - characterises conventional implicatures as encoded meanings, as shown in the following two notations.

"For example, conventional implicatures will be *non-cancellable* because they do not rely on defeasible assumptions about the nature of the context;"(Levinson 1983: 128)

"It should be noted, however, that in this scheme, what is *coded* by the linguistic system is the sum of what is *said* (roughly the truth-conditional content) and what is *conventionally implicated*." (Levinson 2000: 14)

Let us return to procedural meanings of connectives. Relevance Theorists (e.g. Blakemore 1992) insist that connectives encode only a unitary procedural meaning. The unitary meaning is prerequisite for constraining the interpretation of the contextualisation of the two segments coupled by a given connective such as *so*. However, this monosemy encounters counterexamples such as (30).

> (30) Tom ate the condemned meat. So he fell ill thirteen hours later.
> (Blakemore 1987: 88)

So in (30) involves CAUSAL because 'eating the condemned meat' causes 'falling ill thirteen hours later'. In Blakemore's (1987) account, *so* in (30) has something to do with inferential relation in the sense that (30) is only acceptable on the condition that the hearer assumes that anyone who ate the condemned meat would fall ill thirteen hours later. Here, we consider a notion of 'causation'.

Lacey defines causation as follows.

> "Roughly, the relation between two things when the first is necessary or sufficient or both for the occurrence of the second." (Lacey 1986: 32)

Lacey (1986: 33-34) suggests seven kinds of causes, i.e., objects, events, forces, facts, states, processes and absences. For instance, the object *the dog* in (31)a, the force *gravity* in (31)b and *the absence of oxygen* in (31)c are factors for enabling *the accident*, his falling and *his death* to occur respectively.

> (31) a. The dog caused the accident. (Lacey 1986: 33)
>
>   b. Gravity caused him to fall. (Lacey 1986: 33)
>
>   c. The absence of oxygen caused his death. (Lacey 1986: 34)

This supports the argument that *so* in (30) encodes a concept *as a result of*. In this sense, explicatures such as (32) can be recovered from (30).

> (32) [As a result of Tom's eating the condemned meat] [he fell ill thirteen hours later].

This is supported by H-K. Lee (2001: 188-193). Here, one may say that it is not necessary to reject a procedural analysis, just because an explicit paraphrase, such as "as a result of", can be provided for one of the readings of *so*. However, this poses a serious problem of constraints on the interpretation of two segments.

Thus, the above discussion on 'conventional implicature' and 'procedural meaning' forces us to adopt Gricean-theoretic and neo-Gricean-theoretic term 'conventional implicature' as our non-truth-conditional encoded meanings.[10]

---

[10] The purpose of the discussion on the two notions, 'conventional implicature' and 'procedural meaning', is to explain the rationale for adopting Gricean-theoretic and neo-Gricean-theoretic term 'conventional implicature' as our term 'non-truth-conditional encoded meaning' while raising a problem to Relevance-Theoretic term 'procedural meaning'.

3.2.3 Non-truth-conditional inferred meaning

With respect to connectives, a non-truth-conditional inferred meaning obtains when the given connective disjoins (or does not conjoin) two propositions truth-functionally. As far as connectives are concerned, Gricean theory and Default Semantics accept the existence of non-truth-conditional inferred meanings of connectives. They advocate two different types of meanings: 'GCI' (Gricean theory) and 'inferential meaning' (Default Semantics). GCIs are truth-conditional, as has been discussed in (20).

Unlike Default Semanticists who argue that there are non-truth-conditional inferred meanings of *and,* we do not accept non-truth-conditional meanings of *and*. Below, we discuss 'inferential meanings' of connectives *and* and *because.*

According to Default Semanticists (e.g. H-K. Lee 2001, 2002), the so-called 'sentence-initial *and'* such as (33)b has an inferential meaning.

(33) Sally: a. What was the first job that you had, when you got out of school.
            (Question)

     Zelda: I worked in a : um coffee em.....eh coffee manufacturing. They
            used to eh buy the coffee green, and uh- and I worked as the : eh
            billing clerk. (Answer)

     Sally: Uhhuh.
            b. **And** when was that? (Question)

     Zelda: Eh : I gradu- nineteen :- nineteen forty. (Answer)
            (Adapted from Schiffrin 1987: 146)

In (33), *and* couples a non-sentence element, i.e., the interjection *Uhhuh*, and a sentence element, i.e., an interrogative sentence. H-K. Lee (2002: 854) says that *and* marks the continuation of the speaker's action in Schiffrin's (1987: 152) terms, and that *and* in (33)b relates Sally's first question to the second question. However, Schiffrin (1987) argues that *and* in (33)b connects Zelda's first answer and Sally's second question on the basis of a notion of interactional structure, and that Sally's second question is a request for an elaboration on Zelda's first answer. Schiffrin's (1987) explication provides us with a ground for recovering the omitted utterance before *and* in (33)b. This is supported by Relevance Theorists (e.g. Blakemore and Carston 2005: 583). They argue that elliptical segments before connectives are recovered by pragmatic inferences. According to them, the propositions communicated by the previous utterance are stored as parts of contextual assumptions in the hearer's encyclopaedic entries. In their sense, in (33) the hearer gains access to propositions inferred from Zelda's first answer and recovers the missing utterance before *and*. ENUMERATION obtains between the implicit and explicit utterances coupled by *and* in (33)b. This shows that *and* in (33)b is truth-conditional. So, we do not consider 'inferential meaning' of *and*.

Let us consider inferential meaning of *because* in (34).

(34)   John loves his wife, because he comes home early. (H-K. Lee 2001: 67)

From (34) two propositions, such as (35)a-b can be recovered.

(35) a. John comes home early.

     b. John loves his wife.

The propositions (35)a-b have INFERENTIAL in that (35)a functions as evidence for the speaker's belief that (35)b is true. According to H-K. Lee (2001), *because* in (34) has one Default-Semantic meaning: 'inferential meaning' in that the higher-order semantic representation such as (36) is recovered from (34).

(36) The speaker believes that John loves his wife, because John comes home early. (H-K. Lee 2001: 68)

However, the non-truth conditional semantic representation (36) does not make the meaning of *because* in (34) clear. Nevertheless, the representation implicates that the notion of 'a causal relation in a belief world' has something to do with a notion of 'an evidence for the speaker's belief'. That is to say, the utterance after *because* in (34) is identified as an evidence for the utterance before *because*, whose content is the speaker's belief. This means that the inferential meaning of *because* in (34) equates to INFERENTIAL that obtains between two disjoined utterances. Relevance Theorists identify the INFEREITAL as an inferred contextual implication.

If 'inferential meaning' of *because* in (34) is an inferred contextual implication, how are the two notions of 'evidence' and 'belief' defined within Relevance Theory? First, we introduce the Relevance-Theoretic definition of 'belief'. Sperber and Wilson (1986/1995: 15-16) consider beliefs as constituents of contexts and argue that a context is a subset of the assumptions about the world (e.g. information about the immediate physical environment, the immediately preceding utterances, expectations about the future, scientific hypothesis, 'religious belief', anecdotal memories, general cultural assumptions, 'beliefs about the mental state of the speaker'). This suggests that Relevance-Theoretic notion of belief is identified as 'contextual assumption'. Second, we introduce the Relevance-Theoretic definition of 'evidence'. Blakemore (1987: 81) considers 'evidence' as 'premise'. According to Wilson (2004), a notion of premise consists of two types of assumptions: explicature and contextual assumption. Blakemore cites (37) for explaining a notion of evidence on the basis of Relevance Theory.

(37) a. Barbara isn't in town.

   b. David isn't here. (Blakemore 1992: 136)

In Blakemore's (1992: 36) account, an assumption, i.e., explicature, recovered from (37)b is identified as the implicated conclusion of (37)a if and only if (37)a "is relevant as evidence for the claim in" (37)b.

In Default-Semantic sense the 'inferential meaning' of *because* in (34) is that 'loving his wife' is the result of the inference, as seen in (38).

(38) The conclusion that John loves his wife *is the result of* the inference from two premises, i.e., *if a husband goes home early, he loves his wife* and *John comes home early*.

Furthermore, the meaning of *because* in (34) does not fall within the scope of the truth-conditional connective *if ... then* in (39).

(39) **If** ..., **then** John and his wife will live happily.

That is to say, this meaning is not embedded in the antecedent of (39). Therefore, we argue that there are non-truth-conditional inferred meanings of *because*.

3.3 The Use of Connectives

The question we try to answer in this section is what the use of connectives is.

The term **use** refers to whether the meanings of a given connective conjoin or disjoin (or do not conjoin) the propositions, which are recovered from two segments coupled by the connective, truth-conditionally. Two notions are important here: truth-functionally conjoining and truth-functionally disjoining. The use of connectives shows that the meanings of a word or words, which make up an utterance, do not necessarily play a part in the utterance's conveying a proposition.

Our truth-functionally conjoining is identical with the truth-functionally conjoining in the Relevance Theory (Carston 2002: 243 Blakemore and Carston 2005: 576-583). Relevance Theorists do not use the term disjoining. However, we choose this term as an antonym of conjoining, for expository convenience. We elaborate these two notions below.

It is a truism that in logical semantics only logical connectives conjoin propositions truth-functionally. However, in linguistic semantics, which Relevance Theorists (Carston 2002: 243, Wilson 2004) accept, non-logical connectives (e.g. *after, before, when*) also conjoin propositions truth-functionally, resulting in two types of conjoining: (1) two propositions truth-functionally conjoined by a logical connective, (2) two propositions truth-functionally conjoined by a non-logical connective. The two types vary depending on the calculus of a single conjoined truth-conditional proposition.

The truth-value of a single conjoined proposition, which logical connectives form, depends on the truth-values of two propositions and truth-tables of the connectives. The truth-values of two propositions rely on whether or not a fact or an event, which the propositions convey, subsists in the world. Consider the following example.

(40)   Bill's hobby is listening to music **and** Tom's hobby is watching movies.

From (40) two propositions, such as (41)a-b, can be recovered.

(41)   a. Bill's hobby is listening to music.
       b. Tom's hobby is watching movies.

The propositional relation that obtains between (41)a and (41)b is ENUMERATION, i.e., the logical relation &. This is because the truth-value of oneconjoined truth-conditional proposition (42)a is identical to that of (42)b where (41)a-b are reversed.

> (41) a. [Bill's hobby is listening to music] & [Tom's hobby is watching
>   movies].
>
> b. [Tom's hobby is watching movies] & [Bill's hobby is listening to
>   music].

And in (40) has a truth-conditional encoded meaning &. This meaning is identified as a logical connective. The two-valued calculus of (42)a-b relies on the truth value of (41)a, that of (41)b, and the following truth-table.

Table 3.1: Truth-Table for &

p q	p & q
T T	T
T F	F
F T	F
F F	F

(*P* and *q* refer to two propositions. Further, T and F stand for 'true' and 'false' respectively.) (Lyons 1977: 144)

If (41)a and (41)b are true, (42)a and (42)b are true under the interpretation of *p* & *q*, for example.

Let us turn into non-logical connectives. The truth-value of a single conjoined truth-conditional proposition, which a given non-logical connective constitutes, depends on whether or not the meanings of the connective affect a fact or an event, which two conjoined propositions convey, causally or temporally. Consider the following example.

> (43) Tom failed the entrance examination **because** he didn't solve many problems.

From (43) two proposition, such as (44)a-b, can be recovered.

> (44) a. Tom did not solve many problems.
>
> b. Tom failed the entrance examination.

The propositional relation that obtains between (44)a and (44)b is CAUSAL in that not solving many problems causes failing the entrance examination. *Because* in (43) has a truth-conditional encoded meaning *as a result of*. This is identified as a non-logical connective. The causal meaning *as a result of* of *because* in (43) truth-functionally conjoins two propositions (44)a-b and makes up a single conjoined truth-conditional proposition, such as (45).

> (45) [As a result of Tom's not solving many problems] [Tom failed the entrance examination].

The two-valued calculus of (45) depends on whether or not the meaning *as a result of* gives a rise to two events depicted by (44)a-b. If Tom's not solving many problems is the cause of his failing the entrance examination, (45) is true. On the contrary, if Tom's failing the entrance examination is caused by his not sitting for the examination, (45) is false.

Finally, let us take up truth-functionally disjoining. Our definition of truth-functionally disjoining is that the meanings of a given connective do not conjoin two propositions, which are recovered from segments linked by the connective, truth-functionally. Consider the following example.

(46)   Tom is thirteen, **because** he is my brother's classmate.

From (46) two propositions, such (47)a-b can be recovered.

(47)   a. Tom is a classmate of the speaker's brother.
       b. Tom is thirteen years old.

The propositional relation that obtains between (47)a and (47)b is INFERENTIAL on the ground that (47)a functions as evidence for the speaker's belief that (47)b is true. *Because* in (46) has a non-truth-conditional inferred meaning that occurs when INFERENTIAL obtains between (47)a and (47)b. The non-truth-conditional inferred meaning of *because* in (46) disjoins (47)a and (47)b and hence does not form a proposition, which (46) including *because* expresses.

4
The Data

The purpose of this chapter is twofold. One is to specify data, i.e., tokens of six Korean conjunctive verbal suffixes, *-ko*, *-nuntey*, *-nikka*, *-se*, *-ciman*, and *-to*. The other is to give reasons for taking up only the [X-target suffix Y] sequence.

4.1 Acquisition of Data

The data were collected in Canberra from the 1st of February to the 10th August in 2003. Participants in the data collection were set up in pairs. Each conversation was recorded for 30 minutes. Participants were Korean students who were undertaking undergraduate courses or postgraduate courses at an Australian university. They were members of groups and/or the Korean Church and/or Korean student meetings, one or more of which we all belonged to. Their ages range from 18 to 27.

We took the following measures in order to protect the participants' privacy. First, we did not deal with the topics that would easily infringe on the participants' privacy according to their cultural and social customs. We adopted the topics 'My Excursion', 'When I Was a Primary School Student' and 'My Hobby' as topics of conversations. Second, we did not identify the participants when their data were exploited but rather used initials for them in the book in order to preserve their anonymity.

The recording was done through in four stages. The first step was to provide the participants with an information sheet and the following was outlined:

(i) a brief description of my Ph. D. study; (ii) details about how I will would properly provide explication; (iii) that participants can could withdraw recording voluntarily (iv) the importance of the Human Research Ethics Committee (HREC); (v) that this study was reviewed and approved by HREC for an ethical clearance.

The second step was to ask the participants to sign the consent form, if they had read and understood the information sheet and agreed to allow me to record their conversations. The third step was to give the participants the information sheet and keep the consent form. The fourth step was to record the participants' conversations. After starting the tape recorder, I left the place in which the recording was conducted and came back half an hour later.

4.2 Data Transcription

The source of data for the book was 360 minutes of audio-taped natural conversations in order to revise functions of the above target verbal suffixes from the perspective of spoken language.

We use three symbols *[ ]*,→, and *( )* (see page xviii). Furthermore, we adopt bold-faces in order to highlight expressions in question.

The data transcripts consist of the following three parts: the top line, which is the romanised utterance following the Yale system (see page xx); the second line containing the italicised morpheme-by-morpheme gloss (see page xix); and the third line providing the free translation, as follows.

(1) (HY & NY From 'When I Was a Primary School Student')
   [Context: HY is telling NY about the types of institute she attended in her
   primary school days.]

HY: →   hakwen   toykey manhi tany-ess-**nuntey**
          *educational institute very   much attend-PST-**NUNTEY***
          'I attended lots of educational institutes.'
          seyey hakwen-twu   tani-kwu
          school for calligraphy-also attend-KO
          'I attended private schools for calligraphy. And.'

NY: um
       'Yeah'

HY: sukheyithu-twu tani-kwu panghak ttay [swuyengcang]-twu
       skate-also   attend-KO holidays time swimming pool-also

NY: [a na-twu]
                              oh I-also
       'Me also.'

HY: tani-kwu
       attend-KO
       'I attended a private school of ice skating. And, in the holidays
       I attended a swimming pool.'

NY: e

'Yeah.'

HY: tto   swuyengcang-ilang

again swimming pool-and

yenge hoyhwa hakwen   tani-kwu

private school for English conversation attend-KO

'And I attended swimming pools and private schools for English conversation.'

4.3 Distributions of Korean Conjunctive Verbal Suffixes

Below, we explain the distributions of tokens of Korean conjunctive verbal suffixes, *-ko*, *-nuntey*, *-nikka*, *-se*, *-ciman*, and *-to*, which are obtained from the 360 minutes of audio-taped natural conversations. The frequencies of tokens of the six suffixes are as follows.

Table 4.1: Frequencies of Tokens of Korean Conjunctive Verbal Suffixes

Suffixes	Frequencies
-ko	1,864 Tokens (55.26%)
-nuntey	840 Tokens (24.90%)
-nikka	380 Tokens (9.13%)
-se	272 Tokens (8.06%)
-ciman	55 Tokens (1.63%)
-to	34 Tokens (1.01%)
Total	3,373 Tokens (100.00%)

4.3.1 Tokens of *-ko*

As shown in Table 4.1 above, there are 1,864 tokens of conjunctive verbal suffix *-ko* in the data. In actual conversations, the vowel *o* in *-ko* is generally changed into the vowel *wu* (Martin 1992: 41). In the book, we adopt *-ko* as the representative form of the two allomorphs, as is the case with in grammar books.

Tokens of *-ko* can be divided into three groups as follows.

(i)   Group (I)

The [X-*ko*Y] sequence (X refers to a segment whose predicate is a non-finite form and Y indicates a segment whose predicate is non-finite or finite);

(ii)   Group (II)

The [X'-*ko issta/nata/malta/siphehata/siphta*] segment;

(iii)   Group (III)

The [X"-*ko*] clause without any segment after *-ko*

Table 4.2: Frequencies of Tokens of *-ko*

Groups		Frequencies
Group (I)		1,156 Tokens (62.02%)
Group (II)	-*ko issta*	52 Tokens (2.79%)
	-*ko nata*	9 Tokens (0.48%)
	-*ko malta*	3 Tokens (0.27%)
	-*ko siphehata*	5 Tokens (0.16%)
	-*ko siphta*	36 Tokens (1.93%)
Group (III)		603 Tokens (32.35%)
Total		1,864 Tokens (100.00%)

Group (I) is the [X-*ko* Y] sequence, in which four kinds of linguistic forms, i.e., main verb, main adjective, the copula *-ita* 'be', and the [main verb-*ko* auxiliary verb/adjective] construction, make up predicates of X and Y. On the one hand, main verbs (e.g. *kata* 'go', etc.), main adjectives (e.g. *caymiissta* 'interesting', etc.) and the copula *-ita* 'be' function as one predicate without help of other verbs and adjectives (Sohn 1994: 221-223). On the other hand, the [main verb-*ko* auxiliary verb/adjective] construction incorporates the [main verb-*ko* *issta/nata/malta/shiphehata/siphta*] construction of Group (II) as a subclass of it.

Consider the following example.

(2)   (HY & JS From 'When I Was a Primary School Student')

JS: ku sensayng-nim kiek   **na-ko**   ceki ohaknyen

        that teacher-HT   memory **come into one's mind-*KO*** *uh fifth grade*

        sensayng-nim-to toykey manhi   kiek   **na**

        teacher-HT-also very   frequently memory **come into one's mind**.*INF*

        'That teacher comes into my mind and I think my class teacher on the fifth grade very often.'

In (2), the main verb *na-* 'come into one's mind' before *-ko* and the main verb *na* 'come into one's mind' after *-ko* are identified as predicates of X and Y in the [X-*ko* Y] sequence, respectively.

Consider another example.

(3)   (SH & YH From 'When I Was a Primary School Student')

YH: sensayng-nim-to toykey **coh**-ass-**ko**   ay-tul-to   toykey **coh**-a

      *teacher-HT-also very   **good**-PST-**KO*** *child-PL-also very   **good**-INF*

'My class teacher and classmates were very good.'

In (3), the main adjective *coh-* 'is good' before *-ko* and the main adjective *coh-* 'is good' at the end are treated as predicates of X and Y in the [X-*ko* Y] sequence, respectively.

Consider one more example.

(4)   (HY & JS From 'My Hobby')

HY: yeki.se-twu manhi   **ha-kwu** hankwuk-eyse-twu maynal
      *here.at-also very often **do-KO**   Korea-at-also   every day*
      syophingha-nun   ke.y   na-uy chwimi-**y**-ess-ci
      *do the shopping-MD thing.NM I-GN hobby-**be**-PST-SUP*
      'Here I enjoy shopping and in Korea it was my hobby.'

In (4), the main verb *ha-* 'do' before *-ko* and the copula *-y-* 'be' after *-ko* are considered as predicate words of X and Y in the [X-*ko* Y] sequence, respectively.[11]

Group (II) is the [X'-*ko issta/nata/malta/siphehata/siphta*] segment, in which *issta, nata, malta* and *siphehata* are auxiliary verbs and *siphta* is an auxiliary adjective. It is possible for a token, which belongs to this group, to form the predicate of X. It is part of Korean grammar that a main verb constitutes a predicate in combination with an auxiliary verb/adjective that follows the suffix *-ko* (Martin et al. 1967: 133; Martin 1992: 226-228, 259;

---

[11] The stem vowel *i* of the copula *-ita* can be changed into *y* when the past tense suffix *-ess* is subsequent to this stem (Martin 1992: 217).

K-D. Lee 1993: 475-479; Sohn 1994: 212, 221-223, 332-333, 364-367). Let us consider some examples. First, in (5) *-ko iss-* indicates the progressive aspect, i.e., be doing, of the main verb *chyetapo-* 'look up'.

(5)   (HY & NY From 'When I Was a Primary School Student')

NY: kulayse kyeysok   tta.n   tey-man   menghani

     so   continuously different.MD place-only blankly

     chyetapo-ko iss-ess-ta

     ***look up-KO ISSTA**-PST-DC*

     'So, I was blankly looking up only other place.'

Second, in (6) *-ko na-* designates the transitional aspect, i.e., just did, come from doing, of the main verb *ha-* 'do'.

(6)   (HY & NY From 'When I Was a Primary School Student')

     [Context: NY is telling HY about an experience when her class played a *phikwu* 'a ball game that Korean children enjoy' match against another class in her primary school days.]

NY: wenlay   pan tayhang mwe **ha-kwu na**-myen ku pan-ilang

     *originally class rivalry what **do-KO NATA**-if   that class-with*

     sai-ka   nappacy-e

     relationship-NM get worse-INF

     'If my class played a *phikwu* match against other class, my class got into bad terms with that class.'

Third, in (7) *-ko mal-* indicates the terminative aspect, i.e., finish doing, of the main verb *ile-* 'say like this'.

(7) (HY & NY From 'When I Was a Primary School Student')
     [Context: HY is telling NY about an experience when HY prepared for a
     costume procession in her primary school days. HY explained that her
     class teacher broke her classmate's wooden sword.]

HY: a   ppwuleci-ney
             oh be broken-FML
             'Oh, it's broken.'

   →   **ile-kwu mal**-ass-nuntey   toykey
             say like this-KO MALTA-PST-NUNTEY *very*
             pwulssanghay-ss-e
             pitiful-PST-INF
             'He just said like this. He looked very pitiful.'

Fourth, in (8) *-ko ship-* designates the desiderative mood, i.e., want to do, of
the main verb *cwu-* 'give'.

(8) (HY & NY From 'My Hobby')
     [Context: HY is telling NY about hobbies that HY wants in her future. HY
     explained that HY wanted to make something like bags and pencil cases
     for her future baby.]

HY: nay-ka mantul-ese nay-ka ayki-hanthey **cwu-kwu siph**-e
     I-NM   make-SE   I-NM   baby-to   ***give-KO SIPHTA-INF***
     'I want to give them to my baby after making them.'

Group (III) is the [X"-*ko*] clause in which the segment after -*ko* does not
exist. First, the speaker deliberately does not articulate the segment after -*ko*.
For example, in (9) DS is telling HK that C is one of pastors of the church DS

attends instead of not uttering the segment after *-ko*.

(9)   (DS & HK From 'My Excursion')

DS: →   yuni chechi   kkuthna-**ko**

        *Uniting Church end-**KO***

        'After the worship of Uniting Church.'

        C al-ci

          know-SUP

        'You know C, aren't you?'

        C C ku   maynnal aph-eyse selkyoha-si-nun pwun

          that every day front-at   preach-SH-MD esteemed person

        iss-e

        exist-INF

        'C is a pastor of Uniting Church.'

Second, the speaker does not articulate the segment after *-ko* because he/she is interrupted by the other speech participant. For instance, in (10) JS does not utter the segment after *-ko* in order to answer the other speech participant HY's question.

(10)   (HY & JS From 'My Excursion')

        [Context: JS is telling HY about an experience when he visited a certain death camp that was built by Nazis. JS explained that he met an old guide who was in the death camp in World War II, and that the guide's older sister was executed.]

JS: →   palo ceki chongsaltangha-**ko**

*right there be excecuted-**KO***

'She was executed over there and.'

HY: po-nun aph-eyse

see-MD front-at

'In front of him?'

JS: e

'Yes.'

4.3.2 Tokens of *-nuntey*

There are 840 tokens of conjunctive verbal suffixe *-nuntey*, as shown in Table 4.1 above. The suffix *-nuntey* alternates with *-ntey* and *-untey* and the selection of each suffix is made on the following conditions. First, *-nuntey* follows non-finite forms of verbs, as follows (Suh et al. 2005: 413).

(11) a. *ka-ta* 'go' + *-nuntey* → *ka-nuntey*

   b. *mek-ta* 'eat' + *-nuntey* → *mek-nuntey*

   c. *iss-ta* 'exist' + *-nuntey* → *iss-nuntey*

Second, *-ntey* follow non-finite forms of the copula *-ita* 'be' and adjectives whose stems end in a vowel, as follows (Suh et al. 2005: 332).

(12) a. *-i-ta* 'be' + *-ntey* → *-i-ntey*

   b. *ssa-ta* 'cheap' + *-ntey* → *ssa-ntey*

Third, *-untey* follows non-finite forms of adjectives whose stems end in a consonant, as follows (Suh et al. 2005: 332).

(13) *kem-ta* 'black' + *-untey* → *kem-untey*

In the book, we adopt *-nuntey* as the representative form of the above three allomorphs. Tokens of *-nuntey* can be classified into the following two groups.

Table 4.3: Frequencies of Tokens of *-nuntey*

Groups	Frequencies
Group (I)	503 Tokens (59.88%)
Group (II)	337 Tokens (40.12%)
Total	840 Tokens (100.00%)

Group (I) is the [X-*nuntey* Y] sequence, where X refers to a segment whose predicate is a non-finite form and Y indicates a segment whose predicate is non-finite or finite.

Consider the following example.

(14) (HY & NY From 'My Hobby')

[Context: HY and NY are talking about Korean translations of foreign novels. NY is telling HY that she likes the detective stories English novelist Agatha Christie wrote, and that she has great difficulty in memorising characters of those novels because each character is named in the English style.]

NY: kulayse nayyong-un ta **a-nuntey**   ilum-un kiek-ul   mos

*so   content-TC all **know-NUNTEY** name-TC memory-AC cannot*

ha.y

do.INF

'So, I completely know contents of those novels but I cannot remember characters' names.'

In (14) the first segment, where the predicate, i.e. *a-* 'know', is non-finite and the second segment, where the predicate, i.e., *ha.y* 'do', is finite, constitute the [X-*nuntey* Y] sequence.

Group (II) is the [X'-*nuntey*] clause where the segment after -*nuntey* does not exist. First, the speaker deliberately does not articulate the segment after -*nuntey*. For example, in (15) NY does not fully utter the segment after -*nuntey*. Instead, NY tells HY that she learned fine arts.

(15) (HY & NY From 'When I Was a Primary School Student')
      [Context: HY and NY are talking about private schools they attended in their school days.]

HY: phiano hakwen-twu tani-kwu   phullwus-twu
            school for piano-also attend-KO flute-also
            'I attended music schools for piano and flute.'
            phullwus-un cwunghakkyo ttay hay-ss-na
            flute-TC   middle school time do-PST-Q
            'Did I learn flute in my middle school days?'

NY: na cwunghakkyo ttay
            I middle school time
            'When I was a middle school student.'

HY: um taycheylo manhi manhi tani-n   ke   kath-ay
            yeah generally much much attend-PST-MD fact same-INF
            'I think I attended many private schools in general.'

NY: um   na-nun thay[kwento   tani-kwu]

yeah I-TC   Korean art of bare-handed self-defence attend-KO

'I attended a *Thaykwento* 'Korean art of bare-handed

self-defence' hall, and ... '

HY: [thaykwento   tani-kwu]

Korean art of bare-handed self-defense attend-KO

'I attended a *Thaykwento* 'Korean art of bare-handed

self-defence' hall. And.'

NY: →   ku   taum-ey seyey-twu   tany-ess-**nuntey**

*that next-at   calligraphy-also attend-PST-**NUNTEY***

seyey hakwen   nay-ka cin(cca)

calligraphy institute I-NM   really

'And then, I also attended a school for calligraphy ... '

a   miswul hakwen-twu tany-ess-ta

oh fine art school-also   attend-PST-DC

'Oh, I also attended fine art schools.'

Second, the speaker does not articulate the segment after *-nuntey* because he/she is interrupted by the other speech participant. For instance, in (16) HY breaks in when NY tries to utter the segment after *-nuntey* and causes NY not to articulate the segment Y.

(16) (HY & NY From 'When I Was a Primary School Student')

      [Context: NY is telling HY about an event that NY experienced when she attended educational institutes in her primary school days.]

NY: ku ttay solcikhi kule-n   hakwen mak

      that time frankly be like that-MD institute much

      tany-ess-c.an.h.a

      attend-PST-NOM.not.do.INF

      'We attended fine art classes very much.'

      seyey hakwen-itun miswul hakwen-itun

      calligraphy institute-or fine art school-or

      tany-ess-nuntey pyello towum-un an

      attend-PST-NUNTEY particularly aid-TC not

      toy-n   kes kath-ay

      become-MD fact same-INF

      'I attended schools for calligraphy and fine art schools, but they

      weren't very useful to me.'

HY → na-nun coh-**untey**

      *I-TC good-**NUNTEY***

      'They were useful to me (Lit., They were good to me).'

NY: na coh-ass-nuntey an kuli-nikka tasi tto

      I good-PST-NUNTEY not draw-NIKKA again again

      kuleh-key toy-te-la

      be like that-AD become-RT-DC

      'I did quite well in fine art and calligraphy when I attended

      those schools. But, I didn't after I left them.'

      kulaytwu se(yey)

      nevertheless calligraphy

      'Nevertheless, calligraphy.'

HY: kulentey kulaytwu hak(kyo) hankwuk-eyse hakkyo

      by the way nevertheless school Korea-at school

      tani-myen miswul sikan-ey seyey-twu mak iss-kwu

      attend-if fine art class-at calligraphy-also much exist-KO

'By the way, if you attend a primary school in Korean, you can learn calligraphy at fine art classes.'

4.3.3 Tokens of *-nikka*

As shown in Table 4.1 above, there are 308 tokens of suffixes *-nikka*. The suffix *-nikka* alternates with *-unikka* and the selection of each suffix is made on the following conditions. First, *-nikka* follows non-finite forms of the copula *-ita* 'be' and verbs and adjective whose stems end with a vowel, as follows (Suh, et al. 2005: 418).

    (17) a. *-i-ta* 'be' + *-nikka* → *-i-nikka*

          b. *o-ta* 'come' + *-nikka* → *o-nikka*

          c. *ttattusha-ta* 'warm' + *-nikka* → *ttattusha-nikka*

Second, *-unikka* follows non-finite forms of verbs and adjectives whose stems end with a consonant, as follows (Suh et al. 2005: 1338).

    (18) a. *mek-ta* 'eat' + *-unikka* → *mek-unikka*

          b. *coh-ta* 'good' + *-unikka* → *coh-unikka*

In the book, we adopt *-nikka* as the representative form of the above two allomorphs. Tokens of *-nikka* can be divided into two groups, as follows.

Table 4.4: Frequencies of Tokens of *-nikka*

Groups	Frequencies
Group (I)	234 Tokens (75.97%)
Group (II)	74 Tokens (24.03%)
Total	308 Tokens (100.00%)

Group (I) is the [X-*nikka* Y] sequence; X refers to a segment whose predicate is a non-finite form and Y indicates a segment whose predicate is non-finite or finite. It is notable that there are 42 tokens, in which the order of X-*nikka* and Y is reversed.[12]

Consider the following example.

(19) (SH & YH From 'My Hobby')

[Context: SH is explaining why many people enjoy playing squash.]

YH: **cohaha-nikka ha**-nun ke.ci

***like-NIKKA   do**-MD fact.be.SUP*

'Because they like it, they do it.'

In (19), two segments *cohaha*- 'like' and *ha*- 'do' are both non-finite and constitute the [X-*nikka* Y] sequence.

Consider another example.

(20) (DS & HK From 'My Excursion')

[Context: DS is telling about a movie that he saw yesterday.]

DS: ttak   **kkuthna-kwu na-nikka** sey   si   pan-**i-ya**

*exactly **end-KO NATA-NIKKA** three o'clock half-**be-INF***

'When the movie ended, it was half past 3 o'clock.'

In (20), *kkuthna-ko na*- 'ended', which is non-finite, and *-i-ya* 'is', which is finite, make up the [X-*nikka* Y] sequence.

---

[12] H-J. Lee and C-H. Lee (1999: 124; 2001: 261-262) suggest that in the [Y X-*nikka*] sequence, X is read as a cause for Y or as an evidence for the belief in Y.

Consider another example.

(21)   (SH & YH From 'My Excursion')

[Context: SH and YH are talking about how students and teachers arrived at the excursions. YH is telling SH how most teachers went to the excursions.]

YH: caki cha tha-ko   **o-ci**

own car ride-KO ***come-SUP***

'They went there by their car.'

→   kuke.y   te   **phyenha-nikka**

that.NM more ***convenient-NIKKA***

'Because that was more convenient.'

In (21), the convenience of going by car, which is communicated by Y, is a cause for most teachers' going to the excursions by their car, which is communicated by X.

Group (II) is the [X'-*nikka*] clause where there is no segment Y. First, the speaker deliberately does not articulate the segment Y after -*nikka*. For instance, in (22) YH is telling SH that there is one story related to Kwachen in his middle school days instead of not uttering the segment after -*nikka*.

(22)   (SH & YH From 'My Excursion')

[Context: SH and YH are talking about excursions that they went on in their middle school days. YH explained that Kwachen was mainly adopted as a destination for excursions in that it was not far from his middle school.]

YH: →   mwe Kwachen-un kakkawu-**nikka**

*what   -TC near-**NIKKA***

'Because Kwachen was near to my school.'

kuntey   cwunghakkyo-ttay Kwachen ha-myen

by the way middle school-time   say-if

sayngkakna-nun   ke.y   hana iss-ci

come to one's mind-MD fact.NM one   exist-SUP

'By the way, if I hear the place Kwachen, one event of my middle school days comes to mind.'

Second, the speaker does not articulate the segment Y after *-nikka* because he/she is interrupted by the other speech participant. For example, in (23) SH does not utter the segment after *-nikka* in order to agree with YH that physical education was taught by his/her class teacher rather then by specialised teachers such as music teachers teaching music.

(23) (SH & YH From 'When I Was a Primary School Student')

[Context: SH and YH are talking about courses they joined in a primary school. YH is telling SH that most courses were conducted by class teachers but only two courses - music and the fine arts - were taught by teachers who had majored in them respectively. SH is pointing out that music and the fine arts are ...]

SH: →   supheysephikha-**nikka**

*specific-**NIKKA***

'Because it was specialised.'

YH: e   supheysephikha-kwu

yeah specific-KO

'Yeah. It was specialised and.'

cheyyuk-twu   sensayng-nim-i hay-ss-e

physical education-also teacher-HT-NM do-PST-INF

kunayng

as it is

'Physical education was conducted by class teachers.'

SH: e   cheyyuk-to   sensayng-nim hay-ss-e

yeah physical education-also teacher-HT   do-PST-INF

'Yeah. Class teachers taught physical education.'

4.3.4 Tokens of *-se*

There are 272 tokens of conjunctive verbal suffixes *-se*, as shown in Table 4.1 above. The suffix *-se* alternates with *-ase*, *-ese* and *-y(e)se* and the choice of each suffix is made on the following conditions. First, *-se* follows non-finite forms of verbs and adjectives whose stems end with a vowel, except for the verb *hata* 'do' and *-hata* that combines with verbal and adjectival nouns, as follows (Suh et al. 2005: 978).

(24) a. *ka-ta* 'go' + *-se* → *ga-se*

b. *pissa-ta* 'expensive' + *se* → *pissa-se*

Second, *-ase* follows non-finite forms of verbs and adjectives, whose last stem vowels are *a* and *o*, which end in one or more consonants, as follows (Suh et al. 2005: 1130).

(25) a. *cak-ta* 'small' + *-ase*→ *cak-ase*

b. *o-ta* 'come' + *-ase* → *w-ase*

Third, *-ese* follows non-finite forms of the copula *-ita* 'be' and verbs and adjectives whose last stem vowels are *e, ay, oy, wu, wi, u, uy* and *i* except for *a, o* and *ye*, as follows (Suh et al. 2005: 1180). Here, the last stem vowel *i* is selectively changed into the vowel *y* when the suffix *-ese* follows non-finite forms of verbs whose stems end with the vowel *i* (Martin 1992: 465).

(26)   a. *-ita* 'be' + *-ese* → *i-ese*

   b. *pel-ta* 'earn' + *-ese* → *pel-ese*

   c. *may-ta* 'bind' + *-ese* → *may-ese*

   d. *toy-ta* 'become' + *-ese* → *toy-ese*

   e. *twu-ta* 'put' + *-ese* → *twu-ese*

   f. *ttwi-ta* 'run' + *-ese* → *ttwi-ese*

   g. *hulu-ta* 'flow' + *-ese* → *hull-ese*

   h. *kil-ta* 'long' + *-ese* → *kil-ese*

   i. *kitali-ta* 'wait' + *ese* → *kitali-ese* or *kitaly-ese*

Fourth, *-y(e)se* follows non-finite forms of the verb *hata* 'do' or *-hata* that combines with verbal and adjectival nouns, as follows (Suh et al. 2005: 1857-1859):

(27)   a. *ha-ta* 'do' + *-y(e)se* → *ha-y(e)se*

   b. *kongpwu-ha-ta* 'study' + *-y(e)se* → *kongpwu-ha-y(e)se*

   c. *kenkang-ha-ta* 'healthy' + *-y(e)se* → *kenkang-ha-y(e)se*

In the book, we adopt *-se* as the representative form of the above four allomorphs. Tokens of *-se* can be divided into two groups as follows.

Table 4.5: Frequencies of Tokens of *-se*

Groups	Frequencies
Group (I)	230 Tokens (84.56%)
Group (II)	42 Tokens (15.44%)
Total	272 Tokens (100.00%)

Group (I) is the [X-*se* Y] sequence; X refers to a segment whose predicate is a non-finite form and Y indicates a segment whose predicate is non-finite or finite.

Consider the following example.

(28) (SH & YH From 'My Excursion')
[Context: YH is telling SH about how he went on excursions in his school days.]

YH: kwankwang pesu **pilly-ese** kathi   **ka-ci**
sightseeing bus   rent-SE together go-SUP
'After school authorities rented sightseeing buses, we went to excursions by bus.'

In (28) two segments *kwankwang pesu pilly-* 'rent sightseeing buses', whose predicate is non-finite, and *kathi ka-ci* 'go together', whose predicate is finite, constitute the [X-*se* Y] sequence.

Group (II) is the [X'-*se*] clause where the segment after *-se* does not exist, as follows. First, the speaker deliberately does not articulate the segment after *-se*. For instance, in (29) DS is pointing out the difference between two notions of naivety and purity instead of not uttering the segment after *-se*.

(29) (DS & HK From 'My Hobby')

[Context: DS is telling HK about his girl friend whom he had been separated from before he came to Australia.]

DS: → nemwu swuncinha-**y(e)se**

very   naive-SE

'She was so naive.'

swunswuha-n ke.lang-un   tall-e

pure-MD   thing.with-TC different-INF

'Naivety is different from purity.'

Second, the speaker does not articulate the segment after *-se* because he/she is interrupted by the other speech participant. For example, in (30) JS does not articulate the segment after *-se* in order to answer the other speech participant HY's question.

(30) (HY & JS From 'My Excursion')

[Context: JS is telling HY about how he went on excursions in his school days.]

HY: a [oppa]

oh elder brother

'Oh, JS.'

JS: → [keki] ga-**se**

there go-SE

'I went there.'

HY: Sinka chotung hakkyo tany-ess-ta-kwu

primary school attend-PST-DC-QT

kulay-ss-ci

say like that-PST-SUP

'Did you say that you had attended Sinka Primary School?'

JS: e

'Yes.'

4.3.5 Tokens of *-ciman*

As shown in Table 4.6 below, there are 54 tokens of the conjunctive verbal suffix *-ciman*, and they can be classified into two groups, as follows.

Table 4.6: Frequencies of Tokens of *-ciman*

Groups	Frequencies
Group (I)	32 Tokens (58.18%)
Group (II)	23 Tokens (41.82%)
Total	55 Tokens (100.00%)

Group (I) is the [X-*ciman* Y] sequence; X refers to a segment whose predicate is a non-finite form and Y indicates a segment whose predicate is non-finite or finite.

Consider the following example.

(31) (DS & HK From 'My Hobby')

[Context: DS is telling HK about his girl friend whom he was separated from before coming to Australia.]

DS: →   a yeyswu-nim mit-kwu   ileh-key   cheum

oh Jesus-HT   believe-KO be like that-AD at first

manna-n   yeca-hakwu **sakwi-e**

*meet-PST-MD woman-with **make friends-INF***

pw-ass-ciman

try-PST-CIMAN

HK: um

'Yeah.'

DS: nemwu   **moll-ass-ci**

*too much **not know-PST-SUP***

'I tried making friends with a woman whom I came to know

first at a church, after accepting Jesus, but I didn't know too

much about her.'

In (31) the first segment, where the predicate, i.e., *sakwi-e pw-ass-* 'tried

making friends', is non-finite, and the second segment, where the predicate,

i.e., *moll-ass-ci* 'did not know', is finite, make up the [X-*ciman* Y] sequence.

Group (II) is the [X-*ciman*] clause where the segment after -*ciman* does

not appear. First, the speaker deliberately does not articulate the segment

after -*ciman*. For example, in (32) YH is explaining that he made a study trip

to mud flats in Yengchongto when he was a sixth year student, and he does

not utter the segment after -*ciman*.

(32)   (SH & YH From 'When I Was a Primary School Student')

       [Context: YH is telling SH about where how his school travelled in his

       sixth year.]

YH: yukhaknyen   ttay kiek-ey   nam-nun ke.y

                   the sixth year time memory-in abide-MD fact.NM

                   mwe.nya.myen-un

                   what.be.Q.QT.say.if-TC

                   'If anyone asks me what abides in memory on my sixth year.'

wuli Yengcongto-lo ka-ss-e

we   -to go-PST-INF

'We went to Yengcongto.'

→   Yengcongto cikum konghang-i toy-se   cikum keuy

now   airport-NM become-SE now   almost

ku   pwupwun-i cikum epsecy-ess-**ciman**

*that part-NM   now   disappear-PST-**CIMAN***

'Because Yengcongto became an airport, the place

disappeared, but.'

wuli yukhaknyen ttay swu(hak yehayng) yukhaknyen

we   the sixth year time study trip   the sixth year

ttay ka-ss-ess-nuntey

time go-PST-PST-NUNTEY

'We travelled there on the sixth year.'

kayspel-ul   ka-ss-ess-ketun

mud flat-AC go-PST-PST-KETUN

'We went to mud flats.'

Second, the speaker does not articulate the segment after *-ciman* because he/she is interrupted by the other speech participant. For instance, in (33) NY is cutting HY short; as a consequence, HY cannot articulate the segment after *-ciman*.

(33) (HY & NY From 'My Excursion')

     [Context: HY and NY are talking about heritage villages where they went on excursions during their school days.]

NY: kuntey   minsokchon   umsik cincca masiss-e
by the way heritage village food   really delicious-INF
'By the way, food and drink sold in heritage villages are
delicious.'

HY: mak   tongtongcwu   ile-n   ke
at random liquor with floating grains be like this-MD thing
sse   noh-kwu kule.c.an.h.a
write.INF put-KO   do like that.NOM.not.do.INF
'*Tongtongcwu* 'liquor with floating grains' is written on cards of
restaurants in heritage villages.'

NY: e   e
'Yeah. Yeah.'

HY: →   ku ttay-nun haksayng-i-ese mak tongtongcwu
that time TC student-be-SE hard rice wine
ile-n   ke.nun   mos   masy-ess-keyss-**ciman**
*be like that-MD thing.TC cannot drink-PST-may-**CIMAN***
'Because I was a student I couldn't drink something like
Tongtongcwu 'rice wine', but.'

NY: kulikwu   kule-n   tey-ka   pap masiss-ci
and be like that-MD place-NM meal delicious-SUP
'Meals sold in those places are delicious.'
mwe solcikhi Yongin kath-un   tey-nun   nelp-ese
what really   same-MD place-TC wide-SE
po-l   ke.la-twu   manh-ci
see-PRS-MD thing.be.DC-also many-SUP
'There are many things to see and enjoy, because the heritage
village in Yongin is big.'

> Lostey Weltu minsokchon-un   cincca ccoykumah-ketun
> *heritage village-TC really   small-KETUN*
> 'The heritage village in Lostey Weltu is really small.'

HY: um

'Yeah.'

NY: kekilo way sophwung-ul ka-l   sayngkak

there   *why excursion-AC go-MD thinking*

hay-ss-ess-nun-ci   molu-keyss-e

do-PST-PST-MD-NOM not know-may-INF

'And I don't know why we made an excursion to the heritage

village in Lostey Weltu.'

HY: kulaytwu weynmakhum khu-ci   an.h.nya

but   to some extent big-NOM not.be.Q

'But, it's somewhat big, is it?'

4.3.6 Tokens of *-to*

As shown in Table 4.1 above, there are 34 tokens of conjunctive verbal

suffixes *-to*. There are two points that we have to bear in mind. One is that the

vowel *o* of the suffix *-to* is generally replaced by the vowel *wu* in actual

conversations (Martin 1992: 41). The other is that the suffix *-to* alternates

with *-ato*, *-eto* and *-y(e)to*, and the choice of each suffix is made on the

following conditions. First, *-to* follows verbs and adjectives whose stems

end with a vowel, except for the verb *hata* 'do' and *-hata* that combines with

verbal and adjectival nouns, as follows (Suh et al. 2005: 489).

(34) a. *ka-ta* 'go' + *-to* → *ka-to*

b. *pissa-ta* 'expensive' + *-to* → *pissa-to*

Second, *-ato* follows non-finite forms of verbs and adjectives whose last stem vowels are *a* and *o*, which end in one or more consonants, as follows (Suh et al. 2005: 1125).

(35) a. *phal-ta* 'sell' + *-ato* → *phal-ato*
      b. *coh-ta* 'goo' + *-ato*→ *coh-ato*

Third, *-eto* follows the copula *-ita* and non-finite forms of verbs and adjectives whose last stem vowels are *e, ay, oy, wu, wi, u, uy*, and *i* except for *a, o* and *ye*, as follows (Suh et al. 2005: 1174). Here, the last stem vowel *i* is optionally changed into the vowel *y* when the suffix *-eto* follows non-finite forms of verbs whose stems end with the vowel *i* (Martin 1992: 465).

(36) a. *-i-ta* 'be' + *-eto* → *-i-eto*
      b. *mek-ta* 'eat' + *-eto* → *mek-eto*
      c. *nay-ta* 'pay' + *-eto* → *nay-eto*
      d. *toy-ta* 'become' + *-eto* → *toy-eto*
      e. *pwul-ta* 'blow' + *-eto* → *bwul-eto*
      f. *ttwi-ta* 'run' + *-eto* → *ttwi-eto*
      g. *tul-ta* 'lift' + *-eto* → *tul-eto*
      h. *huy-ta* 'white' + *-eto* → *huy-eto*
      i. *kil-ta* 'long' + *-eto* → *kil-eto*
      j. *kitali-ta* 'wait' + *-eto* → *kitali-eto* or *kitaly-eto*

Fourth, *-y(e)to* follows non-finite forms of the verb *hata* 'do' *-hata* that combines with verbal and adjectival nouns, as follows (Suh et al. 2005: 1857-1859).

(37) a. *ha-ta* 'do' + *-y(e)to* → *ha-y(e)to*

　　　b. *kongpwu-ha-ta* 'study' + *-y(e)to* → *kongpwu-ha-y(e)to*

　　　c. *kenkang-ha-ta* 'healthy' + *-y(e)to* → *kenkang-ha-y(e)to*

In the book, we adopt *-to* as the representative form of the above four allomorphs. Tokens of *-to* can be divided into the following two groups:

Table 4.7: Frequencies of Tokens of *-to*

Groups	Frequencies
Group (I)	27 Tokens (79.41%)
Group (II)	7 Tokens (20.59%)
Total	34 Tokens (100.00%)

Group (I) is the [X-*to* Y] sequence, X refers to a segment whose predicate is a non-finite form and Y indicates a segment whose predicate is non-finite or finite.

Consider the following example.

(38) (SH & YH From 'My Excursion')

　　　[Context: SH and YH are talking about their school days. They agree that they couldn't go on picnics as many times as they wanted while at school in Korea because they had to study hard. They hoped to go on more outings at anytime when they grew up.]

YH:　　　　　mos　nol-ci　　sayngkaktaylo

　　　　　　　cannot play-SUP as one thinks

　　　　　　　'I can't go on a picnic as much as I expected.'

SH: [um]

             Yeah.

YH: [ku]nyang sayngkakchelem ileh-key   no-n

             as it is   as one thinks   be like that-AD play-PST-MD

             cek-un eps-ess-ci

             time-TC lack-PST-SUP

             'I didn't go on a picnic as much as I expected.'

SH: →   kuntey   **khe-twu**   kuke.y kuleh-key   tto

             *by the way **grow up-TO** that.NM be like that-AD again*

             an **toy**-nun   ke   kath-ay

             *not **become**-MD fact same-INF*

             'Although I've grown up, I don't go on a picnic so frequently.'

In (38), two predicates, i.e., *khe-* 'is big' before *-to* and *toy* 'become' after *-to*, are respectively non-finite, and they constitute the [X-*to* Y] sequence. Consider another example.

(39) (SH & YH From 'My Hobby')

      [Context: SH and YH are talking about the definition of hobby. YH says that gambling is identified as a hobby if people consider hobby as everything that they enjoy.]

SH: ku chwimi-la-n   cachey-ka illikel-**i-etwu** amwu sangkwan-i

     *that hobby-DC-MD itself-NM illegal-**be-TO** any   relation-NM*

     eps-ney

     lack-FML

     'Although the hobby is illegal, you don't mind it.'

In (39), the first segment, in which the predicate, i.e., the copula *-i-* 'be', is non-finite, and the second segment, in which the predicate *eps-ney* 'is lack', is finite, make up the [X-*to* Y] sequence.

Group (II) is the [X-*to*] clause where the segment after *-to* does not exist. First, the speaker deliberately does not articulate the segment after *-to*. For example, in (40) DS does not utter the segment after *-to* but explains that he focused on members and guidelines of the missionary unit rather than uttering the other parts of this segment.

(40) (DS & HK From 'When I Was a Primary School Student')
[Context: DS is telling HK how he established a Christian Student Association with other students in his university.]

DS: hakkyo senkyo tanchey   tayphyo   ha-kwu
Christian Student Association representation do-KO
ha-ta(ka) po-nikka   thim lituha-nun ke.nun
do-while view-NIKKA team lead-MD   thing.TC
kulay-twu   kunyang   cal toy-nun   ke.ya
do like that-TO all the time well become-MD fact.be.INF
'I somehow could manage to lead the Christian Student Association after I became the president.'

→ hananim-kkeyse ku   ccok-ulo
God-NM   that direction-to
ssu-si-l-le-n-ci-nun   moll-**atwu**
use-SH-PRS-IN-MD-whether-TC not know-TO
'Although God may use me that way.'
kunyang thim cocikha-kwu thim-i   mewl-lo enu
as it is   team organise-KO team-NM what-to what

kil-lo   ka-ya   toy-nun-ka

road-to go-if only become-IN-Q

'How will this unit have to be organised and managed?'

Second, the speaker does not articulate the segment Y after -*to* because he/she is interrupted by the other speech participant. For instance, in (41) HY cuts in when DS starts to utter the segment, i.e., *kunyang* 'as it is', after -*to*; as a result, DS fully does not articulate it.

(41) (HY & JS From 'When I Was a Primary School Student')
      [Context: HY and JS share the view that the life in their primary school days was very happy, and that exams in a primary school were not so difficult to prepare for them.]

HY: ka-se maynal   nol-kwu kule-nikka

              go-SE every day play-KO do like that-NIKKA

JS: um

              'Yeah.'

HY: toykey caymiiss-e

              very   interesting-INF

              'Because every day I played at a school, the school life was very interesting.'

JS: →   kunikka mwe pyello   kongpwu-to an ha-**y(e)to**

              *so   what particularly study-also   not do-**TO***

HY: e

              'Yeah.'

JS: kunayng

              without doing anything

	'Although we didn't study hard.'
HY:	kongpwu elyew-n kes-to eps-c.an.h-a
	study difficult-MD thing-also lack-NOM.not.be-INF
	'Courses of a primary school were not difficult.'
JS:	e
	'Yeah'

So far, we have provided explanations and descriptions of the data. While counting the number of tokens of Korean conjunctive verbal suffixes *-ko*, *-nuntey*, *-nikka*, *-se*, *-ciman*, and *-to* was not difficult, we did have a few difficulties in illustrating the data. First, we encountered ungrammatical tokens, as seen in (42).

(42) **phullwus**-twu **khi**-l   cwul   al-a
     flute-also   play-PRS-MD the how know-INF
     'She is able to play the flute also.'

(42) is not grammatical because in Korean language the transitive verb *khi*- 'play' does not require the object *phullwus* 'flute', which refers to a 'wind instrument', but an object such as *kitha* 'guitar', which designates a string instrument. Second, we ran into tokens that take an incomplete sentence structure, as shown in (43).

(43) kunyang mek-**ko** w-ass-e
     *just   eat-**KO** come-PST-INF*
     'I came back to the dormitory after eating dishes in my friend's house.'

In (43), there are not expressions that refer to *dormitory, food,* and *my friend's house*. However, we analysed (43) based on the contexts, such as (44)a-b, and our intuition as a Korean native speaker.

> (44) a. The speaker lives at the dormitory.
>
>   b. The speaker joined a party in his friend's house.
>
>   c. Dishes of the party were not delicious.

Finally, we had great difficulty in identifying propositional relations that obtain between segments coupled by the six suffixes. This is because there were a lot of relations, which the previous studies on the six suffixes did not characterise.

4.4 The Elliptical Y

As has been pointed out in Section 4.3., tokens of six conjunctive verbal suffixes *-ko, -se, -nikka, -ciman, -to* and *-nuntey* are divided into the following two groups, according to whether or not the segment Y after these suffixes is explicit.

> (i) Group (I)
>
>   The [X-target suffix Y] sequence (X refers to a segment whose predicate is a non-finite form and Y indicates a segment whose predicate is non-finite or finite);

(ii) Group (II)

The [X'-target suffix] clause without any segment after the target suffix

In this section, we look over the recovery of the omitted segment Y' in the [X'-*nuntey*] clause and state the reason why in Chapter 5 we will take up only the propositional relations, which obtain between X and Y in the [X-target suffix Y] sequence.

According to Blakemore and Carston (2005: 583), elliptical segments before English connectives, which are counterparts of the target suffixes, are recovered by pragmatic inferences because previous utterances are stored as parts of contextual assumptions in the hearer's encyclopaedic entries. Now, we apply their approach to the recovery of the completely or partially unsaid segment Y', which follows the [X'-*nuntey*] clause.

Consider the following example. It appeared as (16) but we repeat below.

(16') (HY & NY From 'When I Was a Primary School Student')

 [Context: NY is telling HY about an event that NY experienced when she attended educational institutes in her primary school days.]

NY: ku ttay solcikhi kule-n hakwen mak

   that time frankly be like that-MD institute much

   tany-ess-c.an.h.a

   attend-PST-NOM.not.do.INF

   'We attended fine art classes very much.'

→ seyey hakwen-itun miswul hakwen-itun

   calligraphy institute-or fine art school-or

tany-ess-nuntey   pyello   towum-un an

attend-PST-NUNTEY particularly aid-TC   not

toy-n   kes kath-ay

become-MD fact same-INF

'I attended schools for calligraphy and fine art schools, but they weren't very useful to me.'

HY   →   na-nun coh-**untey**

I-TC   good-NUNTEY

'They were useful to me (Lit., They were good to me).'

NY: na coh-ass-nuntey   an kuli-nikka   tasi tto

I good-PST-NUNTEY not draw-NIKKA again again

kuleh-key   toy-te-la

be like that-AD become-RT-DC

'I did quite well in fine art and calligraphy when I attended those schools. But, I didn't after I left them.'

kulaytwu   se(yey)

nevertheless calligraphy

'Nevertheless, calligraphy.'

In (16'), the hearer can recover the following implicit segment Y after -*nuntey* by the deduction between the arrowed [X'-*nuntey*] clause and the arrowed previous utterance (Park 1996, 1997, 1998, 1999).

(45) ne-nun an coh-ass-ci

you-TC not good-PST-SUP

'They weren't useful to you.'

Hence, it is possible to identify the [X'-*nuntey*] clause in (16') as the

[X-*nuntey* Y] sequence such as (46).

(46) na-nun coh-**untey**   ne-nun an coh-ass-ci
      *I-TC   good-**NUNTEY** you-TC not good-PST-SUP*
      'They were useful to me, but they weren't useful to you.'

However, it is no simple matter to identify the elliptical segment Y' subsequent to the [X'-*nuntey*] clause. Consider (15'). It also appeared as (15). However, we repeat below.

(15') (HY & NY From 'When I Was a Primary School Student')
       [Context: HY and NY are talking about private schools they attended in their school days.]

HY: phiano hakwen-twu tani-kwu   phullwus-twu
                 school for piano-also attend-KO flute-also
                 'I attended music schools for piano and flute.'
                 phullwus-un cwunghakkyo ttay hay-ss-na
                 flute-TC   middle school time do-PST-Q
                 'Did I learn flute in my middle school days?'

NY: →   na cwunghakkyo ttay
                 I middle school time
                 'When I was a middle school student.'

HY: um   taycheylo manhi manhi tani-n   ke   kath-ay
                 yeah generally much   much attend-PST-MD fact same-INF
                 'I think I attended many private schools in general.'

NY: →   um na-nun
                 yeah I-TC

             thay[kwento   tani-kwu]

             Korean art of bare-handed self-defense attend-KO

             'I attended a Thaykwento hall, and ... '

HY: [thaykwento   tani-kwu]

             Korean art of bare-handed self-defense attend-KO

             'I attended a Thaykwento hall. And.'

NY: →   ku taum-ey seyey-twu   tany-ess-**nuntey**

             *that next-at calligraphy-also attend-PST-**NUNTEY***

             seyey hakwen   nay-ka cin(cca)

             calligraphy institute I-NM   really

             'And then, I also attended a school for calligraphy ... '

             a   miswul hakwen-twu tany-ess-ta

             oh fine art school-also   attend-PST-DC

             'Oh, I also attended fine art schools.'

In (15'), the hearer might not recover the unsaid part of the segment after
-nuntey. This is because the arrowed prior utterances do not provide the
hearer with any information for inferring that part.

   Consider another example.

(47) (SH & YH From 'My Excursion')

      [Context: YH is telling about an event that YH experienced in Yongin
      Natural Park at during his school days.]

YH: na cwunghakkyo ttay han pen keki ka-n   cek

             I   middle school time one time there go-MD experience

             iss-ta

             exist-DC

             'I went there once at my middle school days.'

SH: eti

  where

  'Where?'

→ eti   ka-ss-**nuntey**

  *where go-PST-**NUNTEY***

  'Where did you go?'

YH: Yongin cayen nongwen Eypelaynd

  natural part

  'Yongin Natural Park, Ever Land.'

In (47) *-nuntey* is considered as a sentence-final verbal suffix rather than a conjunctive verbal suffix in the sense that this suffix functions as a quotation marker, i.e., an interrogative sentence-type suffix, that involves the speaker's desire to know where SH went (Han 1986, 1991, 2004; H-J. Lee and C-H. Lee 1999, 2001). This means that any implicit segment Y' does not follow the [X'-*nuntey*] clause such as (47).

Han (1986, 1991, 2004) considers the following *wh*-interrogatives, which include the suffix *-nuntey*, as the speaker's question about precedent utterances or given circumstances and identifies this suffix as a sentence-final suffix.

(48) a. kuke.y   mwe.ntey

  that.NM what.be.NUNTEY

  'What is it?'

  b. chelswu-ka   nwukwu-i-ntey

  -NM who-be-NUNTEY

  'Who is Chelswu?'

    c. chelswu-ka eti   ka-nuntey

       -NM where go-NUNTEY

      'Where is Chelswu going?' (Han 2004: 182)

According to Itani (1996: 77), the *wh*-interrogative communicates the speaker's desire to know a certain kind of information. In her sense, the answers to *wh*-interrogatives such as (48)a-c, i.e., *mwe* 'what', *nwukwu* 'who' and *eti* 'where', are information which the speaker desires. So, the suffix *-nuntey* in (48)a-c is identified not as a conjunctive verbal suffix but as a sentence-final suffix.

Theoretical approaches on to the [X'-target suffix] clause are split into three groups of scholars in terms of whether or not the elliptical segment Y can be recovered, as follows:

Group (A): The sentence-final suffix *-nuntey*

           (e.g. Ko 1974; Han 1986, 1991, 2004; Kwon 1984, 1992, 1994; Kim

           1998, 2001)

Group (B): The conjunctive suffix *-nuntey*

           (e.g. H-S. Lee 1991, 2000; Y-Y. Park 1996, 1997, 1998, 1999; Jung

           2001)

Group (C): The sentence-final suffix *-nuntey* and the conjunctive suffix *-nuntey*

           (e.g. H-J. Lee and C-H. Lee 1999, 2001)

First, Group (A) excludes the elliptical segment Y. Second, Group (B) argues that the implicit segment Y is recovered by inference. Third, Group (C) proposes some cases in which the omitted segment Y is not recovered.

In this book, we take up only the [X-target suffix Y] sequence. We set aside the [X'-target suffix] clause for two reasons. One is that in the book we focus on propositional relations that obtain between X and Y in the [X-target suffix Y] sequence. The other is that the recovery of the elliptical segment after the six suffixes requires an entirely different scope of discussion, i.e., divergence between the conjunctive verbal suffix and the sentence-final verbal suffix.

5

Propositional Relations

In this chapter, we present the results of our data analysis. In particular, our focus is to characterise propositional relations that obtain between two separate 'propositions', i.e., the proposition recovered from the segment X (hereafter P_x) and the proposition recovered from the segment Y (hereafter P_y). In pursuit of this aim, fourteen propositional relations are identified from the data as follows.

Table 5.1: Propositional Relations (The [X-Target Suffix Y] Sequence)

Sequences	Propositional Relations
The [X-*ko* Y] Sequence	ENUMERATION, FORWARD SEQUENTIAL, CAUSAL, SIMULTANEITY, REPETITION
The [X-*nuntey* Y] Sequence	TIME, CAUSAL, CONTRAST, DENIAL OF EXPECTATION, INTRODUCTION, INFERENTIAL, BACKWARD INFERENTIAL, REPETITION, REFORMULATION, EXEMPLIFICATION
The [X-*nikka* Y] Sequence	TIME, CAUSAL, INFERENTIAL, REPETITION, REFORMULATION
The [X-*se* Y] Sequence	FORWARD SEQUENTIAL, CAUSAL, REPETITION, REFOMULATION
The [X-*ciman* Y] Sequence	CONTRAST, DENIAL OF EXPECTATION
The [X-*to* Y] Sequence	CONDITION, CONTRAST, DENIAL OF EXPECTATION

5.1 The [X-*ko* Y] Sequence

The [X-*ko* Y] sequence involves five propositional relations: ENUMERATION, FORWARD SEQUENTIAL, CAUSAL, SIMULTANEITY, and REPETITION. Table 5.2 below shows the frequencies of the five propositional relations in the data.

Table 5.2: Frequencies of Propositional Relations (The [X-*ko* Y] Sequence)

Propositional Relations	Frequencies
ENUMERATION	409 Tokens (35.38%)
FORWARD SEQUENTIAL	253 Tokens (21.88%)
CAUSAL	35 Tokens (3.03%)
SIMULTANEITY	103 Tokens (8.91%)
REPETITION	356 Tokens (30.80%)
Total	1,156 Tokens (100.00%)

Below we provide explanations of the five propositional relations together with relevant examples.

ENUMERATION

As far as *-ko* is concerned, ENUMERATION is one of the three propositional relations identified most significantly in the data.

Consider the following example.

(1)   (HY & NY From 'My Hobby')

[Context: NY is telling HY of NY's friend who has a talent for music.]

NY: →   paiolin-twu khi-l   cwul   al-**kwu**
            *violin-also play-PRS-MD the how know-**KO***
            'She is able to play the violin and.'
HY: a
            'Oh.'
NY: phullwus-twu khi-l   cwul   al-a
            flute-also   play-PRS-MD the how know-INF
            'She is able to play the flute also.'

In (1) NY is saying that her friend can play the flute as well as the violin. A single conjoined proposition, such as (2), can be recovered from the [X-*ko* Y] sequence.

(2)   [NY's friend is able to play the piano] & [NY's friend is able to play the flute].

Notice that the truth-value of (2) is identical with the truth-value of (3) where P_x and P_y in (2) are reversed.

(3)   [NY's friend is able to play the flute] & [NY's friend is able to play the piano].

ENUMERATION refers to the logical relation & where the truth-values of two propositions P_x and P_y involved are constant, regardless of the ordering of the propositions (Suh 2006: 1124).

FORWARD SEQUENTIAL

FORWARD SEQUENTIAL involves two sequenced events, where the event conveyed by the first proposition P_x precedes that conveyed by the second proposition P_y (Carston 2002: 231). (This relation refers to a relation where the first proposition without any causal relationship precedes that conveyed by the second proposition.) As far as *-ko* is concerned, FORWARD SEQUENTIAL is the third most frequent propositional relations found in the data. Consider (4).

(4)　　(DS & HK From 'My Excursion')

　　　　[Context: HK knows that DS lives at the dormitory. DS tells HK about what he experienced when he joined a party at his friend's house.]

DS:　　　　mek-ul　　ke.n　　pyello　　eps-ess-e

　　　　eat-PRS-MD thing.TC particularly lack-PST-INF

　　　　'There was nothing delicious.'

　　　　pyello　　masiss-key　an mek-ess-e

　　　　particularly delicious-AD not eat-PST-INF

　　　　'Dishes were not delicious.'

→　　　kunyang mek-**ko** w-ass-e

　　　　*just　　eat-**KO**　come-PST-INF*

　　　　'I came back to the dormitory after eating them.'

In (4) DS is saying that he came home right after eating dishes at his friend's party. P_x and P_y, such as (5)a-b, can be recovered from the [X-*ko* Y] sequence in (4).

(5) a. DS ate dishes at DS's friend's party at t.

   b. DS came back to DS's dormitory at t+n.

In (5) DS's eating dishes in clause (a) precedes DS's going to his dormitory in clause (b). We take this propositional relation as FORWARD SEQUENTIAL.

CAUSAL

CAUSAL refers to the propositional relation where the event depicted by the first proposition P_x causes the event depicted by the second proposition P_y (Carston 2002: 227).

Consider the following example.

(6)   (HY & NY From 'My Excursion')
      [Context: HY and NY are talking about what kinds of items booth keepers sold at the excursions in their school days.]

HY: sophwung-ul encey.n   cwul   al-**kwu**   kwisin-kathi
     *excursion-AC when.be.MD assumed fact know-**KO** ghost-like*
     w-a
     come-INF
     'Booth keepers went there because they already knew when and where we would go on excursions.'

In (6) HY is explaining that booth keepers could attend excursions because they collected information on dates and destinations of excursions. P_x and P_y, such as (7)a-b, can be recovered from the [X-*ko* Y] sequence in (6).

(7) a. Booth keepers knew when and where HY and NY would go on excursions
         at t.

     b. Booth keepers went to the excursions at t+n.

In (7) booth keepers' knowing dates and destinations of excursions in clause
(a) causes booth keepers'going to the excursions in clause (b). In this sense,
the propositional relation between (7)a and (7)b is CAUSAL.

SIMULTANEITY

SIMULTANEITY refers to the propositional relation where events depicted
by two propositions P_x and P_y occur at the same time (Tsai 1985: 35).
   Consider the following example.

(8) (HY & JS From 'My Hobby')
     [Context: JS is telling HY an event that JS experienced when he fished in
        the sea in Australia. JS explained that he stopped fishing at sunset in order
        to arrive home before midnight.]
JS: cha-lul mol-**ko**   mak   cip-ulo ka
     *car-AC drive-**KO** unhesitatingly house-to go.INF*
     'I went home while driving a car.'

In (8) JS is saying that he drove home from the seashore. P_x and P_y, such as
(9)a-b, can be recovered from the [X-*ko* Y] sequence in (8).

(9) a. JS drove a car at t.
     b. JS went home at t.

In (9) JS's driving a car in clause (a) temporally overlaps with JS's going home in clause (b).

REPETITION

REPETITION obtains when the second proposition P_y is identical with to the first proposition P_x (Blakemore 1993: 116).[13] The number of this relation is the second most frequent propositional relations found in the data.

The frequencies of REPETITION with in different environments are as follows.

Table 5.3: Frequencies of REPETITION (The [X-*ko* Y] Sequence)

REPETITION		Frequencies
Where predicates of X and Y are identical		50 Tokens (14.05%)
Deictic Verbs	*ileta/ilehata*	34 Tokens (9.55%)
	kuleta/kulehata	235 Tokens (66.01%)
Deictic Adjective	*kulehta/kulehata*	37 Tokens (10.39%)
Total		356 Tokens (100.00%)

---

[13] According to Blakemore (1993), REPETITION obtains when the propositions recovered from the two adjacent utterances such as (i) are identical to each other.

(i)   They ran, ran up the hill. (Blakemore 1993: 116)

In Blakemore's account, the hearer has access to contextual assumptions related to the word *run* in his/her encyclopaedic entries and recovers the same propositions such as (ii) and (iii) from these utterances in (i) that contain the word *ran*.

(ii)   They ran up the hill.
(iii) They ran up the hill.

She adds that (i) has a reading of the continuance of running.

Let us consider (10), where REPETITION involves a repetition of the predicate; subjects of X and Y are identical to each other and the predicate of Y is a repetition of the predicate of X. H-J. Lee and C-H. Lee (1999: 17, 2001: 54-55) argue that in this type Y strengthens the mental state conveyed by X.

 (10) (SH & YH From 'My Hobby')

   [Context: SH and YH are talking about kinds of hobbies.]

 YH: um nemwu **manh-ko manh**-ci

   well very ***many-KO many***-*SUP*

   'Well, there are many hobbies. There are many hobbies.'

In (10) YH is saying that many hobbies exist in the world. P_x and P_y, such as (11)a-b can be recovered from the [X-*ko* Y] sequence in (10).

 (11) a. There exist multitudinous hobbies.

   b. There exist multitudinous hobbies.

In (11) clause (b) is identical to clause (a).

Let us turn to another environment, where REPETITION employs deictic verbs *ileta/ilehata* 'do like this', *kuleta/kulehata* 'do like that', and the deictic adjective *kulehta/kulehata* 'be like that' subjects of X and Y are identical and the predicate, i.e., deictic verbs/adjective, of Y deictically refers to the predicate of X. Yi (1999) and K-Y. Park (2001), who focus on this environment, do not provide any relevant account for discriminating between -*ko ileta/ilehata* and -*ko kuleta/kulehata*. Yi (1999: 183) takes up only two predicates *kuleta/kulehata* 'do like that' and *kulehta/kulehata* 'be like that', and Yi (1999: 183 footnote) considers functions of the expressions *-ko kuleta/kulehata* and *-ko kulehta/kulehata* as redundant on the ground that the omission of these expressions does not affect the reading of this type. By contrast, K-Y. Park (2001: 102-103) claims that the two deictic verbs, i.e., *ileta/ilehata* 'do like this' and *kuleta/kulehata* 'do like that' have an anaphoric function, and that the subject of *kuleta/kulehata* can be any person but the subject of *ileta/ilehata* can only be the speaker or the hearer. This syntactic constraint on *-ko ileta/ilehat* is not the case with our data. There are numerous counterexamples; the subject of 10 tokens of *ileta/ilehata* is the third party.

Sohn discriminates the anaphoric use of two kinds of demonstratives, i.e., the *i*-series and the *ku*-series, as follows.

"The *i*-series is used to refer to a referent which is known to the speech participants from the speaker's perspective ... The *ku*-seires, which is used most often, refers to a referent known to the speaker and addressee from the same perspective." (Sohn 1994: 295)

Hence, this reminds us of the following two points. First, *kuleta/kulehata* of the [X-*ko kuleta/kulehata*] sequence refers to the predicate of X from the speaker's and hearer's same perspective, whereas *ileta/ilehata* of the [X-*ko ileta/ilehata*] sequence refers to the predicate of X from the speaker's perspective. Second, each of the deictic predicates strengthens the mental state communicated by X in that it is a repetition of the predicate of X. Consider (12).

(12) (HY & JS From 'My Hobby')

[Context: JS is telling HY about his childhood in Seoul. JS explained that he put up a tent on the top of his house and passed a hot summer in the tent.]

JS: keki.se saynghwalha-**ko kulay**-ss-ess-e

*there.at live-**KO KULETA**-PST-PST-INF*

'I passed hot summer there.'

In (12) JS is saying that he enjoyed living in the tent every summer when he was a child. P_x and P_y, such as (13)a-b, can be recovered from the [X-*ko* Y] sequence in (12) in that in (12) *kulay-* 'do like that' of Y refers to *keki.se saynghwalha-* 'live there' of X.[14]

(13) a. JS lived in the tent of the top of his house.

b. JS lived in the tent of the top of his house.

In (13) clause (b) is identical to clause (a). Thus, (13)a and (13)b establish REPETITION. Here, it is possible to say that the deictic verb *kulay-* 'do like that' of Y in (12) is more than an anaphor (K-Y. Park 2001: 102-103).

5.2 The [X-*nuntey* Y] Sequence

The [X-*nuntey* Y] sequence involves ten propositional relations: TIME, CAUSAL, CONTRAST, DENIAL OF EXPECTATION, INTRODUCTION, INFERENTIAL, BACKWARD INFERENTIAL, REPETITION,

---

[14] The word *kulay-* is the abbreviated linguistic form for the stem of the deictic verb *kuleta* 'do like that' (Martin 1992: 652).

REFORMULATION, and EXEMPLIFICATION. Table 5.4 below shows the frequencies of the ten propositional relations in the data.

Table 5.4: Frequencies of Propositional Relations (The [X-*nuntey* Y] Sequence)

Propositional Relations	Frequencies
TIME	63 Tokens (12.52%)
CAUSAL	27 Tokens (5.37%)
CONTRAST	88 Tokens (17.50%)
DENIAL OF EXPECTATION	166 Tokens (33.00%)
INTRODUCTION	52 Tokens (10.34%)
INFERENTIAL	8 Tokens (1.59%)
BACKWARD INFERENTIAL	10 Tokens (1.99%)
REPETITION	31 Tokens (6.16%)
REFORMULATION	45 Tokens (8.95%)
EXEMPLIFICATION	13 Tokens (2.58%)
Total	503 Tokens (100.00%)

Below we provide brief explanations of the ten propositional relations together with relevant examples.

TIME

TIME refers to the propositional relation where the event communicated by the first proposition P_x represents the temporal situation in which the event communicated by the second proposition P_y occurs, occurred, or will occur (Tsai 1985: 163).

Consider the following example

(14) (DS & HK From 'My Excursion')

[Context: DS is telling HK of his experience when his front teeth were broken during his childhood. DS says that his two front teeth were broken and fell out when he was eating shrimp crisps. However, HK expresses the feeling that she cannot understand why his teeth fell out.]

DS: ani saywukkang-ul   mek-**nuntey**   ippal-i   ppacy-ess-e

*no shrimp crisps-AC eat-**NUNTEY** tooth-NM lose-PST-INF*

'No. When I ate shrimp crisps, I really lost my teeth.'

In (14) DS is saying that his teeth dropped out while he was chewing shrimp crisps. P_x and P_y, such as (15)a-b, can be recovered from the [X-*nuntey* Y] sequence in (14).

(15) a. DS ate shrimp crisps.

b. DS's front teeth dropped out.

In (15) DS's losing his front milk teeth occurs on the time at which DS ate shrimp crisps; (15)a and (15)b have TIME.

CAUSAL

Consider the following example, where CAUSAL obtains between P_x and P_y.

(16) (HY & NY From 'My Hobby')

[Context: NY is telling HY about a CD she lent someone. NY says that she does not remember to whom she lent her CD. However, she suddenly remembers it ...]

> NY: um ani a nwukwu pillyecwu-ess-nun-ci al-kyess-**nuntey**
> *well no oh who   lend-PST-MD-NOM know-may-**NUNTEY***
> com   ku salam-ul   manna-llyekwu
> *a little that person-AC meet-to*
> 'Oh. Because I know who I lent it, I will meet her.'

In (16) NY is saying that she will ask someone to return her CD to her because she remembers that she let the person use the CD. P_x and P_y, such as (17)a-b, can be recovered from the [X-*nuntey* Y] sequence in (16).

> (17) a. NY knows to whom she lent her CD.
> b. NY will meet the person to whom she lent her CD.

In (17), NY's knowing to whom she lent her CD in clause (a) causes NY's meeting that person in clause (b).[15] CAUSAL refers to the propositional relation where the event depicted by the first proposition P_x causes the event depicted by the second proposition P_y (Carston 2002: 227).

CONTRAST

CONTRAST obtains when two propositions P_x and P_y are in contrast with each other (Blakemore 1987: 125-131). There are cases where the propositions derived from P_x that derived from P_y are in contrast with each other. However, these cases only obtain in the [X-*nuntey* Y] sequence.

There are two different environments where CONTRAST obtains. One is

---

[15] This relation may or may not be labelled as INTRODUCTION. However, speaker NY docs not introduce any object or event.

where CONTRAST is marked by the topic-contrast particle *-un/nun* or the conditional *myen*-clause or both. The two markers focus on the foregoing word or phrase or segment in order to highlight the point of contrast between other parts that follow these markers.[16] Another one is where the two markers are not present. The frequencies of CONTRAST with different environments are as follows.

Table 5.5: Frequencies of CONTRAST (The [X-*nuntey* Y] Sequence)

CONTRAST	Frequencies
With *-un/nun* or *-myen*	66 tokens (75.00%)
None of both	22 tokens (25.00%)
Total	88 tokens (100.00%)

Let us consider (18), where X and Y have the topic-contrast particle *-un*.

(18) (SH & YH From 'My Excursion')

[Context: SH and YH are talking about how students and teachers arrived at the excursions. They state that students had to arrive for their excursions early as the appointment time was usually 9 o'clock and they could not be late. Y describes how teachers travelled to the destination and compares

---

[16] Martin describes the function of *-un/nun* as follows.

"marks the theme, subdues the focus on the preceding word or phrase in order to foreground the rest of the sentences for various reasons, ... Two items in contrast are backgrounded so as to play up the points of contrast." (Martin 1992: 896-897)

The use of *-un* and *-nun* hinges on whether they are after consonants or vowels; *-un* is subsequent to consonants, whereas *-nun* follows vowels (Martin 1992: 896).

ordinary teachers with class teachers.]

YH: tamim-tul-i   ilpwule   ay-tul-ilang   kathi   kal-lyeko

class teacher-PL-NM on purpose child-PL-with together go-to

kule-n   ay-tul   sen(sayng) sensayng-nim-tul

do like that-MD child-PL teacher   teacher-HT-PL

iss-e kacikwu   sensayng-nim-tul-**un** kathi   cihachel tha-ko

*exist-with the result of teacher-HT-PL-**TC**   together subway ride-KO*

ka-key toy-**nuntey**   keuy   taypwupwun sensayng-nim-tul-**un**

*go-AD become-**NUNTEY** almost most   teacher-HT-PL-**TC***

cacenke caki cha tha-ko   o-ci

bicycle   own car ride-KO come-SUP

kuke.y te   phyenha-nikka

that.NM more convenient-NIKKA

'Class teachers went there by subway to go with their students, but most
teachers went there by their car for convenience.'

In (18) YH is saying that class teachers went to the destination by subway but
other teachers went to the place by their car. The topic-contrast particle *-un*
of X and Y in the [X-*nuntey* Y] sequence in (18) highlights the point of
contrast between class teachers of X and other ordinary teachers of Y. P_x and
P_y, such as (19)a-b, can be recovered from the [X-*nuntey* Y] sequence in
(18).

(19) a. Class teachers went to the excursions by subway so that their students
          would not be late.

      b. Ordinary teachers went to the excursions by their car because they do not
          think it convenient to go to excursions by subway.

Moreover, two propositions, such as (20)a and (20)b, can be derived from (19)a and (19)b respectively.

> (20) a. A subway is one means of public transportation.
>
>   b. A private car is not public transportation.

(20)a and (20)b establish CONTRAST; (20)a contrasts to (20)b.

Let us consider another (21), where neither of the topic-contrast particle *-un/nun* nor the conditional *myen*-clause is present.

> (21) (HY & JS From 'My Excursion')
>
> [Context: JS is telling HY of his experience when he was a soldier. JS says that he joined one week's military drill ...]
>
> JS: sal   manhi ppacy-ess-ess-**nuntey**
>
> *flesh much lose weight-PST-PST-NUNTEY*
>
> tto   tasi   ccy-ess-e
>
> *again again gain weight-PST-INF*
>
> 'I lost weight very much, but I gained weight again.'

In (21) JS is saying that he lost weight during one week's military drill but he gained weight after the drill. In (21) no marker stresses the viewpoint of contrast between two periods of time, i.e., during and after the military drill. P_x and P_y can be recovered from in the [X-*nuntey* Y] sequence in (22) as follows.

> (22) a. JS lost weight during one week's military drill.
>
>   b. JS gained weight after one week's miliary drill.

In (22) JS's losing weight in clause (a) presents a striking contrast with his gaining weight in clause (b). In this sense, (22)a and (22)b establish CONTRAST.

DENIAL OF EXPECTACTION

DENIAL OF EXPECTACTION refers to the propositional relation where an expectation derived from the first proposition P_x is denied by the second proposition P_y (Blakemore 1987: 131-141).

Consider the following example.

 (23) (HY & JS From 'My Excursion')

   [Context: JS is telling HY about an experience when he visited a certain death camp that was built by Nazis. JS explained that he met an old guide who was in the death camp in World War II, and that the guide's older sister was executed in front of him.]

  JS: → solcikhi na-to sulph-ess-**nuntey**

     honestly I-also sad-PST-NUNTEY

     na-n kuleh-key an na-te

     I-TC be like that-AD not drop-RT

     'To be frank, I was also sad, but I didn't cry.'

     [an] na-ss-nuntey

     not drop-PST-NUNTEY

     'I didn't cry.'

  HY: [um]

     'Yeah.'

     na-twu kule-n   ke.ey nwunmwul cal an

     I-also be like that-MD thing.at tear well not

> hully-e
>
> *shed-INF*
>
> 'I don't cry about that.'

In (23) JS is saying that he heard the sad story from the old guide but he did not cry at all. P_x and P_y, such as (24)a-b, can be recovered from the [X-*nuntey* Y] sequence in (23).

(24) a. JS was saddened by the story that a poor Jewish girl was executed by Nazis in front of her brother.

     b. JS did not cry.

The expectation, such as (25), can be derived from clause (24)a.

(25) JS cried.

Here, (24)b denies the expectation (25); (24)a and (24)b and thus establish DENIAL OF EXPECTATION.

INTRODUCTION

Consider the following example, which involves INTRODUCTION.

(26) (DS & HK From 'My Excursion')

    [Context: HY is telling DS episodes about butter she picked up from a certain pub.]

HK: → enni ku kathi ka-ss-te-n **hankwuk**

    *big sister that together go-PST-RT-MD **Korea***

enni-ka iss-**nuntey**   **ku enni**-ka   ku bethe

big sister-*NM exist*-**NUNTEY** *that big sister*-*NM that butter*

com   caki chayngky-e ka-ya   toy-keyss-ta

a little self pick up-INF go-if only become-may-DC

'I had a Korean friend - she calls her my elder sister - who went

to the pub with me and she said "I will take the butter."'

ileh-key   ileh-key   cokuma.n bethe

be like that-AD be like that-AD small.MD butter

'A small packet of butter as small as this.'

ileh-key   iss.c.an.h.a.yo   ileh-key

be like that-AD exist.NOM.not.do.INF.POL be like that-AD

neymonah-key

square-AD

'Like this, the square shaped one.'

DS: al-e

know-INF

'I know.'

In (26) HK is saying that she went to the pub with one of her friends and that

very person took a packet of butter from the pub. P_x and P_y, such as (27)a-b,

can be recovered from the [X-*nuntey* Y] sequence in (26).

    (27) a. One of HK's friends went to a certain pub with her.

        b. The same friend told HK that she would take a packet of butter from the

        pub.

In (27), clause (a) introduces *One of HK's friends* on which the speaker focuses in clause (b). INTRODUCTION refers to the relation where the first proposition P_x introduces a certain object or an event on which the speaker focuses in the second proposition P_y (K-D. Lee 1979: 123-135).

INFERENTIAL

INFERENTIAL refers to the propositional relation where the first proposition P_x functions as evidence for the speaker's belief that the second proposition P_y is true (H-K. Lee 2001: 195).

Consider the following example.

(28) (DS & HK From 'My Excursion')

[Context: DS tells HK about what he is cooking at in his dormitory in Australia. DS is expressing the a feeling when he eats *kimchi* 'Korean pickled vegetables' made by him.]

HK: a kimchi.**ntey**   eti   ka-na   ku

*oh Korean pickled vegetables.be.**NUNTEY** where go-although that*

mas-i   nao-nun-ke.n   tangyenha-ci

flavour-NM come-MD-fact.TC natural-SUP

'*Kimchi* 'Korean pickled cabbage' is *kimchi*. So, it makes sense that everywhere *kimchi* tastes the same flavour because *kimchi* is *kimchi*.'

In (28) DS is saying that he tastes the same flavour as he did in his home in Korea when he eats *kimchi,* 'Korean pickled vegetables', made by him. P_x and P_y, such as (29)a-b, can be recovered from the [X-*nuntey* Y] sequence in (28).

(29) a. The thing which DS is making in his dormitory is *kimchi*.

     b. DS tastes the same flavour of *kimchi* wherever he eats it.

If it is assumed that anyone tastes the same flavour of *kimchi*, i.e., Korean pickled cabbage, everywhere, (29)a and (29)b are identified as premise and conclusion respectively. In this sense, (29)a and (29)b have establish INFERENTIAL.[17]

BACKWARD INFERENTIAL

BACKWARD INFERENTIAL refers to the propositional relation where the second proposition P_y is identified as evidence for the speaker's belief that the first proposition P_x is true (Carston 2002: 228).

Consider the following example.

(30) (HY & NY From 'My Hobby')

    [Context: NY is explaining why she likes being alone at home.]

NY: → wenlay honca iss-nun ke cohaha-ki-n ha-**ntey**

      *originally alone exist-MD fact like-NOM-TC do-**NUNTEY***

      'Originally, I like being alone.'

      maynnal honcase mak kongsangha-kwu [mak]

      every day alone   much daydream-KO   much

      'Every day, I daydream very much.'

HY: [um]

      'Yeah'

---

[17] This relation may be labelled as INTRODUCTION, but speaker DS does not introduce any object or event.

NY:	omankaci	sayngkak ta ha-kwu

various kinds of thinking   all do-KO

'And I imagine lots of things. And.'

HY: [um]

'Yeah.'

NY: [ku]le-ta(ka)   po-myen sikan hwuttak ka-kwu

do like that-while see-if   time   quickly go-KO

mak kule-nun   ke   kath-ay

much do like that-MD fact same-INF

'Meantime, time seems to pass very quickly.'

In (30) NY is saying that she likes being alone at home because she imagines a lot of things and it helps her to forget an insipid life. P_x and P_y, such as (31)a-b, can be recovered from the [X-*nuntey* Y] sequence in (30).

(31) a. NY likes being alone at home.

b. [NY daydreams very much at home] & [she imagines a lot of things at home].

If it is assumed that people, who daydream very much and imagine a lot of things, can forget the tedium of everyday affairs and that people like to forget the tedium of everyday affairs, then (31)b and (31)a are identified as premise and conclusion respectively; BACKWARD INFERENTIAL is obtained between (31)a and (31)b.[18]

---

[18] This relation may be labelled as REFORMULATION. However, this is not the case because in (31) clause (a) and clause (b) do not resemble each other.

REPETITION

Consider the following example, where REPETITION is obtained.

(32) (HY & NY From 'My Excursion')
  [Context: HY is telling an episode related to bugs when she went on an excursion in her school days. HY says that she went to places of nature and amusement parks on excursions rather than places in cities, and that she had difficulty in eating ice cream and soft drink because of bugs.]

HY: e   na pelley toykey silheha-**nuntey**   nemwu silh-un   ke.ya
  *well I bug   very   dislike-**NUNTEY** very   dislike-MD fact.be.INF*
  'Well, I hate bugs very much. Very much.'

In (32) HY stresses that she hates bugs intensely. In (32) subjects of X and Y in the [X-*nuntey* Y] sequence are identical and the predicate *silh-* 'dislike' of Y is a synonym of the predicate *silheha-* 'dislike' of X. P_x and P_y, such as (33)a-b, can be recovered from the [X-*nuntey* Y] sequence in (32).

(33) a. HY hates bugs intensely.
  b. HY hates bugs intensely.

In (33) clause (b) is identical to clause (a). REPETITION obtains when the second proposition P_y is identical to the first proposition P_x (Blakemore 1993: 116).

REFORMULATION

REFORMULATION refers to the propositional relation where two propositions P_x and P_y resemble each other, in which elaboration, specification, and/or strengthening result (Blakemore 1997: 10).[19]

Consider the following example.

> (34) (DS & HK From 'My Excursion)
>
> [Context: DS is explaining how he writes assignments. HK says that she cannot understand why DS summarises repeatedly the same article given as an assignment. DS explains how he summarises articles. He is talking about articles he summarised recently.]
>
> DS: pulapepul inpeyicyen-ey kwanlyentoy-n ke.**ntey**
>
> *probable invasion-to   relate-MD   thing.be.**NUNTEY***
>
> makheys ilon-uy   olientheyisyen-i ettehkey talu-n   kos-ey
>
> *market theory-GN orientation-NM   how   different-NM place-to*

---

[19] According to Blakemore (1993, 1997, 2002), reformulation obtains when the propositions recovered from two utterances conjoined by English connectives, which are counterparts of the target suffixes, resemble each other. She (1997: 10) considers 'reformulation' as resemblance of utterances because "…between propositional representations of states of affairs in the world which holds in virtue of resemblances in propositional form." She (1997, 2002) suggests two types of reformulation as follows.

(i) (a) At the beginning of this piece there is an example of an anacrusis. (b) That is, it begins with an unaccented note which is not part of the first full bar. (Blakemore 1997: 8)

(ii) A WELL-GROOMED CAR REFLECTS ITS OWNER
The car you drive says a lot about you. (Adopted from Mann and Thompson 1988: 277)

First, she says that the reformulation such as (ib) helps the hearer understand the original such as (ia) on condition that the hearer is unfamiliar with the word *anacrusis* in (ia). Second, in her (1997: 9-10) account, the original such as the first utterance in (ii) provides the hearer with a puzzle, and the reformulation such as the second utterance in (ii) interprets the original and gives a solution to that puzzle.

yenghyang-ul michi-na   kiep sengkong-ey   ile-n   ke.ey

effect-AC   happen-Q enterprise success-to do like this-MD thing.to

kwanlyentoy-n ke.ta

relate-MD   thing.be.DC

'It relates to 'probable invasion'[20]. It relates to 'how the orientation of
market   theory affects other parts, that is, the success of enterprises.'

In (34) DS is explaining that the article for his assignment takes up 'probable
invasion', i.e., how the orientation of market theory contributes to the
success of enterprises. In (34), the subjects of X and Y of the [X-*nuntey* Y]
sequence are also identical to each other, and Y communicates what the
expression *pulapepul inpeyicyen* 'probable invasion' of X means. P_x and
P_y , such as (35)a-b, can recovered from the [X-*nuntey* Y] sequence in (34).

(35) a. The article that DS summarised as an assignment recently is related to
          probable invasion.
      b. The article that DS summarised as an assignment recently is related to
          how the orientation of market theory affects the success of enterprises.

In (35) *how the orientation of market theory affects the success of
enterprises* in clause (b) resembles *probable invasion* in clause (a); (35)a
and (35)b have establish REFORMULATION.

---

[20] According to informant DS, the term "probable invasion" is one of the terms of
business.

EXEMPLIFICATION

EXEMPLIFICATION refers to the propositional relation where the second proposition P_y gives instances of the first proposition P_x (Carston 1992: 164).[21]

Consider the following example.

    (36) (HY & NY From 'When I Was a Primary School Student')

        [Context: HY is telling NY about the types of institute she attended in her primary school days.]

    HY: →   hakwen   toykey manhi tany-ess-**nuntey**

                     *educational institute very   much attend-PST-**NUNTEY***

                     'I attended lots of educational institutes.'

                     seyey hakwen-twu   tani-kwu

                     school for calligraphy-also attend-KO

                     'I attended private schools for calligraphy. And.'

    NY: um

                     'Yeah'

    HY: sukheyithu-twu tani-kwu   panghak ttay

                     skate-also   attend-KO holidays time

---

[21] Carston (1992: 164) and Blakemore (1997: 12-14) postulate that two adjacent utterances such as (i) involve EXEMPLIFICATION when the second utterance is identified as an instance of the first utterance, and that this instance is to provide an evidence for supporting a claim communicated by the first utterance.

    (i)   Wars are breaking out all over; Champaign and Urbana have begun having border skirmishes. (Bar-Lev and Palacas, 1980: 144)

In Carston's accounts, in (i) an instance, i.e., border skirmishes between Champaign and Urbana, gives evidence for the speaker to believe that wars are breaking out all over.

[swuyengcang]-twu tani-kwu

swimming pool-also attend-KO

'I attended a private school of ice skating. And, in the holidays
I attended a swimming pool.'

NY: [a na-twu]

oh I-also

'Me also.'

e

'Yeah.'

HY: tto   swuyengcang-ilang

again swimming pool-and

yenge hoyhwa hakwen   tani-kwu

private school for English conversation attend-KO

'And I attended swimming pools and private schools for
English conversation.'

In (36) HY is listing private schools she attended in her primary school days.
P_x and P_y, such as (37)a-b, can be recovered from the [X-*nuntey* Y] sequence
in (36).

(37) a. HY attended many educational institutes in her primary school days.

b. [HY attended private schools for calligraphy] & [HY attended a private
school for ice skating] & [HY attended a swimming pool in the
holidays].

In (37), *a swimming pool and private schools for calligraphy* and *ice
skating* in clause (b) are identified as concrete examples of *educational*

institutes in clause (a). In this sense, (37)a and (37)b establish EXEMPLIFICATION.

5.3 The [X-*nikka* Y] Sequence

The [X-*nikka* Y] sequence holds five propositional relations: TIME, CAUSAL, INFERENTIAL, REPETITION, and REFORMULATION. Table 5.6 below shows the frequencies of the five propositional relations in the data.

Table 5.6: Frequencies of Propositional Relations (The [X-*nikka* Y] Sequence)

Propositional Relations	Frequencies
TIME	23 Tokens (9.83%)
CAUSAL	161 Tokens (68.80%)
INFERENTIAL	42 Tokens (17.95%)
REPETITION	3 Tokens (1.28%)
REFORMULATION	5 Tokens (2.14%)
Total	234 Tokens (100.00%)

Below we explicate the five propositional relations together with relevant examples.

TIME

TIME refers to the propositional relation where the event communicated by the first proposition P_x represents the temporal situation in which the event communicated by the second proposition P_y, occurs, occurred, or will occur (Tsai 1985: 163).

Consider the following example, where TIME is obtained.

(38) (DS & HK From 'My Excursion')
      [Context: DS is telling HK how he did his assignment last Saturday.]
      DS: ku pam-ey twu si   toy-**nikka**   ta
           *that night-at two o'clock become-**NIKKA** everything*
           sse-ss-te-la-kwu
           write-PST-RT-DC-QT
           'When it was 2 o'clock in the morning, I completed my assignment.'

In (38) DS is saying that he did completed his assignment at 2 o'clock in the morning. P_x and P_y, such as (39)a-b, can be recovered from the [X-*nikka* Y] sequence in (38).

(39) a. The time was 2 o'clock in the morning last Sunday.
      b. DS completed his assignment.

In (39) the time at which DS finished his assignment was 2 o'clock in the morning last Sunday.

CAUSAL

CAUSAL refers to the propositional relation where the event depicted by the first proposition P_x causes the event depicted by the second proposition P_y (Carston 2002: 227). Consider (40).

(40) (NY & HY From 'My Hobby')
      [Context: HY tells NY about her friend who likes Barbie dolls very much.]

HY: →   khulisumasu ttay-mata   emma-twu papi inhyeng-ul
               Christmas   time-every mother-also Barbie doll-AC
               ilpwule   kyay-ka papi inhyeng-ul nemwu cohaha-**nikka**
               *specially she-NM Barbie doll-AC very   like-**NIKKA***
NY: um
               'Yeah.'
HY: senmwul ha.y   cwu-kwu
               present   do.INF give-KO
               'Because she likes Barbie dolls very much, every year her
               mother gives her a Barbie doll as a Christmas gift. And.'

In (40) HY is saying that her friend likes Barbie dolls very much and this compels the person's mother to buy a Barbie doll for her every Christmas. P_x and P_y, such as (41)a-b, can be recovered from the [X-*nikka* Y] sequence in (40).

(41) a. HY's friend likes Barbie dolls very much.
      b. Every year HY's friend's mother gives HY's friend a Barbie doll as a Christmas gift.

In (41) the daughter's liking Barbie dolls very much in clause (a) is a cause for the mother to buy a Barbie doll every Christmas in clause (b).

INFERENTIAL

Consider the following example, which involves INFERENTIAL.

(42) (NY & HY From 'My Hobby')

[Context: YH and SH are talking about cases of confectionery that they liked in their primary school days. YH says that he liked *Homlenpol*, which was a brand of biscuits produced in Korea, and that ...]

YH: → kuke.n ccikuleci-**nikka**   mak kak-i   com   phocang-i

*that.TC be crushed-**NIKKA** hard case-NM a little packing-NM*

an toy-e   iss-c.an.h.[a]

not become-INF is-NOM.not.be.INF

'The box of biscuits was badly packed, because it was crushed.'

SH: [um]

'Yeah.'

mac-e

right-INF

'That's right.'

In (42) YH is saying that the box's being poorly packed is based on the fact that it was crushed. P_x and P_y, such as (43)a-b, can be recovered from the [X-*nikka* Y] sequence in (42).

(43) a. The box of biscuits was crushed.

  b. The box of biscuits was badly packed.

If it is assumed that boxes of biscuits, which are well packed, are not crushed, in (43) 'being crushed' in clause (a) provides an evidence for the belief in clause (b), i.e., that the box of biscuits was badly packed. In (43) clause (a) and clause (b) are identified as a premise and an implicated conclusion. INFERENTIAL refers to the propositional relation where the first proposition P_x functions as evidence for the speaker's belief that the second proposition P_y is true (H-K. Lee 2001: 195).

REPETITION

REPETITION obtains when the second proposition P_y is identical with the first proposition P_x (Blakemore 1993: 116).

Consider the following example.

(44) (HY & NY From 'When I Was a Primary School Student')
[Context: NY is telling of her experience when her class teacher checked the homework of her classmates and herself in her primary school days. On that day, NY did not do her homework. So, in order not to be penalised, NY completed her homework while her teacher was checking other students'.]

NY: → chotunghakkyo ttay-nun il   i   sam sa   pwuntan-kkaci
primary school time-TC one two three four division-up to
iss-**unikka**
*exist-**NIKKA***
'There were four *pwuntan*s 'divisions according to which writing tables were arranged' at each classroom.'

HY: um
'Yeah.'

NY: sa   pwuntan-i-nikka   to-nun   tey sikan-i
four divisions-be-NIKKA take a walk round-MD case time-NM
kelly-ese
take-SE
'Because there were four *pwuntan*s divisions at each

classroom, it took some time for my teacher to take walk

around the classroom for checking our homework.'

kulayse nay-ka ku ttay ta hay-ss-nuntey

so   I-NM   that time all do-PST-NUNTEY

'So, I finished my homework while he was checking other

students' homework.'

In (44) NY stresses that she bought time because there were four divisions in each classroom, and that she did her homework before her class teacher arrived at her desk to check it. Here, it is important that in (44) NY is not interrupted by HY, who utters "um". P_x and P_y, such as (45)a-b, can be recovered from the [X-*nikka* Y] sequence in (44).

(45) a. There were four *pwuntan*s in each classroom when NY

attended a primary school.

b. There were four *pwuntan*s in each classroom when NY

attended a primary school.

In (45) clause (b) equals to clause (a); (45)a and (45)b establish REPETITION.[22]

---

[22] One can say that in (45) clauses (a) and (b) do not establish REPETITION in the sense that in (44) the [X-*nikka*] clause is repeated. However, this does not seem to be the case. The arrowed [X-*nikka* Y] sequence in (44) belongs to Group (ii) of those suggested in Chapter 4.

Groups of tokens of -*nikka*
Group (i): The [X-*nikka* Y] sequence (X refers to a segment whose predicate is a
              non-finite form and Y indicates a segment whose predicate is **finite**).
Group (ii) The [X-*nikka* Y] sequence (X refers to a segment whose predicate is

REFORMULATION

Consider the following example, where REFORMULATION is obtained.

(46) (SH & YH From 'My Excursion')

[Context: SH and YH are talking about events of the excursions in their school days. YH is explaining how the leader who performed the events was chosen.]

YH: → kuntey   olakpwuchang kath-un   ke   ppop-**unikka**

by the way leader   same-MD thing appoint-NIKKA

hakkyo-eyse

school-at

'By the way, because my class teacher appointed a leader.'

SH: kule-ci

do like that-SUP

'That's right.'

YH: → ceyil cal no-nun   ay-tul-i-la-tunci   mwue.l pwunwiki

best well play-MD child-PL-be-DC-or what.AC atmosphere

cal kku-nun ay-tul   kule-n   ay-tul

well draw-MD child-PL do like that-MD child-PL

ppop-unikka   kule-n   ay-tul-i   no-nun

appoint-NIKKA do like that-MD child-PL-NM play-MD

ke.ci

fact.be.SUP

'Because the teacher appointed a student who had the best talent of entertainment in the class to a leader, the chosen leader performed events of the excursions.'

---

a non-finite form and Y indicates a segment whose predicate is **non-finite**).

In (46) YH is explaining that her class teacher appointed a student with the best entertainment talent as a leader of events of the excursions. P_x and P_y, such as (47)a-b, can be recovered from the [X-*nikka* Y] sequence in (46).

> (47) a. The class teacher appointed a leader who would perform events of the excursions.
>
> b. The class teacher appointed a student who had the best entertainment talent in the class as a leader to perform events of the excursions.

In (47) clause (b) resembles clause (a).[23] REFORMULATION refers to the propositional relation where two propositions P_x and P_y resemble each other, in which elaboration, specification, and/or strengthening result (Blakemore 1997: 10).

5.4 The [X-*se* Y] Sequence

The [X-*se* Y] sequence has four propositional relations: FORWARD SEQUENTIAL, CAUSAL, REPETITION, and REFORMULATION. Table 5.7 below shows the frequencies of the four propositional relations in the data.

---

[23] Note that this relation may be seen as CAUSAL. However, the event depicted by (47)a is not the cause of the event depicted by (47)b.

Table 5.7: Frequencies of Propositional Relations (The [X-*se* Y] Sequence)

Propositional Relations	Frequencies
FORWARD SEQUENTIAL	137 Tokens (59.57%)
CAUSAL	83 Tokens (36.09%)
REPETITION	3 Tokens (1.30%)
REFORMULATION	7 Tokens (3.04%)
Total	230 Tokens (100.00%)

Below we provide explanations of the four propositional relations together with relevant examples.

FORWARD SEQUENTIAL

Consider (48), where RORWARD SEQUENTIAL is obtained between X and Y.

(48) (DS & HK From 'When I Was a Primary School Student')

[Context: DS is explaining why he received a scholarship from his university.]

DS: tayhak   tulew-**ase** kyelcengcekulo ches hakki-ey swusek-ul

university enter-SE definitely   first term-at top-AC

hay-ss-ketun

do-PST-KETUN

'I was at the top on the first term after entering the university.'

In (48) DS is saying that he was at the head on the first term in the first academic year. P_x and P_y, such as (49)a-b, can be recovered from the [X-*se* Y] sequence in (48).

(49) a. DS entered the university at t.

b. DS was at the top on the first term at t+n.

In (49) DS's entering the university in clause (a) precedes DS's being at the top on the first term. FORWARD SEQUENTIAL involves two sequenced events, where the event conveyed by the first proposition P_x precedes the the event conveyed by the second proposition P_y (Carston 2002: 231).

CAUSAL

CAUSAL refers to the propositional relation where the event depicted by the first proposition P_x causes the event depicted by the second proposition P_y (Carston 2002: 227). Consider (50).

(50) (DS & HK From 'When I Was a Primary School Student')
    [Context: DS is explaining why he passed an entrance examination for a university.]

DS: kunayang chayk manhi   pw-**ase**
    *as it is   book   in large numbers see-**SE***
    sengcek naw-ass-te-n   ke kath-ay
    result   come out-PST-RT-MD fact same-INF
    'It seems that I was marked very well because I had read many books.'

In (50) DS is saying that reading was an important factor for his good result in an entrance examination. P_x and P_y, such as (51)a-b, can be recovered from the [X-*se* Y] sequence in (50).

(51) a. DS read a large number of books at t.

b. DS obtained a good result in an entrance examination for a university

at t+n.

In (57) DS's reading multitudinous books in clause (a) causes DS's obtaining

a good result from an entrance examination in clause (b).

REPETITION

REPETITION obtains when the second proposition P_y is identical to the first

proposition P_x (Blakemore 1993: 116).

Consider the following example.

(52) (DS & HK From 'When I Was a Primary School Student')

[Context: DS is telling HK of the relationship between his father and him.

DS says that he did not apologize to his father for his faults because he did

not like his father in his childhood, and that his father and he talked about

this after DS grew up.]

DS: nacwungey khe-**se**   nacwungey khe-se   twul-i

*later   grow-up-**SE** later   grow up-SE two-NM*

kule-n   yeyki-lul hay-ss-ess-nuntey

be like that-MD story-AC do-PST-PST-NUNTEY

'After I grew up, after I grew up, my father and I talked about it.'

In (52) DS is saying that he and his father talked about his fault after he grew

up. P_x and P_y, such as (53)a-b, can be recovered from the [X-*se* Y] sequence

in (52).

(53) a. DS grew up.

b. DS grew up.

In (53) clauses clause (a) and clause (b) are identical to each other (53)a and (53)b establish REPETITION.[24]

REFORMULATION

Consider the following example, which involves REFOMULATION.

(54) (HY & NY From 'My Hobby')

[Context: NY is telling about NY's friend who entered a college of engineering after giving up a teachers' college.]

NY: ipen-ey   hakkyo tasi   tuleka-**se**

*this time-at school again enter-**SE**

kongtay   tuleka-ss-e

a college of engineering enter-PST-INF

'This year, she entered a university again. She entered a college of engineering.'

---

[24] One can say that in (53)a and (53)b REPETITION is not established in that in (52) the [X-*se*] clause is repeated. However, this does not seem to be the case. The arrowed [X-*se* Y] sequence in (52) belongs to Group (ii) of those suggested in Chapter 4.

Groups of tokens of -*se*
Group (i): The [X-se Y] sequence (X refers to a segment whose predicate is a non-finite form and Y indicates a segment whose predicate is **finite**).
Group (ii) The [X-*se* Y] sequence (X refers to a segment whose predicate is a non-finite form and Y indicates a segment whose predicate is **non-finite**).

In (54) NY is saying that her friend, who had given up a teachers' college, entered a university. P_x and P_y, such as (55)a-b, can be recovered from the [X-*se* Y] sequence in (54).

    (55) a. NY's friend entered a university.

           b. NY's friend entered a college of engineering.

In (55) *a college of engineering* in clause (b) resembles *a university* in clause (a). REFORMULATION refers to the propositional relation where two propositions P_x and P_y resemble each other, in which elaboration, specification, and/or strengthening result (Blakemore 1997: 10).

5.5 The [X-*ciman* Y] sequence

The [X-*ciman* Y] sequence involves two propositional relations: CONTRAST and DENIAL OF EXPECTATION. Table 5.8 below provides the frequencies of the two propositional relations in the data.

Table 5.8: Frequencies of Propositional Relations (the [X-*ciman* Y] Sequence)

Propositional Relations	Frequencies
CONTRAST	9 Tokens (28.12%)
DENIAL OF EXPECTATION	23 Tokens (71.88%)
Total	32 Tokens (100.00%)

Below we briefly explicate the two propositional relations together with relevant examples.

CONTRAST

CONTRAST obtains when two propositions are in contrast with each other (Blakemore 1987: 125-131). There are two distinct environments where CONTRAST obtains. One is where the topic-contrast particle *-un/nun* or the conditional *myen*-clause or both are present. As has been described in Section 5.2., the two markers focus on the foregoing word or phrase or segment in order to highlight the point of contrast between other parts that follow these markers. Another one is where X and Y do not have the two markers. The frequencies of CONTRAST with the two environments are as follows.

Table 5.9: Frequencies of Contrast (the [X-*ciman* Y] Sequence)

Contrast	Frequencies
With *-un/nun* or *myen*-clause	7 Tokens (77.78%)
None of both	2 Tokens (22.22%)
Total	9 Tokens (100.00%)

Let us consider (56), which has *myen*-clause.

    (56) (SH & YH From 'My Hobby')

        [Context: SH and YH are talking about the definition of hobby. SH is telling YH that most people are not interested in the subject of hobbies, and hence that they hesitate to answer when asked what kinds of hobby they have.]

    SH: salam-hanthey a ilum-i   mwe.ey.yo   kule-n   ke

        person-to   oh name-NM what.be.Q.POL be like that-MD thing

mwul-e po-**myen** ilum kath-un   ke   swip-key taytapha.y
ask-INF try-if   name same-MD thing easy-AD   answer.INF
cwu-kwu nai kath-un   ke   swip-key taytapha-l   swu
give-KO   age same-MD thing easy-AD answer-PRS-MD way
iss-**ciman**   a chwimi-ka mwe.ey.yo   ttak   kule-**myen**
exist-CIMAN oh hobby-NM what.be.Q.POL suddenly do like that-if
kapcaki ttak   makhi-nun ke   kath-ay
suddenly suddenly stick-MD   fact same-INF
'I can easily answer them if anyone suddenly asks me my name and age,
  but I can't easily answer it if he suddenly asks me my hobby.'

In (56) SH is explaining that his name and age are things to say to strangers at once but his hobbies are things he cannot say to them immediately. The conditionals of X and Y in the [X-*ciman*Y] sequence in (56) put emphasis on contrast between name and age of X and hobby of Y. P_x and P_y, such as (57)a-b, can be recovered from the [X-*ciman* Y] sequence in (56).

(57) a. If people suddenly ask SH his name and age, hecan easily supply the
         answer.
      b. If people suddenly ask SH of about his hobby, he cannot easily supply
         the answer.

In (57) SH's provision of his name and age in clause (a) presents a contrast with SH's answering hobby in clause (b). In this sense, (57)a and (57)b establish CONTRAST.[25]

---

[25] One may take this relation as DENIAL OF EXPECTATION without looking

Let us consider (58), where CONTRAST is marked by the topic-contrast particle and the conditional clause.

(58) (SH & YH From 'My Hobby')

[Context: YH is telling SH about sports that he is interested in.]

YH: cikum tangcang   ha-kwu iss-nun   ke.**n**   sukhwesi-lang e

*now   the present do-KO ISSTA-MD thing.**TC** squash-and   well*

cim   tani-nun   ke.ki-n   ha-**ciman**   kihoy-ka

*fitness centre attend-MD thing.be.NOM-TC do-**CIMAN** chance-NM*

toy-n-ta-**myen-un**   theynisu-twu payw-e   po-kwu siph-kwu

*become-IN-DC-**if-TC** tennis-also   learn-INF try-KO SIPHTA-KO*

'I now play squash and attend a fitness centre, but if I have a chance I'd like

to learn tennis as well.'

In (58) YH is saying that he is playing squash at present but he wants to learn tennis if he gains an opportunity to do so. In (58) the topic-contrast particle -*n* of X and the topic-contrast particle -*un* plus the conditional of Y place emphasis on contrast between the present and a possible future.[26] P_x and P_y, such as (59)a-b, can be recovered from the [X-*ciman* Y] sequence in (58).

(59) a. YH plays squash and attends a fitness centre now.

b. If YH has a chance in the future he would like to learn tennis.

---

closely at the context. However, since the context of (56) does not show the expectation that the question of hobby is easy to answer, it cannot be DENIAL OF EXPECTATION.

[26] -*N* is the shortened form of the topic-contrast particle -*nun* (Martin 1992: 896).

In (59) YH's playing squash and attending a fitness centre in clause (a) is in contrast to YH's learning tennis in clause (b).[27]

Let us consider(60), where CONTRAST obtains without any marker.

(60) (SH & YH From 'My Hobby')

[Context: YH is telling SH about how he learned *hapkito* 'aikido' in his middle school days.]

YH: mwullon   tocang   ga-se yensupha-nun kes-to   iss-**ciman**

undoubtedly training hall go-SE practice-MD   fact-also exist-CIMAN

mayil   kuke oyey-twu   cip-eyse-twu   mak yensupha-kwu

every day that besides-also house-at-also hard practice-KO

'Of course, every day I learned motions of *hapkito* 'aikido' at the training hall, but in addition to that official training I practiced at home by myself.'

In (60) YH is saying that he learned the motions of aikido at the drill hall but he practiced them at home by himself. In (60) no marker stresses the point of contrast between the exercise hall of X and YH's house of Y. P_x and P_y, such as (61)a-b, can be recovered from the [X-*ciman* Y] sequence in (60).

(61) a. YH learned *hapkito* 'aikido' from his master at the training hall.

b. YH practiced *hapkito* 'aikido' by himself at home.

---

[27] One may take this relation as DENIAL OF EXPECTATION without looking closely at the context. However, since the context of (60) does not show the expectation that YH does enough sporting activities and does not need to do more, it cannot be DENIAL OF EXPECTATION.

In (61), YH's learning *hapkito* from his master in clause (a) is in contrast to YH's practicing *hapkito* by himself in clause (b).[28]

DENIAL OF EXPECTATION

Consider the following example, where DENIAL OF EXPECTATION is obtained.

(62) (DS & HK From 'When I Was a Primary School Student')
[Context: DS is telling HK about human relations with his classmates in his school days. DS is explaining that he made friends with his classmates after he became a year ten student.]

DS: ku cen-ey-nun keuy mwe nol-ki-nun   nol-ass-**ciman**
*that past-at-TC almost what play-NOM-TC play-PST-**CIMAM***
salam-tul-hanthey maum-ul yel-ci   an.h.ass-e
person-PL-to   mind-AC open-NOM not.do.PST-INF
'Before that time I played with my classmates, but I didn't open up my mind to them.'

In (62) DS is saying that he did not bare his heart to his classmates although he played with them. P_x and P_y, such as (63)a-b, can be recovered from the [X-*ciman* Y] sequence in (62).

(63) a. DS played with his classmates before he was a year ten student.

---

[28] One may take this relation as DENIAL OF EXPECTATION without looking closely at the context. However, since the context of (60) does not show the expectation that HY learned all he needed to know about *hapkito* 'aikido' from his master at the training hall, it cannot be DENIAL OF EXPECTATION.

b. DS did not open up his mind to his classmates before he was a y e a r ten student.

Moreover, the expectation, such as (64), can be derived from (63)a.

(64)   DS would open up his mind to his classmates.

Here, (64) is denied by (63)b. DENIAL OF EXPECTATION refers to the propositional relation where an expectation derived from the first proposition P_x is denied by the second proposition P_y (Blakemore 1987: 131-141).

5.6 The [X-*to* Y] sequence

The [X-*to* Y] sequence holds three propositional relations: CONDITION, CONTRAST, and DENIAL OF EXPECTATION. Table 5.10 below shows the frequencies of the three propositional relations in the data.

Table 5.10: Frequencies of Propositional Relations (the [X-*to* Y] Sequence)

Propositional Relations	Frequencies
CONDITION	6 Tokens (22.22%)
CONTRAST	1 Token (3.70%)
DENIAL OF EXPECTATION	20 Tokens (74.07%)
Total	27 tokens (100.00%)

Below we provide explanations of the three propositional relations together with relevant examples.

CONDITION

CONDITION refers to the relation where the first proposition P_x represents a protasis and the second proposition P_y depicts an apodosis (Jeon 1989: 93). Consider (65):

(65) (HY & JS From 'When I was a Primary School Student')
       [Context: HY and JS are talking about teachers in their primary schools.]

JS: cikum sayngkakha-**y(e)to** cincca ippe-ss-e
       now   think-TO   really beautiful-PST-INF
       'If I think of her, she was really beautiful.'

In (65) JS is saying that one of his assistant teachers is was beautiful. P_x and P_y can be recovered from the [X-*to* Y] sequence in (65) as follows.

(66) a. JS thinks of one of his female assistant teachers in his primary school.
       b. JS is sure of that the assistant teacher was beautiful.

In (66) the thinking of the assistant teacher in clause (a) and the assurance of that she was beautiful are identified as 'antecedent' and 'consequent' respectively (66)a and (66)b establish CONDITION.

CONTRAST

CONTRAST obtains when the two propositions P_x and P_y are in contrast with each other (Blakemore 1987: 125-131).

Consider the following example:

(67) (SH & YH From 'My Hobby')

[Context: SH and YH are talking about the definition of hobby. SH restricts the scope of a hobby within narrow limits only useful to self-culture. However, YH considers a hobby as everything that relieves mental stress.]

YH: ne-**nun** ni-ka   kuleh-key   sayngkak an ha-**y(e)to** na-**nun**
you-TC you-NM be like that-AD thinking not do-TO   I-TC
kuleh-key   sayngkakha-l   swu iss-ta.nun   ke.ci
be like that-AD think-PRS-MD way exist-DC.QT.say.MD fact.be.SUP
'You don't think so, but I think so.'

In (67) YH is saying that he considers a hobby as a relief of mental stress but SH does not. The topic-contrast particle *-nun* of X and Y in the [X-*to* Y] sequence in (67) puts emphasis on contrast between SH of X and YH of Y. P_x and P_y, such as (68)a-b, can be recovered form the [X-*to* Y] sequence in (67).

(68) a. SH does not think that a hobby is everything that relieves mental stress.
      b. YH thinks that a hobby is everything that relieves mental stress.

In (68) SH's not thinking of a hobby as relieving mental stress in clause (a) presents a contrast to YH's considering a hobby as relieving mental stress in clause (b).[29]

---

[29] Unfortunately, this is the only token of *-to* expressing CONTRAST. We cannot put too much emphasis on it.

DENIAL OF EXPECTATION

Consider the following example, where DENIAL OF EXPECTATION is obtained.

(69) (DS & HK From 'When I Was a Primary School Student')
[Context: DS is telling HK that the relationship between his father and him was not good before he became a Christian. DS now explains that he did not show his report card after year 7.]

DS: sengcekphyo an kac-kwu w-**ato**   amwu mal an ha-kwu
*report card   not take-KO come-**TO** any   word not do-KO*
'Although I didn't show him my report card, he didn't tell me anything.'

In (69) DS is saying that he did not show his father the result of an examination but received no response. P_x and P_y, such as (70)a-b, can be recovered from the [X-*to* Y] sequence in (69).

(70) a. DS did not show his father his report card.
      b. DS's father did not say anything to DS about DS's not showing him DS's report card.

Further, the expectation, such as (71), can be derived from (70)a.

(71) DS's father would say something about, or seven scold DS, for DS's not showing him DS's report card.

Here, (71) is denied by (70)b. DENIAL OF EXPECTATION refers to the propositional relation where an expectation derived from the first proposition P_x is denied by the second proposition P_y (Blakemore 1987: 131-141).

So far, we have shown propositional relations that Korean conjunctive verbal suffixes *-ko, -nuntey, -nikka, -se, -ciman,* and *-to* involve. The establishment of the propositional relations is important for judging whether the meanings of the six suffixes are encoded or inferred. In Chapter 6, we will take up the **use** of the six suffixes, i.e., truth-functionally conjoining and truth-functionally disjoining.

6

The Use of Korean Conjunctive Verbal Suffixes

In this chapter we continue to present the results of our data analysis.

Our focus here is to identify whether or not the propositional relations that obtain between the two linked segments are encoded by the conjunctive verbal suffix, by using the scope test.

Second, we show that truth-conditional encoded meanings of Korean conjunctive verbal suffixes *-ko*, *-nuntey*, *-nikka*, *-se*, *-ciman*, and *-to*, conjoin P_x and P_y truth-functionally, and that non-truth-conditional inferred meanings of Korean conjunctive verbal suffixes, *-ko*, *-nuntey*, *-nikka*, and *-se*, disjoin P_x and P_y truth-functionally.

6.1 A Single Conjoined Truth-Conditional Proposition

The aim of this section is to show that truth-conditional encoded meanings of six suffixes *-ko*, *-nuntey*, *-nikka*, *-se*, *-nikka*, *-ciman*, and *-to* conjoin P_x and P_y truth-functionally and yield a single conjoined truth-conditional proposition.

In Chapter 5, we have shown propositional relations that obtain between P_x and P_y. Encoded meanings of the six suffixes refer to propositional relations that are encoded by the suffixes. Encoded meanings of a given suffix can be defined as meanings simply carried by the connective.

We will adopt the scope test, which was taken by Rouchota (1990), as a yardstick when deciding whether or not meanings of the six suffixes are encoded. The test refers to judging whether or not meanings of conjunctive verbal suffixes fall within the scope of the truth-conditional connective *if...then*. That is, meanings of conjunctive verbal suffixes fall within the scope of the connective *if... then* if and only if they are encoded by these suffixes. Let us take *-ciman*, for example. Consider (1).

(1) Tom-un khi-ka   cak-**ciman**   John-un khi-ka   khuta
      *TC height-NM short-**CIMAN**   TC height-NM tall*
     'Tom is short, but John is tall.'

From (1) two propositions, such as (2)a-b can be recovered.

(2)   a. Tom is short.
      b. John is tall.

The propositional relation between (2)a and (2)b is a contrast relation because Tom's being short in (2)a and John's being tall in (2)b are in contrast with each other (Tsai 1985: 111-120; Jeong 1986: 24-25; Choi 1989: 69, 1991: 75; Jeon 1989: 64, 66-67; Yoon 1989: 59, 61, 2005: 256-257; Suh 2006: 1147, 1149). In Rouchota's sense, *-ciman* in (1) has two encoded meanings: & and a contrast meaning. This is because the two meanings are embedded in the antecedent of (3).

(3)   If Tom is short-*ciman* John is tall then Mary will not marry either of them.

Encoded meanings of the six suffixes are split into truth-conditional and non-truth-conditional, as shown in Table 6.1 below. Note that Contrast Meaning, Denial of Expectation Meaning, and Introduction Meaning in Table 6.1 below respectively refer to CONTRAST, DENIAL OF EXPECTATION, and INTRODUCTION encoded by suffixes.

Table 6.1: Encoded Meanings of Korean Conjunctive Verbal Suffixes

Suffixes	Encoded Meanings	
	Truth-Conditional	Non-Truth-Conditional
-ko	&	
-nuntey	*&, when, as a result of*	Contrast Meaning, Denail of Expectation Meaning, Introduction Meaning
-nikka	*when, as a result of*	
-se	*after, as a result of*	
-ciman	&	Contrast Meaning, Denial of Expectation Meaning
-to	$\rightarrow$, &	Contrast Meaning, Denial of Expectation Meaning

Our truth-conditional encoded meanings of Korean conjunctive verbal suffixes are identical with conceptual meanings of English connectives in Relevance Theory (Carston 2002: 243; Wilson 2004).[30] Furthermore, our

---

[30] In personal communication, Wilson(2004) replied to our question about meanings of connectives, which in effect says:

> "We need to distinguish connectives (like 'and', 'or', 'if ⋯ then', 'because') which make a difference to truth conditions, and connectives (like 'but', 'moreover', 'nevertheless') which don't make a difference to truth conditions. According to relevance theory, truth-conditional

non-truth-conditional encoded meanings of Korean conjunctive verbal suffixes are essentially the conventional implicature found in Gricean and neo-Gricean theories but with some modification.

The truth-conditional encoded meanings of the six suffixes in Table 6.1 above are divided into two types according to whether or not the meanings have truth-tables. First, two meanings $\&$ and $\to$ have truth-tables as follows.

Table 6.2: Truth-Tables for & and $\to$

p	q	p $\&$ q	p $\to$ q
T	T	T	T
T	F	F	F
F	T	F	T
F	F	F	T

(P and q refer to two propositions. Further, T and F stand for 'true' and 'false' respectively.) (Lyons 1977: 144)

Let us take *-ko*, for instance. Consider (4).

(4)   onul-un   kumyoil-i-**ko** nayil-un   thoyoil-i-ta
      *Today-TC Friday-be-**KO** tomorrow-TC Saturday-be-DC*
      'Today is Friday, and tomorrow is Saturday.'

From (4) two propositions, such as (5)a-b can be recovered.

(5)   a. Toda is Friday.

      b. Tomorrow is Saturday.

---

connectives can be seen as encoding concepts, while non-truth-conditional connectives can't."

The propositional relation between (5)a and (5)b is ENUMERATION because the truth-values of (5)a and (5)b are constant, regardless of the ordering of the propositions (Suh 2006: 1124). The truth-values of (5)a and (5)b hinge on whether or not a fact or an event, which they convey, exists in the world. *-Ko* in (4) has a truth-conditional encoded meaning &. The truth-conditional encoded meaning & of *-ko* (4) conjoins (5)a and (5)b truth-functionally and yields a single conjoined truth-conditional proposition, such as (6).

(6)   [Today is Friday] & [tomorrow is Saturday].

The truth-value of a single conjoined proposition (6) depends on the truth-values of two propositions (5)a-b and the truth-table for & in Table 6.2 above. Second, three meanings, *when, after,* and *as a result of,* do not have any truth-table for them. The truth-value of a single conjoined proposition, which contains these three meanings, relies on whether or not they affect facts or events, which two propositions P_x and P_y convey causally. Consider (7):

(7)   Tom-un stheyikhu-ul mek-**ese** paythal-i   na-ss-ta
          -TC steak-AC   eat-SE   stomach trouble-MN occur-PST-DC
          'Because Tom ate a steak, he suffered from stomach trouble.'

Two propositions, such as (8)a-b, can be recovered from (7).

(8)   a. Tom ate a steak.
       b. Tom suffered from a stomach trouble.

In (8) eating a steak in clause (a) caused suffering from stomach trouble in clause (b); clauses (a) and (b) have CAUSAL. This relation is encoded by *-se* in (7) (Yang 1972: 5; Tsai 1985: 40; Choi 1989: 156, 1991: 164; Jeon 1989: 53; K-D. Lee 1993: 453; Yi 1996: 177, 2000: 226; H-J. Lee and C-H. Lee 1999: 343, 2001: 655; Yoon 2005: 203; Suh 2006: 1177). *-Se* in (7) has a truth-conditional encoded meaning *as a result of*. In terms of Relevance Theory, the truth-conditional encoded meaning *as a result of* of -se in (7) conjoins (8)a and (8)b truth-functionally and forms a single conjoined proposition, such as (9).

> (9)   [As a result of Tom's eating a steak] [Tom suffered from a stomach trouble].

The truth-value of a single conjoined truth-conditional proposition (9) relies on whether or not the truth-conditional encoded meaning *as a result of* -se in (7) causally affects the event 'eating a steak' depicted by (8)a and the event 'suffering from stomach trouble' depicted by (8)b.

In Table 6.1 above, we provided three non-truth-conditional encoded meanings: a contrast meaning, a denial of expectation meaning, and an introduction meaning. The three meanings do not conjoin two propositions P_x and P_y truth-functionally but comments on the two propositions. First, a the contrast meaning refers to the signalling that P_x contrasts with P_y or the signalling that the proposition derived from P_x contrasts with that derived from P_y. Second, a denial of expectation meaning designates the signalling that the proposition, which is derived from P_x, contrasts with P_y. Third, an introduction meaning stands for the signalling that P_x introduces a certain object or an event on which the speaker focuses in P_y. One can say that the signalling is a procedure, which instructs the hearer how to interpret P_x and P_y. However, this encounters a problem because three suffixes *-nuntey*, *-ciman*, and *-to*, which have the signalling, encode more than two meanings, as seen in Table 6.1 above. Blakemore (1987, 1992, 2002), who introduced the notion 'procedure', postulates that a procedure encoded by a connective constrains the hearer's interpretation of two propositions, and hence that a unitary procedure is a prerequisite of the constraint of the interpretation. In this sense, we do not adopt the notion 'procedure'. In Section 7.1., we will take up this in detail.

The frequencies of a single conjoined truth-conditional proposition in our data are given in Table 6.3 below. This table provides the following two points: the first is that in the data the number of examples that cite encoded meanings of the suffix is bigger than the number of examples that cite inferred meanings of the suffixes; the second is that in the data the two suffixes have only encoded meanings.

Table 6.3: Frequencies of a Single Truth-Conditional Conjoined Proposition

Suffixes	Frequencies	
	A Single Conjoined Truth-Conditional Proposition	Propositional Relations between P_x and P_y
-ko	800 Tokens (48.22%)	1,156 Tokens (52.98%)
-nuntey	396 Tokens (23.87%)	503 Tokens (23.05%)
-nikka	184 Tokens (11.09%)	234 Tokens (10.72%)
-se	220 Tokens (13.26%)	230 Tokens (10.54%)
-ciman	32 Tokens (1.93%)	32 Tokens (1.47%)
-to	27 Tokens (1.63%)	27 Tokens (1.24%)
Total	1,659 Tokens (100.00%)	2,182 Tokens (100.00%)

What follows in this section shows, with examples, that the truth-conditional encoded meanings of a given suffix conjoin two propositions P_x and P_y truth-functionally and yield a single conjoined truth-conditional proposition.

6.1.1 Encoded meanings of *-ko*

As shown in Table 6.4 below, the [X-*ko* Y] sequence involves five propositional relations.

Table 6.4: Frequencies of Propositional Relations (the [X-*ko* Y] Sequence)

Propositional Relations	Frequencies
ENUMERATION	409 Tokens (35.38%)
FORWARD SEQUENTIAL	253 Tokens (21.88%)
CAUSAL	35 Tokens (3.03%)
SIMULTANEITY	103 Tokens (8.91%)
REPETITION	356 Tokens (30.80%)
Total	1,156 Tokens (100.00%)

These appeared in Table 5.2, but we provide it here again for expository convenience.

In this section, we will take up four propositional relations: ENUMERATION, FORWARD SEQUENTIAL, CAUSAL, and SIMULTANEITY. These four relations involve the following encoded meanings. We exclude REPETITION as it involves a non-truth-conditional inferred meaning (see Section 6.2.1.).

Table 6.5: Encoded Meanings of *-ko*[31]

Propositional Relations	Encoded Meanings	
	Truth-Conditional	Non-Truth-Conditional
ENUMERATION	&	
FORWARD SEQUENTIAL	&	
CAUSAL	&	
SIMULTANEITY	&	

ENUMERATION

Consider the following example.

(10) (HY & NY From 'My Hobby')

[Context: NY is telling HY of NY's friend who has a talent for music.]

a. P_x: NY's friend is able to play the piano.

b. *-ko*

c. P_y: NY's friend is able to play the flute.

---

[31] One can say that in Table 6.5 CAUSAL, FORWARD SEQUENTIAL, and SIMULTANEITY, which the [X-*ko* Y] sequence involves, are identified as an inferred causal meaning, an inferred forward sequential meaning, and an inferred simultaneity meaning of *-ko*, respectively. However, this is not the case, based on the following points.

The three pragmatic theories, Gricean theory (e.g. Grice 1975), neo-Gricean theory (e.g. Levinson 1983, 1995, 2000), and Default Semantics (e.g. H-K. Lee 2001, 2002), argue that the connective *and*, which is the counterpart of *-ko*, has inferred meanings (e.g. forward sequential meaning, causal meaning, and simultaneity meaning). But, their ways of explaining these meanings bring problems to their own theoretical framework. (See Chapter3 for more details.)

Furthermore, Moon (1994), who applied Carston (1988) to Korean conjunctive verbal suffixes, supports our analysis of the [X-*ko* Y]sequence.

The propositional relation between (10)a and (10)c is ENUMERATION. This is because the truth-value of (11)a equals the truth-value of (11)b where (10)a and (10)c are reversed (Suh 2006: 1105, 1124).

(11)   a. [NY's friend is able to play the piano] & [NY's friend is able to play the flute].

   b. [NY's friend is able to play the flute] & [NY's friend is able to play the piano].

In Rouchota's (1990) sense, *-ko* in (10)b has one enocded meaning: &. This is because of the meaning of *-ko* in (10)b is embedded in the antecedent of (12).

(12) If P_x-***ko*** P_y then NY's friend will like music teachers.

In terms of Relevance Theory, *-ko* in (10)b has one type of meaning: truth-conditional encoded meaning (&). From the viewpoint of Moon (1994: 66), who applies Relevance Theory to *-ko*, the truth-conditional encoded meaning of *-ko* in (10)b conjoins (10)a and (10)c truth-functionally and yields a single conjoined truth-conditional proposition (11)a.

FORWARD SEQUENTIAL

Consider the following example.

(13) (DS & HK From 'My Excursion')
      [Context: HK knows that DS lives at the dormitory. DS tells HK about what he experienced when he joined a party at his friend's house.]

a. P_x: DS ate dishes in DS's friend's party at t.

b. *-ko*

c. P_y: DS came back to DS's dormitory at t+n.

The propositional relation between (13)a and (13)c is FORWARD SEQUENTIAL because DS's eating dishes in clause (13)a precedes DS's going to his dormitory in (13)c. In Rouchota's (1990) sense, *-ko* in (13)b encodes & in that this meaning is embedded in the antecedent of (14).

(14)   If P_x-*ko* P_y then DS will go to sleep.

So, *-ko* in (13)b has one type of meaning: truth-conditional encoded meaning (&). In terms of Relevance Theory, the truth-conditional encoded meaning of *-ko* in (13)b conjoins (13)a and (13)c truth-functionally and forms a single conjoined truth-conditional proposition (15).

(15)   [DS ate dishes at DS's friend's party at t] & [DS came back to DS's dormitory at t+n].

How does FORWARD SEQUENTIAL obtain in a single conjoined truth-conditional proposition that contains the truth-conditional encoded meaning & of *-ko* in (13)b? From Moon's (1994: 67) point of view, the hearer realises that in (10) the time indexical *t* is ahead of the other time indexical *t+n* and infers FORWARD SEQUENTIAL. Our analysis is identical to Moon's (1994: 67).

CAUSAL

Consider the following example.

(16) (HY & NY From 'My Excursion')

[Context: HY and NY are talking about what kinds of items booth keepers sold at the excursions in their school days.]

a. P_x: Booth keepers knew when and where HY and NY would go on excursions at t.

b. *-ko*

c. P_y: Booth keepers went to the excursions at t+n.

The propositional relation between (16)a and (16)c is CAUSAL in that in (16) booth keepers' knowing dates and destinations of excursions in clause (a) causes booth keepers' going to the excursions in clause (c). In Rouchota's (1990) sense, *-ko* in (16)b has one type of meaning: truth-conditional encoded meaning (&). This is because the meaning of *-ko* in (16)b is embedded in the antecedent of (17).

(17) If P_x-*ko* P_y then booth keepers will sell goods at the excursions.

Let us illustrate how CAUSAL obtains in a single conjoined truth-conditional proposition that contains the non-truth-conditional encoded meaning & of *-ko* in (16)b. In terms of Relevance Theory, & of (16)b conjoins (16)a and (16)c truth-functionally and makes up a single conjoined truth-conditional proposition (18).

(18)   [Booth keepers knew when and where HY and NY would go on excursions at t]p & [as a result of p booth keepers went to the excursions at t+n].

From Moon's (1994: 67) standpoint, the hearer gains access to contextual assumptions, such as (19)a-b, and recovers *as a result of p*, such as in (18), while realising that *p* is a cause, and infers CAUSAL.

(19)   a. Booth keepers sold many kinds of items at the excursions in HY and NY's school days.
       b. The information about the date and destination of excursions is a prerequisite for selling items at the excursions.

Our analysis is what Moon (1994: 67) adopted.

SIMULTANEITY

Consider the following example.

(20)   (HY & JS From 'My Hobby')
       [Context: JS is telling HY an event that JS experienced when he fished in the sea in Australia. JS explained that he stopped fishing at sunset in order to arrive home before midnight.]
       a. P_x: JS drove a car at t.
       b. *-ko*
       c. P_y: JS went home at t.

The propositional relation between (20)a and (20)c is SIMULTANEITY in the sense that JS's driving a car in (20)a and JS's going home in (20)c overlap temporally. In Rouchota's (1990) sense, *-ko* in (20)b encodes & because this meaning is embedded in the antecedent of (21).

    (21) If P_x-**ko** P_y than JS will eat a dinner at home.

The truth-conditional encoded meaning & *-ko* in (20)b conjoins (20)a and (20)c truth-functionally and shapes a single conjoined truth-conditional proposition (22).

    (22) [JS drove a car at t] & [JS went home at t].

From the Relevance Theorists' angle, SIMULTENITY, which obtain in (22), is not encoded by & but drawn by inference on the ground that the hearer perceives that the two time indices *t*'s of (22) refer to the same point in time and infers SIMULTANEITY.

6.1.2 Encoded meanings of *-nuntey*

As seen in Table 6.6 below, the [X-*nuntey* Y] sequence involves ten propositional relations.

Table 6.6: Frequencies of Propositional Relations (the [X-*nuntey* Y] Sequence)

Propositional Relations	Frequencies
TIME	63 Tokens (12.52%)
CAUSAL	27 Tokens (5.37%)
CONTRAST	88 Tokens (17.50%)
DENIAL OF EXPECTATION	166 Tokens (33.00%)
INTRODUCTION	52 Tokens (10.34%)
INFERENTIAL	8 Tokens (1.59%)
BACKWARD INFERENTIAL	10 Tokens (1.99%)
REPETITION	31 Tokens (6.16%)
REFORMULATION	45 Tokens (8.95%)
EXEMPLIFICATION	13 Tokens (2.58%)
Total	503 Tokens (100.00%)

These appeared in Table 5.4, but we repeat it hear here for convenience's sake.

In this section, we will choose five relations: TIME, CAUSAL, CONTRAST, DENIAL OF EXPECTATION, and INTRODUCTION. These five relations involve the following encoded meanings. We do not deal with the other five relations in Table 6.6 above because they involve non-truth-conditional inferred meanings (see Section 6.2.2.).

Table 6.7: Encoded Meanings of -*nuntey*

Propositional Relations	Encoded Meanings	
	Truth-Conditional	Non-Truth-Conditional
TIME	*when*	
CAUSAL	*as a result of*	
CONTRAST	*&*	Contrast Meaning
DENIAL OF EXPECTATION	*&*	Denial of Expectation Meaning
INTRODUCTION	*&*	Introduction Meaning

TIME

Consider the following example.

> (23)   (DS & HK From 'My Excursion')
>
> [Context: DS is telling HK of his experience when his front teeth were broken during his childhood. DS says that his two front teeth were broken and fell out when he was eating shrimp crisps. However, HK expresses the feeling that she cannot understand why his teeth fell out.]
>
> a. P_x: DS ate shrimp crisps.
>
> b. ***-nuntey***
>
> c. P_y: DS's front teeth dropped out.

The propositional relation between (23)a and (23)c is TIME because DS's losing his front milk teeth in (23)c occurs at the time at which DS ate shrimp crisps in (23)a. In Rouchota's (1990) sense, a time meaning is encoded by *-nuntey* in (23)b because this meaning is embedded in the antecedent of (24).

> (24)   If P_x-***nuntey*** P_y then DS will put the fallen teeth into a wastebasket.

In terms of Relevance Theory, *-nuntey* in (23)b has one type of meaning: truth-conditional encoded meaning (*when*). From the Relevance Theorists' angle, the truth-conditional encoded meaning *when* of -*nuntey* in (23)b conjoins (23)a and (23)c truth-functionally and makes up a single conjoined truth-conditional proposition, such as (25).

> (25)   [When DS was eating shrimp crisps], [DS's front teeth dropped out].

CAUSAL

Consider the following example.

> (26) (HY & NY From 'My Hobby')
>
> [Context: NY is telling HY about a CD she lent someone. NY says that she does not remember to whom she lent her CD. However, she suddenly remembers it ...]
>
> a. P_x: NY knows to whom she lent her CD.
>
> b. ***-nuntey***
>
> c. P_y: NY will meet the person to whom she lent her CD.

The propositional relation between (26)a and (26)c is CAUSAL in that NY's knowing to whom she lent her CD in (26)a causes NY's meeting that person in (26)c. In Rouchota's (1990) sense, a causal meaning is encoded by *-nuntey* in (26)b in that this meaning is embedded in the antecedent of (27).

> (27) If P_x-***nuntey*** P_y then the person will give back the CD.

In terms of Relevance Theory, *-nuntey* in (26)b has one type of meaning: truth-conditional encoded meaning (*as a result of*). From a Relevance Theorist's standpoint, the truth-conditional encoded meaning *as a result of* of *-nuntey* in (26)b conjoins (26)a and (26)c truth-functionally and forms a single conjoined truth-conditional proposition, such as (28).

> (28) [As a result of NY's knowing to whom she lent her CD] [NY will meet the person to whom she lent her CD].

CONTRAST

Consider the following example.

> (29) (HY & JS From 'My Excursion')
>
> [Context: JS is telling HY of his experience when he was a soldier. JS says that he joined one week's military drill ...]
>
> a. P_x: JS lost weight during one week's military drill.
>
> b. ***-nuntey***
>
> c. P_y: JS gained weight after one week's military drill.

The propositional relation between (29)a and (29)c is CONTRAST in that JS's losing weight in (29)a presents a striking contrast with his gaining weight in (29)c. In Rouchota's (1990) sense, *-nuntey* in (29)b encodes & and a contrast meaning in that these two meanings are embedded in the antecedent of (30).

> (30) If P_x-***nuntey*** P_y then JS will buy new clothes.

In terms of Gricean and neo-Gricen theories, *-nuntey* in (29)b has two types of meaning: (1) truth-conditional encoded meaning (&); (2) non-truth-conditional encoded meaning (contrast meaning). First, from Gricean and neo-Gricean theorists' points of view, the truth-conditional encoded meaning & of *-nuntey* of (29)b conjoins (29)a and (29)c truth-functionally and shapes a single conjoined truth-conditional proposition, such as (31).

(31) [JS lost weight during one week's military drill] & [JS gained weight after one week's military drill].

Second, from their angle, the contrast meaning of *-nuntey* of (29)b signals that (29)a contrasts to (29)c.

DENIAL OF EXPECTATION

Consider the following example.

(32) (HY & JS From 'My Excursion')
[Context: JS is telling HY about an experience when he visited a certain death camp that was built by Nazis. JS explained that he met an old guide who was in the death camp in World War II, and that the guide's older sister was executed in front of him.]
a. P_x: JS was saddened by the story that a poor Jewish girl was executed by the Nazis in front of her brother.
b. ***-nuntey***
c. P_y: JS did not cry.

The propositional relation between (32)a and (32)c is DENIAL OF EXPECTATION. This is because the expectation, such as (33), which is derived from (32)a, is denied by (32)c.

(33) JS cried.

-Nuntey in (32)b encodes two meanings, & and a denial of expectation meaning. This is because these meanings are embedded in the antecedent of

(34) (cf. Rouchota 1990: 71).

    (34)   If P_x-***nuntey*** P_y then JS will go to other death camp.

In terms of Gricean and neo-Gricean theories, -*nuntey* in (32)b has two types of meanings: (1) truth-conditional encoded meaning (&); (2) non-truth-conditional encoded meaning (denial of expectation meaning) First, from Gricean and neo-Gricean theorists' viewpoints, the truth-conditional encoded meaning & of -*nuntey* in (32)b conjoins (32)a and (32)c truth-functionally and yields a single conjoined truth-conditional proposition, such as (35).

    (35)   [JS was saddened by the story that a poor Jewish girl was executed by the Nazis in front of her brother] & [JS did not cry].

Second, from their standpoint, the denial of expectation meaning of -*nuntey* in (32)b signals that (33) contrasts with (32)c.

INTRODUCTION

Consider the following example.

    (36)   (DS & HK From 'My Excursion')
         [Context: HY is telling DS episodes about butter she picked up from a certain pub.]
         a. P_x: One of HK's Korean friends went to a certain pub with her.
         b. -***nuntey***

c. P_y: The same friend told HK that she would take packets of butter from the pub.

The propositional relation between (36)a and (36)c is INTRODUCTION in the sense that (36)a introduces *One of HK's friends* on which the speaker focuses in (36)c. *-Nuntey* in (36)b encodes & and an introduction meaning in that these meanings are embedded in the antecedent of (37) (cf. Rouchota 1990).

(37) If P_x-***nuntey*** P_y then the friend will eat them.

Let us analyse *-nuntey* in (36)b in terms of Gricean and neo-Gricean theories. The two theories do not take up INTRODUCTION, which obtains between two propositions, but they are applicable to *-nuntey* in (36)b for the two rationales. One is that *-nuntey* in (36)b is a "coordinate conjunctive ending" (Kwon 1984: 46, 1985: 46, 1992: 258). The other is that the introduction meaning of *-nuntey* in (36)b is a higher-order speech act that comments on the two propositions (36)a and (36)c. In this sense, *-nuntey* in (36)b has two types of meanings: (1) truth-conditional encoded meaning (&); (2) non-truth-conditional encoded meaning (introduction meaning). First, from the angles of Gricean and neo-Gricean theorists, the truth-conditional encoded meaning & of *-nuntey* in (36)b conjoins (36)a and (36)c truth-functionally and constructs a single conjoined truth-conditional proposition, such as (38).

(38)   [One of HK's Korean friends went to a certain pub with her] & [the same friend told HK that she would take packets of butter from the pub].

Second, from their point of view, the introduction meaning of *-nuntey* in (36)b signals that (36)a introduces *One of HK's friends* on which the speaker focuses in (36)c.[32]

6.1.3 Encoded meanings of *-nikka*

As shown in Table 6.8 below, the [X-*nikka* Y] sequence involves five propositional relations.

Table 6.8: Frequencies of Propositional Relations (the [X-*nikka* Y] Sequence)

Propositional Relations	Frequencies
TIME	23 Tokens (9.83%)
CAUSAL	161 Tokens (68.80%)
INFERENTIAL	42 Tokens (17.95%)
REPETITION	3 Tokens (1.28%)
REFORMULATION	5 Tokens (2.14%)
Total	234 Tokens (100.00%)

---

[32] One may say that INTRODUCTION, which the conjunctive verbal suffix *-nuntey* involves, seems more like a function than a meaning. That is to say, his or her point is that certain expressions are **used** to introduce topics in a discourse, but that does not entail that they encode a conceptual meaning to this effect; a procedural analysis would seem more appropriate. However, this is not the case because according to Relevance Theory the procedural meaning is not a function but a **meaning**. Furthermore, we have great difficulty in seeing any theoretical basis in Relevance Theory for the analysis of an introduction meaning of *-nuntey* in(36). See Section 7.1. for more details.

These appeared in Table 5.6, but we proffer it here again for the convenience of exposition.

In this section, we will adopt two relations: TIME and CAUSAL. The two relations involve the following encoded meanings. We set aside the other three relations in that they involve non-truth-conditional inferred meanings (see Section 6.2.3.).

Table 6.9: Encoded Meanings of *-nikka*

Propositional Relations	Encoded Meanings	
	Truth-Conditional	Non-Truth-Conditional
TIME	*when*	
CAUSAL	*as a result of*	

TIME

Consider the following example.

    (39) (DS & HK From 'My Excursion')

        [Context: DS is telling HK how he did his assignment last Saturday.]

        a. P_x: The time was 2 o'clock in the morning last Sunday.

        b. ***-nikka***

        c. P_y: DS completed his assignment.

The propositional relation between (39)a and (39)c is TIME because the time at which DS finished his assignment was 2 o'clock in the morning last Sunday. In Rouchota's (1990) sense, a time meaning is encoded by *-nikka* in (39)b in that this meaning is embedded in the antecedent of (40).

(40)   If P_x-**nikka** P_y then DS will play tennis.

In terms of Relevance Theory, *-nikka* in (39)b has one type of meaning: truth-conditional encoded meaning (*when*). From the Relevance Theorists' standpoint, the truth-conditional encoded meaning *when* of *-nikka* in (29)b conjoins (39)a and (39)c truth-functionally and forms a single conjoined truth-conditional proposition, such as (41).

(41)   [When the time was 2 o'clock in the morning last Sunday], [DS completed his assignment].

CAUSAL

Consider the following example.

(42)   (NY & HY From 'My Hobby')
       [Context: HY tells NY about her friend who likes Barbie dolls very much.]
       a. P_x: HY's friend likes Barbie dolls very much.
       b. *-nikka*
       c. P_y: Every year HY's friend's mother gives HY's friend a Barbie doll as a Christmas gift.

The propositional relation between (42)a and (42)c is CAUSAL in that the daughter's liking Barbie dolls very much in (42)a is a cause for the mother to buy a Barbie doll every Christmas in (42)c. In Rouchota's (1990) sense, *-nikka* in (42)b encodes a causal meaning because this meaning is embedded in the antecedent of (43).

(43)   If P$_x$-***nikka*** P$_y$ then the friend will play with them.

In terms of Relevance Theory, *-nikka* in (42)b has one type of meaning: truth-conditional encoded meaning (*as a result of*). From a Relevance Theorist's point of view, the truth-conditional encoded meaning *as a result of* of *-nikka* in (42)b conjoins (42)a and (42)c truth-functionally and yields a single conjoined truth-conditional proposition, such as (44).

(44)   [As a result of HY's friend's liking Barbie dolls very much] [every year HY's friend's mother gives HY's friend a Barbie doll as a Christmas gift].

6.1.4 Encoded meanings of *-se*

As seen in Table 6.10 below, the [X-*se* Y] sequence involves four propositional relations.

Table 6.10: Frequencies of Propositional Relations (the [X-*se* Y] Sequence)

Propositional Relations	Frequencies
FORWARD SEQUENTIAL	137 Tokens (59.57%)
CAUSAL	83 Tokens (36.09%)
REPETITION	3 Tokens (1.30%)
REFORMULATION	7 Tokens (3.04%)
Total	230 Tokens (100.00%)

These appeared in Table 5.7, but we show it here again for convenience's sake.

In this section, we will take up two relations: FORWARD SEQUENTIAL and CAUSAL. The two relations involve the following encoding meanings. We exclude the other two relations as they involve non-truth-conditional inferred meanings (see Section 6.2.4.).

Table 6.11: Encoded Meanings of *-se*

Propositional Relations	Encoded Meanings	
	Truth-Conditional	Non-Truth-Conditional
FORWARD SEQUENTIAL	*after*	
CAUSAL	*as a result of*	

FORWARD SEQUENTIAL

Consider the following example.

    (45) (DS & HK From 'When I Was a Primary School Student')
        [Context: DS is explaining why he received a scholarship from his university.]
        a. P_x: DS entered the university.
        b. *-se*
        c. P_y: DS was at the top on the first term.

The propositional relation between (45)a and (45)c is FORWARD SEQUENTIAL because DS's entering the university in (45)a precedes DS's being at the top on the first term in (45)c. In Rouchota's (1990) sense, a forward sequential meaning is encoded by *-se* in (45)b in that this meaning is embedded in the antecedent of (46).

    (46) If P_x-*se* P_y then DS will receive a scholarship from his university.

In terms of Relevance Theory, *-se* in (45)b has one type of meaning: truth-conditional encoded meaning (*after*). From the Relevance Theorists' standpoint, the truth-conditional encoded meaning *after* of *-se* in (45)b conjoins (45)a and (45)c truth-functionally and yields a single conjoined truth-conditional proposition, such as (47).

(47)　[After DS entered the university at t], [DS was at the top on the first term at t+n].

CAUSAL

Consider the following example.

(48)　(DS & HK　From 'When I Was a Primary School Student')
　　　[Context: DS is explaining why he passed an entrance examination for a university.]
　　　a. P_x: DS read a large number of books.
　　　b. *-se*
　　　c. P_y: DS obtained a good result from an entrance examination for a university.

The propositional relation between (48)a and (48)c is CAUSAL in that DS's reading multitudinous books in (48)a causes DS's obtaining a good result from an entrance examination (48)c. In Rouchota's (1990) sense, *-se* in (48)b encodes a causal meaning because this meaning is embedded in the antecedent of (49).

(49)   If P_x-*se* P_y then DS will pass an entrance examination for a university.

In terms of Relevance Theory, -*se* in (48)b has one type of meaning: truth-conditional encoded meaning (*as a result of*). From the Relevance Theorists' point of view, the truth-conditional encoded meaning *as a result of* of -*se* in (48)b conjoins (48)a and (48)c truth-functionally and forms a single conjoined truth-conditional proposition, such as (50).

(50)   [As a result of DS's having read a large number of books] [DS obtained a good result from an entrance examination for a university].

6.1.5 Encoded meanings of -*ciman*

As shown in Table 6.12 below, the [X-*ciman* Y] sequence involves two propositional relations.

Table 6.12: Frequencies of Propositional Relations (the [X-*ciman* Y] Sequence)

Propositional Relations	Frequencies
CONTRAST	9 Tokens (28.13%)
DENIAL OF EXPECTATION	23 Tokens (71.87%)
Total	32 Tokens (100.00%)

These appeared in Table 5.8 but we repeat it here for expository convenience.

In this section, we will take up two relations: CONTRAST and DENIAL OF EXPECTATION. The two relations involve the following encoded meanings.

Table 6.13: Encoded Meanings of *-ciman*

Propositional Relations	Encoded Meanings	
	Truth-Conditional	Non-Truth-Conditional
CONTRAST	&	Contrast Meaning
DENIAL OF EXPECTATION	&	Denail of Expectation Meaning

CONTRAST

Consider the following example.

(51) (SH & YH From 'My Hobby')

[Context: SH and YH are talking about the definition of hobby. SH is telling YH that most people are not interested in the subject of hobbies, and hence that they hesitate to answer it when asked what kinds of hobby they have.]

a. P_x: If people suddenly ask SH his name and age, he can easily supply the answer.

b. *-ciman*

c. P_y: If people suddenly ask SH of about his hobby, he cannot easily supply the answer.

The propositional relation between (51)a and (51)c is CONTRAST because providing name and age easily in (51)a forms a striking contrast to not easily answering hobby in (51)c. In Rouchota's (1990) sense, *-ciman* in (51)b encodes & and a contrast meaning in that these meanings are embedded in the antecedent of (52).

(52) If P_x-*ciman* P_y then people will not easily answer what kinds of hobby they have.

In terms of Gricean and neo-Gricean theories, *-ciman* in (37)b has two types of meanings: (1) truth-conditional encoded meaning (&); (2) non-truth-conditional encoded meaning (contrast meaning). First, from the angle of Gricean and neo-Gricean theorists, the truth-conditional encoded meaning & of *-ciman* in (51)b conjoins (51)a and (51)c truth-functionally and yields a single conjoined truth-conditional proposition, such as (53).

(53)   [If people suddenly ask SH his name and age, he can easily answer them] & [if people suddenly ask SH his hobby, he cannot easily answer it].

Second, from their point of view, the contrast meaning of *-ciman* in (51)b signals that (51)a is in contrast with (51)c.

DENIAL OF EXPECTATION

Consider the following example.

(54)   (DS & HK From 'When I Was a Primary School Student')
[Context: DS is telling HK about human relations with his classmates in his school days. DS is explaining that he made friends with his classmates after he became a year ten student.]
a. P_x: DS played with his classmates before he was a year ten student.
b. *-ciman*
c. P_y: DS did not open up his mind to his classmates before he was a year ten student.

The propositional relation between (54)a and (54)c is DENIAL OF

EXPECTATION in that the expectation, such as (55), which is derived from (54)a, is denied by (54)c.

(55)   DS opened up his mind to his classmates before he was a year ten student.

-Ciman in (54)b encodes & and a denial of expectation meaning. This is because the two meanings of *-ciman* in (54)b are embedded in the antecedent of (56) (cf. Rouchota 1990: 71).

(56)   If P_x-***ciman*** P_y then DS will not have a good friend.

In terms of Gricean and neo-Gricean theories, *-ciman* in (54)b has two types of meanings: (1) truth-conditional encoded meaning (&); (2) non-truth-conditional encoded meaning (denial of expectation meaning). First, from the angle of Gricean and neo-Gricean theorists, the truth-conditional encoded meaning & of *-ciman* in (54)b conjoins (54)a and (54)c truth-functionally and forms a single conjoined truth-conditional proposition, such as (57).

(57)   [DS played with his classmates before he was a year ten student] & [DS did not open up his mind to his classmates before he was a year ten student].

Second, from their point of view, the denial of expectation meaning of *-ciman* in (54)b signals that (55) is in contrast with (54)c.

6.1.6 Encoded meanings of *-to*

As seen in Table 6.14 below, the [X-*to* Y] sequence involves three propositional relations.

Table 6.14: Frequencies of Propositional Relations (the [X-*to* Y] Sequence)

Propositional Relations	Frequencies
CONDITION	6 Tokens (22.22%)
CONTRAST	1 Token (3.70%)
DENIAL OF EXPECTATION	20 Tokens (74.07%)
Total	27 Tokens (100.00%)

These appeared in Table 5.10 but we provide it here for convenience's sake.

In this section, we will take up three relations: CONDITION, CONTRAST, and DENIAL OF EXPECTATION. The three relations involve the following encoded meanings.

Table 6.15: Encoded Meanings of *-to*

Propositional Relations	Encoded Meanings	
	Truth-Conditional	Non-Truth-Conditional
CONDITION	$\rightarrow$	
CONTRAST	&	Contrast Meaning
DENIAL OF EXPECTATION	&	Denial of Expectation Meaning

CONDITION

Consider the following example.

(58) (HY & JS From 'When I was a Primary School Student')

[Context: HY and JS are talking about teachers in their primary schools.]

a. P_x: JS thinks of one of his female assistant teachers in his primary school.

b. ***-to***

c. P_y: JS is sure of that the assistant teacher was beautiful.

The propositional relation between (58)a and (58)c is CONDITION because thinking of the female assistants in (58)a and being sure of that she was beautiful in (58)c are identified as 'antecedent' and 'consequent' respectively. In Rouchota's (1990) sense, a condition meaning is encoded by *-to* in (58)b in that this meaning is embedded in the antecedent of (59).

(59) If P_x-***to*** P_y then JS will meet the teacher.

In terms of Relevance Theory, *-to* in (58)b has one type of meaning: truth-conditional encoded meaning ($\rightarrow$). From the Relevance Theorists' point of view, the truth-conditional encoded meaning $\rightarrow$ of *-to* in (58)b conjoins (58)a and (58)c truth-functionally and forms a single conjoined truth-conditional proposition, such as (60).

(60) [JS thinks of one of his female assistant teachers in his primary school] $\rightarrow$ [JS is sure of that the assistant teacher was beautiful].

CONTRAST

Consider the following example.

(61) (SH & YH From 'My Hobby')

[Context: SH and YH are talking about the definition of hobby. SH restricts the scope of a hobby within narrow limits only useful to self-culture. However, YH considers a hobby as everything that relieves mental stress.]

a. P_x: A hobby is not everything that relieves mental stress.

b. *-to*

c. P_y: A hobby is everything that relieves mental stress.

The propositional relation between (61)a and (61)c is CONTRAST in that in (61)a and (61)c the two definitions of hobby are in contrast with each other. In Rouchota's (1990) sense, -*to* in (61)b encodes & and a contrast meaning in the sense that these meanings are embedded in the antecedent of (62).

(62) If P_x-*to* P_y then YH will enjoy his hobbies.

In terms of Gricean and neo-Gricean theories, -*to* in (61)b has two types of meanings: (1) truth-conditional encoded meaning (&); (2) non-truth-conditional (contrast meaning). First, from the standpoint of Gricean and neo-Gricean theorists, the truth-conditional encoded meaning & of -*to* in (61)b conjoins (61)a and (61)c truth-functionally and yields a single conjoined truth-conditional proposition, such as (63).

(63) [A hobby is not everything that relieves mental stress] & [a hobby is everything that relieves mental stress].

Second, the contrast meaning of *-to* in (61)b signals that (61)a is in contrast with (61)c.

DENIAL OF EXPECTATION

Consider the following example.

(64) (DS & HK From 'When I Was a Primary School Student')
      [Context: DS is telling HK that the relationship between his father and him was not good before he became a Christian. DS now explains that he did not show his report card after year 7.]
      a. P_x: DS did not show his father his report card.
      b. *-to*
      c. P_y: DS's father did not say anything to DS about DS's not showing him DS's report card.

The propositional relation between (64)a and (64)c is DENIAL OF EXPECTATION in the sense that the expectation (65), which is derived from (64)a, is denied by (64)c.

(65) DS's father said something about, or even scolded DS, for DS's not showing him DS's report card.

-To in (64)b encodes & and a denial of expectation meaning. This is because the two meanings of *-to* in (64)b are embedded in the antecedent of (66) (cf. Rouchota 1990: 71).

(66) If P_x-*to* P_y then DS will not be a good student.

In terms of Gricean and neo-Gricean theories, *-to* in (64)b has two types of meanings: (1) truth-conditional encoded meaning (&); (2) non-truth-conditional encoded meaning (denial of expectation meaning). First, from the angles of Gricean and neo-Gricean theorists, the truth-conditional encoded meaning & of *-to* in (64)b conjoins (64)a and (64)c truth-functionally and forms a single conjoined truth-conditional proposition, such as (67).

    (67)   [DS did not show his father his report card] & [DS's father did not say anything to DS about DS's not showing him DS's report card].

Second, their standpoint, the denial of expectation meaning of *-to* in (64)b signals that (66) is in contrast with (65)c.

6.2 Two Truth-Functionally Disjoined Propositions

The aim of this section is to show that non-truth-conditional inferred meanings of Korean conjunctive verbal suffixes, *-ko*, *-nuntey*, *-nikka*, and *-se*, truth-functionally disjoin P_x and P_y.

Our non-truth-conditional inferred meanings of Korean conjunctive verbal suffixes are meanings that occur when the following propositional relations are inferred from P_x and P_y. First, the non-truth-conditional inferred meaning of *-ko* occurs when REPETITION is inferred from P_x and P_y. Second, the non-truth-conditional inferred meanings of *-nuntey* occur when INFERENTIAL, BACKWARD INFEREITAL, REPETITION, REFORMULATION, and EXEMPLIFICATION are inferred from P_x and P_y. Third, the non-truth-conditional inferred meanings of *-nikka* occur when INFERENTIAL, REPETITION, and REFORMULATION are inferred from P_x and P_y. Fourth, the non-truth-conditional inferred meanings of *-se* occur when REPETITION and REFORMULATION are inferred from P_x and P_y.

The frequencies of two disjoined truth-functionally propositions in our data are provided in Table 6.16 below. This table says that the number of propositional relations, which have something to do with non-truth-conditional meanings of conjunctive verbal suffixes *-ko*, *-nuntey*, *-nikka*, and *-se*, is significantly smaller than that of propositional relations encoded by these four suffixes, and that the other two suffixes *-ciman* and *-to* do not have any non-truth-conditional inferred meaning.

Table 6.16: Frequencies of Two Truth-Functionally Disjoined Propositions

Suffixes	Frequencies	
	Two Truth-Functionally Disjoined Propositions	Propositional Relations between P_x and P_y
-ko	356 Tokens (68.07%)	1,156 Tokens (52.98%)
-nuntey	107 Tokens (20.46%)	503 Tokens (23.05%)
-nikka	50 Tokens (9.56%)	234 Tokens (10.72%)
-se	10 Tokens (1.91%)	230 Tokens (10.54%)
-ciman		32 Tokens (1.47%)
-to		27 Tokens (1.24%)
Total	523 Tokens (100.00%)	2,182 Tokens (100.00%)

What ensues in this section will show that the inferred meanings of a given suffix truth-functionally disjoin two propositions P_x and P_y.

6.2.1 Inferred meanings of *-ko*

As shown in Table 6.17 below, the [X-*ko*Y] sequence involves five propositional relations. These appeared in Table 5.2, but we repeat it here for expository convenience.

Table 6.17: Frequencies of Propositional Relations (the [X-*ko* Y] Sequence)

Propositional Relations	Frequencies
ENUMERATION	409 Tokens (35.38%)
FORWARD SEQUENTIAL	253 Tokens (21.88%)
CAUSAL	35 Tokens (3.03%)
SIMULTANEITY	103 Tokens (8.91%)
REPETITION	356 Tokens (30.80%)
Total	1,156 Tokens (100.00%)

In Section 6.1.1., we showed that *-ko* in the [X-*ko* Y] sequence, which involve four propositional relations ENUMERATION, FORWARD SEQUENTIAL, CAUSAL, and SIMULTANEITY, has one truth-conditional encoded meaning $\&$, and that this meaning conjoins P_x and P_y truth-functionally and hence makes up a single conjoined truth-conditional proposition. In this section, we will take up other relation: REPETITION.

REPETITION

Consider the following example.

    (68) (SH & YH From 'My Hobby')

        [Context: SH and YH are talking about kinds of hobbies.]

        a. P_x: There exist multitudinous hobbies.

        b. **-ko**

        c. P_y: There exist multitudinous hobbies.

The propositional relation between (68)a and (68)c is REPETITION because in (68) clause (c) is identical to clause (a). In Rouchota's (1990) sense, REPETITION is inferred from (68)a and (68)c in that this relation is not embedded in the antecedent of (69)

    (69) If ... then people will choose may hobbies.

One type of non-truth-conditional inferred meaning occurs when REPETITION obtains between the two segments coupled by *-ko* in (68)b and this meaning disjoins (68)a and (68)c truth-functionally.

6.2.2 Inferred meanings of *-nuntey*

As shown in Table 6.18 below, the [X-*nuntey* Y] sequence involves ten propositional relations. These appeared in Table 5.4, but we provide it here again for convenience's sake.

Table 6.18: Frequencies of Propositional Relations (the [X-*nuntey* Y] Sequence)

Propositional Relations	Frequencies
TIME	63 Tokens (12.52%)
CAUSAL	27 Tokens (5.37%)
CONTRAST	88 Tokens (17.50%)
DENIAL OF EXPECTATION	166 Tokens (33.00%)
INTRODUCTION	52 Tokens (10.34%)
INFERENTIAL	8 Tokens (1.59%)
BACKWARD INFERENTIAL	10 Tokens (1.99%)
REPETITION	31 Tokens (6.16%)
REFORMULATION	45 Tokens (8.95%)
EXEMPLIFICATION	13 Tokens (2.58%)
Total	503 Tokens (100.00%)

In Section 6.1.2., we showed that -*nuntey* in the [X-*nuntey* Y] sequence, which involves five propositional relations TIME, CAUSAL, CONTRAST, DENIAL OF EXPECTATION, and INTRODUCTION, has three truth-conditional encoded meanings &, *when*, and *as a result of*, and that these three meanings conjoin P_x and P_y truth-funcationally and hence makes up a single conjoined truth-conditional proposition. In this section, we will take up another five propositional relations INFERENTIAL, BACKWARD INFERENTIAL, REPETITION, REFORMULATION, and EXEMPLIFICATION.

INFERENTIAL

Consider the following example.

(70) (DS & HK From 'My excursion')

[Context: DS tells HK about what he is cooking in his dormitory in Australia. DS says that he tastes the same flavour as he did in his home in Korea when he eats *kimchi* 'Korean pickled vegetables' made by him.]

a. P_x: The thing that DS is making in his dormitory is *kimchi*.

b. ***-nuntey***

c. P_y: DS tastes the same flavour wherever he eats *kimchi*.

The propositional relation between (70)a and (70)c is INFERENTIAL because hearer HK can derive (70)c from (70)a if she assumes that that anyone tastes the same flavour of *kimchi* 'Korean pickled cabbage' everywhere. In Rouchota's (1990) sense, INFERENTIAL is inferred from (70)a and (70)c in that this relation is not embedded in the antecedent of (71).

(71) If ... then DS will eat *kimchi* very much.

One type of non-truth-conditional inferred meaning occurs when INFERENTIAL obtains between the two segments coupled by *-nuntey* in (70)b. From the Default-Semanticists' angle, this meaning disjoins (70)a and (70)c truth-functionally.

BACKWARD INFERENTIAL

Consider the following example.

(72) (HY & NY From 'My Hobby')

[Context: NY is explaining why she likes being alone at home.]

a. P_x: NY likes being alone at home.

b. *-nuntey*

c. P_y: [NY daydreams very much at home] & [she imagines a lot of things at home].

The propositional relation between (72)a and (72)c is BACKWARD INFERENTIAL in that hearer HY can derive (72)a from (72)c if she assumes that people, who daydream very much and imagine a lot of things, can forget the tedium of everyday affairs and that people like forgetting the tedium of everyday affairs. In Rouchota's (1990) sense, BACKWARD INFERENTIAL is inferred from (72)a and (72)c because this relation is not embedded in the antecedent of (73).

(73)   If ... then NY will go to the movies alone.

One type of non-truth-conditional inferred meaning occurs when BACKWARD INFERENTIAL obtains between the two segments linked by *-nuntey* in (72)b and this meaning disjoins (72)a and (72)c truth-functionally.

REPETITION

Consider the following example.

(74)   (HY & NY From 'My Excursion')
      [Context: HY is telling an episode related to bugs when she went on an excursion in her school days. HY says that she went to places of nature and

amusement parks on excursions rather than places in cities, and that she found it difficult to eat ice cream and soft drink because of bugs.]

a. P_x: HY hates bugs intensely.

b. ***-nuntey***

c. P_y: HY hates bugs intensely.

The propositional relation between (74)a and (74)c is REPETITION in the sense that in (74) clause (c) is identical to clause (a). In Rouchota's (1990) sense, REPETITION is inferred from (74)a and (74)c. This is because this relation is not embedded in the antecedent of (75).

(75) If ... then HY will not tough bugs.

One type of non-truth-conditional inferred meaning occurs when REPETITION obtains between the two segments connected by *-nuntey* in (74)b and this meaning disjoins (74)a and (74)c truth-functionally.

REFORMULATION

Consider the following example.

(76) (DS & HK From 'My Excursion)

[Context: DS is explaining how he writes assignments. HK says that she cannot understand why DS summarises repeatedly the same article given as an assignment. DS explains how he summarises articles. He is telling about articles he summarised recently.]

  a. P_x: The article that DS summarised as an assignment recently is related to probable invasion.

  b. *-nuntey*

  c. P_y: The article that DS summarised as an assignment recently is related to how the orientation of market theory affects the success of enterprises.

The propositional relation between (76)a and (76)c is REFORMULATION in the sense that in (76) clause (c) resembles clause (a). In Rouchota's (1990) sense, REFORMULATION is inferred from (76)a and (76)c in that this relation is not embedded in the antecedent of (77).

  (77) If ... then DS will submit the assignment.

One type of non-truth-conditional inferred meaning occurs when REFORMULATION obtains between the two segments coupled by *-nuntey* in (76)b and this meaning disjoins (76)a and (76)c truth-functionally.

EXEMPLIFICATION

Consider the following example.

  (78) (HY & NY From 'When I Was a Primary School Student')

    [Context: HY is telling NY about the types of institute she attended in her primary school days.]

    a. P_x: HY attended many educational institutes in her primary school days.

    b. *-nuntey*

  c. P_y: [HY attended private schools for calligraphy] & [HY attended a private school for ice skating] & [HY attended a swimming pool in the holidays].

The propositional relation between (78)a and (78)c is EXEMPLIFICATION. This is because in (78) clause (c) provides examples of clause (a). In Rouchota's (1990) sense, EXEMPLIFICATION is inferred from (78)a and (78)c in the sense that this relation is not embedded in the antecedent of (79).

  (79) If ... then HY will be a man of ability.

One type of non-truth-conditional inferred meaning occurs when EXEMPLIFICATION obtains between the two segments linked by *-nuntey* in (78)b and this meaning disjoins (78)a and (78)c truth-functionally.

6.2.3 Inferred meanings of *-nikka*

As was shown in Table 6.19 below, the [X-*nikka*Y] sequence involves five propositional relations. These appeared in Table 5.6, but we repeat it here for expository convenience.

Table 6.19: Frequencies of Propositional Relations (the [X-*nikka* Y] Sequence)

Propositional Relations	Frequencies
TIME	23 Tokens (9.83%)
CAUSAL	161 Tokens (68.80%)
INFERENTIAL	42 Tokens (17.95%)
REPETITION	3 Tokens (1.28%)
REFORMULATION	5 Tokens (2.14%)
Total	234 Tokens (100.00%)

In Section 6.1.3, we showed that *-nikka* in the [X-*nikka* Y] sequence, which involves TIME and CAUSAL, has two truth-conditional encoded meanings *when* and *as a result of*, and that these two meanings conjoin P_x and P_y truth-functionally and hence yield a single conjoined truth-conditional proposition. In this section, we will take up another three relations: INFERENTIAL, REPETITION, and REFORMULATION.

INFERENTIAL

Consider the following example.

(80) (NY & HY From 'My Hobby')

[Context: YH and SH are talking about cases of confectionery that they liked in their primary school days. YH says that he liked *Homlenpol*, which was a brand of biscuits produced in Korea, and that ...]

a. P_x: The box of biscuits was crushed.

b. ***-nikka***

c. P_y: The box of biscuits was badly packed.

The propositional relation between (80)a and (80)c is INFERENTIAL because hearer NY can derive (80)c from (80)a if she assumes that boxes of biscuits, which are well packed, are not crushed. In Rouchota's (1990) sense, INFERENTIAL is inferred from (80)a and (80)c in that this relation is not embedded in the antecedent of (81).

(81) If ... then YH will buy other box of biscuits.

One type of non-truth-conditional inferred meaning occurs when INFERENTIAL obtains between the two segments linked by *-nikka* in (80)b. From H-K. Lee's (2001: 198) point of view, this meaning disjoins (80)a and (80)c truth-functionally.

REPETITION

Consider the following example.

(82) (HY & NY From 'When I Was a Primary School Student')
[Context: NY is telling of her experience when her class teacher checked the homework of her classmates and herself in her primary school days.
On   that day, NY did not do her homework. So, in order not to be penalised, NY finished her homework while her teacher was checking the other students' homework.]
a. P_x: There were four divisions in each classroom when NY attended a primary school.
b. *-nikka*
c. P_y: There were four divisions in each classroom when NY attended a primary school.

The propositional relation between (82)a and (82)c is REPETITION in that in (82) clause (c) is identical to clause (a). In Rouchota's (1990) sense, REPETITION is inferred from (82)a and (82)c because this relation is not embedded in the antecedent of (83).

(83) If ... then NY will finish her homework.

One type of non-truth-conditional inferred meaning occurs when REPETITION obtains between the two segments coupled by -*nikka* and this meaning disjoins (82)a and (82)c truth-functionally.

REFORMULATION

Consider the following example.

> (84) (SH & YH From 'My Excursion')
>
> [Context: SH and YH are talking about events on the excursions in their school days. YH is explaining how the leader who performed the events was chosen.]
>
> a. P_x: The class teacher appointed a leader who would perform events on the excursions.
> b. **-*nikka***
> c. P_y: The class teacher appointed a student who had the best entertainment talent in the class as a leader who would perform events on the excursions.

The propositional relation between (84)a and (84)c is REFORMULATION. This is because in (84) clause (c) resembles clause (a). In Rouchota's (1990) sense, REFORMULATION is inferred from (84)a and (84)b in the sense that relation is not embedded in the antecedent of (85).

> (85) If ... then HY will enjoy the events.

One type of non-truth-conditional inferred meaning occurs when

REFORMULATION obtains between the two segments connected by -*nikka* in (84)b. This meaning disjoins (84)a and (84)c truth-functionally.

6.2.4 Inferred meanings of -*se*

As shown in Table 6.20, the [X-*se* Y] sequence involves four propositional relations. These appeared in Table 5.7, but we show it here again for convenience's sake.

Table 6.20: Frequencies of Propositional Relations (the [X-*se* Y] Sequence)

Propositional Relations	Frequencies
FORWARD SEQUENTIAL	137 Tokens (59.57%)
CAUSAL	83 Tokens (36.09%)
REPETITION	3 Tokens (1.30%)
REFORMULATION	7 Tokens (3.04%)
Total	230 Tokens (100.00%)

In Section 6.1.4, we showed that -*se* in the [X-*se* Y] sequence, which involves FORWARD SEQUENTIAL and CAUSAL, has two truth-conditional encoded meanings *after* and *as a result of*, and that these two meanings conjoin P_x and P_y truth-functionally and hence makes up a single conjoined truth-conditional proposition. In this section, we will take up another two relations: REPETITION and REFORMULATION.

REPETITION

Consider the following example.

(86) (DS & HK From 'When I Was a Primary School Student')
[Context: DS is telling HK of the relationship between his father and him. DS says that he did not apologise to his father for his faults because he did not like his father in his childhood, and that his father and he talked about this after DS grew up.]
a. P_x: DS grew up.
b. *-se*
c. P_y: DS grew up.

The propositional relation between (86)a and (86)c is REPETITION because in (86) clause (c) is identical to clause (a). In Rouchota's (1990) sense, REPETITION is inferred from (86)a and (86)c in that this relation is not embedded in the antecedent of (87).

(87) If ... then DS will not be a good man.

One type of non-truth-conditional inferred meaning occurs when REPETITION obtains between the two segments coupled by *-se* in (86)b and this meaning disjoins (86)a and (86)c truth-functionally.

REFORMULATION

Consider the following example.

(88) (HY & NY From 'My Hobby')
[Context: NY is telling about NY's friend who entered a college of engineering after giving up a teachers' college.]

a. P_x: NY's friend entered a university.

b. ***-se***

c. P_y: NY's friend entered a college of engineering.

The propositional relation between (88)a and (88)c is REFOMULATION. This is because in (88) clause (c) resembles clause (a). In Rouchota's (1990) sense, REFORMULATION is inferred from (88)a and (88)c in the sense that this relation is not embedded in the antecedent of (89).

(89) If ... then NY's friend will study hard in the university.

One type of non-truth-conditional inferred meaning occurs when REFORMULATION obtains between the two segments linked by *-se* in (88)b and this meaning disjoins (88)a and (88)c truth-functionally.

So far, we have adopted the scope test and shown that the truth-conditional encoded meanings of six conjunctive verbal suffixes *-ko, -nuntey, -nikka, -se, -ciman*, and *-to* conjoin two propositions P_x and P_y truth-functionally, and that the non-truth-conditional inferred meanings of four conjunctive verbal suffixes *-ko, -nuntey, -nikka*, and *-se* disjoin the two propositions truth-functionally. From this we found that the use of a given suffix, i.e., whether the meanings of the suffix truth-functionally conjoin or disjoin two propositions, is closely related to whether the meanings of the suffix are encoded or inferred. First, the meanings of a given suffix conjoin the two propositions P_x and P_y truth-functionally if and only if they are encoded by the suffix. One can say that non-truth-conditional encoded meanings do not conjoin P_x and P_y truth-functionally. However, a given suffix, which has a non-truth-conditional encoded meaning, such as a contrast meaning, a denial of expectation meaning, and an introduction meaning has the use of conjoining in that the suffix has simultaneously a truth-conditional encoded meaning $\&$. Second, the meanings of a given suffix disjoin the two propositions P_x and P_y truth-functionally if and only if they are drawn by inference.

In Chapter 7, we will adopt two theories Relevance Theory and Default Semantics as a reasoning tool and will examine encoded and inferred meanings of Korean conjunctive verbal suffixes together with arguments against the two theories.

7

The Nature of the Meanings of
Korean Conjunctive Verbal Suffixes:

Conceptual and Procedural Meanings, and the Scale
of Default-Semantic Meanings

In this chapter, we discuss the nature of the meanings of the suffixes, *-ko*, *-nuntey*, *-nikka*, *-se*, *-ciman*, and *-to*, from the two theoretical standpoints, Relevance Theory and Default Semantics. In particular, we argue against the assumption, held by Relevance Theorists (Blakemore 1992, 2000, 2002; Iten 2000, 2005; Hall 2004), that a connective which has a procedural meaning cannot have a conceptual meaning at the same time. We will also argue that the scale of Default-Semantic meanings of a connective works better with inferred manings that arise with the use of the connective, than with encoded meanings of the connective.

7.1 Conceptual and Procedural Meanings of Korean Conjunctive Verbal Suffixes

Relevance Theorists divide encoded meanings of connectives into two types: conceptual meanings (or concepts) and procedural meanings (or procedures). According to them, when a given connective conjoins two propositions truth-functionally and hence yields a single conjoined truth-conditional proposition, it is the conceptual meaning (in our terms a truth-conditional encoded meaning) of the connective that is responsible. By contrast, the procedural meaning of a given connective does not truth-functionally conjoin the two propositions (and thus it does not yield a single conjoined truth-conditional proposition), but instructs the hearer how to interpret the relationship between the two propositions.

Blakemore (1987, 1992), who introduced the notion of 'procedure', postulates that three English connectives *so, after all, however* encode a procedure in which the hearer identifies the contextualisation of the two segments linked by each of the connectives. That is to say, three connectives *so, after all*, and *however* encode a procedure that instructs the hearer to identify the contextualisation of two segments coupled by the connective as a contextual implication, a strengthening, and a contradiction respectively.

Let us consider the procedure of *so* in (1).

(1)   Barbara isn't in town. So David isn't here. (Blakemore 1992: 136)

According to Blakemore, the procedure of *so* in (1) is identified through three stages. First, the hearer adopts both the proposition, such as (2)a, recovered from the utterance before *so* in (1) and the accessible contextual assumption, like (2)b, as implicated premises and draws an implicated conclusion, such as (2)c.

(2)   a. Barbara is not in town.

    b. If Barbara is not in town, then David will not be in the place of utterance.

    c. David is not in the place of utterance.

Second, the hearer recovers the proposition, such as (3), from the utterance after *so* in (1).

(3)   David is not in the place of utterance.

Third, the hearer identifies the contextualisation of the utterance before *so* in (1) and the utterance after *so* in (1) as a contextual implication; (3) is an implicated conclusion of (2)a.

Let us consider the procedure of *after all* in (4).

(4)   Barbara isn't in town. After all, David isn't here. (Blakemore 1992: 136)

In Blakemore's terms, the procedure of *after all* in (4) is identified through three steps. First, the hearer recovers the proposition, such as (5), from the utterance before *after all* in (4).

(5)   Barbara is not in town.

Second, the hear adopts both the proposition, such as (6)a, recovered from the utterance after *after all* in (4) and the accessible contextual assumption, like (6)b, as implicated premises and draws an implicated conclusion, such as (6)c.

(6)   a. David is not in the place of utterance.

          b. If David is not in the place of utterance, then Barbara will not be in town.

          c. Barbara is not in town.

Third, the hearer identifies the contextualisation of the utterance before *after all* in (4) and the utterance after *after all* in (4) as a strengthening; (6)c strengthens (5).

Let us consider the procedure of *however* in (7).

(7)   Barbara isn't in town. However, David isn't here. (Blakemore 1992: 136)

Blakemore says that the procedure of *however* in (7) is identified through three phases. First, the hearer adopts both the proposition, such as (8)a, recovered from the utterance before *however* in (7) and the accessible contextual assumption, like (8)b, as implicated premises and draws an implicated conclusion, such as (8)c.

(8)   a. Barbara is not in town.

          b. If Barbara is not in town, then David will be in the place of utterance.

          c. David is in the place of utterance.

Second, the hearer recovers the proposition, such as (9), from the utterance after *however* in (7).

(9)   David is not in the place of utterance.

Third, the hearer identifies the contextualisation of the utterance before *however* in (7) and the utterance after *however* in (7) as a contradiction; (9) contradicts (8)c.

Here, it is notable that a difference between early Relevance Theorists (Blakemore 1987, 1989; Rouchota 1990) and late Relevance Theorists (Blakemore 1992, 2000, 2002; Iten 2000, 2005; Hall 2004) provides an opportunity for us to detect a problem in the notion of procedure. The difference is whether or not the connective *but*, which encodes a procedure that instructs the hearer to identify two segments coupled by it as a contradiction, can encode any concept. On the one hand, early Relevance Theorists claim that *but* encodes not only the procedure but also a concept & *as a contrast to p*. On the other hand, late Relevance Theorists argue that *but* encodes only the procedure.

Consider the following example.

(10)   Susan is tall but Mary is short. (Blakemore 1987: 125)

From (10) two propositions, such as (11)a-b, can be recovered.

(11)   a. Susan is tall.
       b. Mary is short.

On Blakemore's (1987) accounts, *but* in (10) encodes a concept & *as a contrast to p*. She says that the concept of *but* in (10) conjoins (11)a and (11)b truth-functionally and yields a single conjoined proposition, such as (12).

(12)   [Susan is tall]$_p$ & [as a contrast to p Mary is short].

Consider another example.

(13)   John is a Republican, but he is honest. (Lakoff 1971: 67)

Blakemore (1987: 125-131) argues that *but* in (13) encodes a procedure, which instructs the hearer to identify the contextualisation of two segments linked by it as a contradiction. In Blakemore's account, this procedure is identified through three stages. First, the hearer adopts both the proposition, such as (14)a, recovered from the segment before *but* in (13) and the accessible contextual assumption, like (14)b, as implicated premises and draws an implicated conclusion, such as (14)c.

(14)   a. John is a member of the Republican Party.

       b. All Republicans are dishonest. (Blakemore 1987: 129)

       c. John is dishonest. (Blakemore 1987: 129)

Second, the hearer recovers the proposition, such as (15), from the segment after *but* in (13).

(15) John is honest.

Third, the hearer identifies the contextualisation of the segment before *but* in (13) and the segment after *but* in (13) as a contradiction: (15) contradicts

(14)c.

As opposed to early Relevance Theorists, late Relevance Theorists persist in a unitary procedural meaning of *but*. Iten (2000: 180), who is one of late Relevance Theorists, follows Foolen's (1991: 51) line and analyses the meaning of *but* in examples like (10) as a procedure. Foolen (1991) argues that the concept & *as a contrast p* of *but* originates from the artificial reading, which is not relevant to context. Consider (16).

(16)   A: John and Bill are both quite tall, aren't they?

B: Actually, John is tall but Bill is short. (Iten 2000: 180)

Iten claims that *but* in (16)B encodes only a unitary procedure. In Iten's (2000) terms, the procedure of *but* in (16)B is identified through three phases. First, the hearer adopts both the proposition, such as (17)a, recovered from the utterance before *but* in (16)B and the accessible contextual assumption, like (17)b, as implicated premises and hence derives an implicated conclusion, such as (17)c.

(17)   a. John is tall.

b. John and Bill are both quite tall.

c. A is right - John and Bill are both quite tall. (Iten 2000: 180)

Second, the hearer adopts both the proposition, such as (18)a, recovered from the utterance after *but* in (16)B and the accessible contextual assumption, like (18)b, as implicated premises and hence draws an implicated conclusion, such as (18)c.

(18) a. Bill is short.

b. John and Bill are both quite tall.

c. A is wrong - John and Bill aren't both quite tall. (Iten 2000: 180)

Finally, the hearer identifies the contextualisation of the segment before *but* in (16)B and the segment after *but* in (16)B as a contradiction: (18)c contradicts (17)c. However, *but* in (16)B encodes a concept *& as a contrast to p* because *are both quite tall* in (17)c contrasts with *aren't both quite tall* in (17)c. Further, *but* can also encode a concept in natural conversation. Consider (19).

(19) [Context: A wants to know John's and Bill's heights.]

A: How tall are John and Bill?

B: John is tall but Bill is short.

From (19)B two propositions, such as (20)a-b can be recovered.

(20) a. John is tall.

b. Bill is short.

But in (19)B encodes a concept *& as a contrast to p* and hence yields a single conjoined proposition, such as (21).

(21) [John is tall]$_p$ *&* [as a contrast to p Bill is short].

This analysis backs up early Relevance Theorists, who argue that *but* has both concept and procedure. Our data also show that three suffixes *-nuntey*, *-ciman*, and *-to* encode not only concepts but also procedures as follows.

Table 7.1: Concepts and Procedures of Suffixes

Suffixes	Concepts	Procedures
-nuntey	TIME	
	CAUSAL	
	CONTRAST	
		DENAIL OF EXPECTATION
		INTRODUCTION*
-ciman	CONTRAST	
		DENIAL OF EXPECTATION
-to	CONDITION	
	CONTRAST	
		DENIAL OF EXPECTATION

Within Relevance-Theoretic framework, the criterion for distinguishing concepts and procedures is whether or not meanings of conjunctive verbal suffixes yield a single conjoined truth-conditional proposition. First, when a given suffix conjoins two propositions truth-functionally and hence yields a single conjoined truth-conditional proposition, it is the concept of the suffix that is responsible. Second, the procedure of a given suffix does not truth-functionally conjoin the two propositions (and thus it does not yield a single conjoined truth-conditional proposition), but instructs the hearer how to interpret the relationship between the two propositions. Here, it is notable that the introduction meaning of *-nuntey* in Table 7.1 above is identified as a procedure that is not analysable by Relevance Theory. Below, we will take up *-nuntey* and will elaborate the following two points. One is that Korean conjunctive verbal suffixes that havea procedure can have concepts. The other is that a notion of procedure is not applicable to all Korean conjunctive verbal suffixes.

Let us consider the time meaning of *-nuntey* in (22).

(22) (DS & HK From 'My Excursion')
      [Context: DS is telling HK of his experience when his front teeth were broken during his childhood. DS says that his two front teeth were broken and fell out when he was eating shrimp crisps. However, HK expresses the feeling that she cannot understand why his teeth fell out.]

DS: ani saywukkang-ul   mek-**nuntey**   ippal-i   ppacy-ess-e
     *no shrimp crisps-AC eat-**NUNTEY** tooth-NM lose-PST-INF*
     'No. When I ate shrimp crisps, I really lost my teeth.'

In (22) DS is saying that his teeth dropped out while he was chewing shrimp crisps. From (22) two propositions, such as (23)a-b,can be recovered.

(23) a. DS ate shrimp crisps.
      b. DS's front teeth dropped out.

The propositional relation between (23)a and (23)b is TIME because in (23) DS's losing his front milk teeth in clause (a) occurs at the time at which DS ate shrimp crisps in clause (b). From the angle of Relevance Theorists, *-nuntey* in (22) encodes a concept *when*. So, this concept conjoins (23)a and (23)b truth-functionally and forms a single conjoined truth-conditional proposition, such as (24).

(24) [When DS was eating shrimp crisps], [DS's front teeth dropped out].

Let us consider the causal meaning of *-nuntey* in (25).

(25) (HY & NY From 'My Hobby')
[Context: NY is telling HY about a CD she lent someone. NY says that she does not remember to whom she lent her CD. However, she suddenly remembers it ...]

NY: um ani a   nwukwu pillyecwu-ess-nun-ci al-kyess-**nuntey**
well no oh who   lend-PST-MD-NOM know-may-NUNTEY
com   ku salam-ul   manna-llyekwu
a little that person-AC meet-to
'Oh. Because I know who I lent it, I will meet her.'

In (25) NY is saying that she will ask someone to return her CD to her because she remembers that she let the person use the CD. From (25) two propositions, such as (26)a-b, can be recovered.

(26) a. NY knows to whom she lent her CD.
b. NY will meet the person to whom she lent her CD.

The propositional relation between (26)a and (26)b is CAUSAL in that in (26) NY's knowing to whom she lent her CD in clause (a) causes NY's meeting that person in clause (b). From a Relevance Theorist's point of view, *-nuntey* in (25) encodes a concept *a result of*. So, this concept conjoins (26)a and (26)b truth-functionally and yields a single conjoined truth-conditional proposition, such as (27).

(27) [As a result of NY's knowing to whom she lent her CD] [NY will meet the person to whom she lent her CD].

Let us consider the contrast meaning of *-nuntey* in (28).

(28) (HY & JS From 'My Excursion')
      [Context: JS is telling HY of his experience when he was a soldier. JS says that he joined one week's military drill ...]

JS: sal   manhi ppacy-ess-ess-**nuntey**

*flesh much lose weight-PST-PST-**NUNTEY***

tto   tasi   ccy-ess-e

again again gain weight-PST-INF

'I lost weight very much, but I gained weight again.'

In (28) JS is saying that he lost weight during one week's military drill but he gained weight after the drill. From (28) two propositions, such as (29)a-b, can be recovered.

(29) a. JS lost weight during one week's military drill.
      b. JS gained weight after one week's military drill.

The propositional relation between (29)a and (29)b is CONTRAST. This is because in (29) JS's losing weight in clause (a) presents a striking contrast with his gaining weight in clause (b), From the standpoint of Relevance Theorists (Blakemore 1987, 1989; Rouchota 1990), *-nuntey* in (28) encodes a concept *& as a contrast to p*. So, this concept conjoins (29)a and (29)b truth-functionally and makes up a single conjoined truth-conditional proposition, such as (30).

(30)　[JS lost weight during one week's military drill]p & [as a contrast to p JS gained weight after one week's military drill].

Let us consider the denial of expectation meaning of the arrowed *-nuntey* in (31).

(31)　(HY & JS From 'My Excursion')

[Context: JS is telling HY about an experience when he visited a certain death camp that was built by Nazis. JS explained that he met an old guide who was in the death camp in World War II, and that the guide's older sister was executed in front of him.]

JS:　　　→　　　solcikhi na-to sulph-ess-**nuntey**

　　　　　　　　*honestly I-also sad-PST-**NUNTEY***

　　　　　　　　na-n kuleh-key　　　an na-te

　　　　　　　　I-TC be like that-AD not drop-RT

　　　　　　　　'To be frank, I was also sad, but I didn't cry.'

　　　　　　　　[an] na-ss-nuntey

　　　　　　　　not drop-PST-NUNTEY

　　　　　　　　'I didn't cry.'

HY:　　　　　　[um]

　　　　　　　　'Yeah.'

　　　　　　　　na-twu kule-n　　　　ke.ey　nwunmwul cal an

　　　　　　　　I-also be like that-MD thing.at tear　　　well not

　　　　　　　　hully-e

shed-INF

'I don't cry about that.'

In (31) JS is saying that he heard the sad story from the old guide but he did not cry at all. From (31) two proposition, such as (32)a-b, can be recovered.

(32) a. JS was saddened by the story that a poor Jewish girl was executed by Nazis in front of her brother.

  b. JS did not cry.

The expectation, such as (33), can be derived from clause (31)a.

(33) JS cried.

The propositional relation between (32)a and (32)b is DENIAL OF EXPECTATION. This is because (32)b denies the expectation (33). From a Relevance Theorist's point of view, the arrowed *-nuntey* in (31) has a procedure that instructs the hearer to identify the contextual effect of (32)a and (32)b as a contradiction. This procedure is identified through two stages. First, HY adopts both the proposition, such as (32)a, and the accessible contextual assumption, such as (34), in her encyclopaedic entries as implicated premises and draws an implicated conclusion, such as (33).

(34) If people are sad, they will cry.

Second, HY identifies the contextual effect of (32)a and (32)b as a contradiction; (32)b contradicts (33).

Finally, let us consider the introduction meaning of *-nuntey*. We find difficulty in seeing any theoretical basis in Relevance Theory for the analysis of an introduction meaning of *-nuntey*. Nevertheless, we attempt to follow Blakemore's (2002) approach on *well* to the introduction meaning of *-nuntey*.

Blakemore (2002: 138-148) renovates a the notion of procedure. She divides procedures, which English connectives encode, into two categories. One is a procedure encoded by such connectives as *but, however, after all* and *so*. The other is a procedure encoded by *well*. She defines the procedure of *well* as follows.

> "a green light for going ahead with the inferential processes involved in the recovery of cognitive effects" (Blakemore 2002: 138)

Consider the following example.

> (35)   Remember Tom? Well, he's just bought a motorbike. (Blakemore 2002: 141)

Blakemore says that *well* in (35) encodes a procedure, which instructs the hearer that in (35) the utterance after *well* is relevant in contextual assumptions derived from the utterance before *well*. According to her, the utterance after *well* in (35) is relevant because *well* in (35) provides the hearer with a sign for the hearer to gain access to the hearer's contextual assumption about Tom in his/her encyclopaedic entries, which he/she does not acknowledge, and hence to identify the contextual effect of the utterance after *well*. However, she does not illustrate which effect is derived from the utterance after *well* in (35). So, we now consider this effect according to Relevance Theory. In a Relevance-Theoretic sense, the effect involves reference assignment. The hearer assigns the referent *he* after *well* in (35) to *Tom* as follows. First, the hearer recovers the proposition, such as (36), from the utterance before *well* in (35).

    (36)   The speaker asks whether or not the hearer remembers Tom.

Second, he/she adopts both the proposition, such as (36), and contextual assumptions, like (37)a-b, as implicated premises and derives the implicated conclusion, such as (37)c.

    (37)   a. The hearer knows that the speaker knows that he/she remembers Tom.
            b. The speaker adopts a question as a preparatory utterance in order to refresh the hearer's memory.
            c. Tom is the name of the person whom the speaker is talking about.

Third, he/she assigns the referent *he* after *well* in (35) to *Tom*.

Let us analyse the meaning of *-nuntey* in (38) on this line.

    (38) (DS & HK From 'My excursion')
         [Context: HY is telling DS episodes about butter she picked up from a certain pub.]

HK: → enni ku kathi ka-ss-te-n **hankwuk**
big sister that together go-PST-RT-MD **Korea**
enni-ka iss-**nuntey** **ku enni**-ka ku bethe
big sister*-NM exist-*NUNTEY* *that big sister*-NM *that butter
com caki com chayngky-e ka-ya toy-keyss-ta
a little self a little pick up-INF go-if only become-may-DC
'I had a Korean friend - she calls her my elder sister - who went
to the pub with me and she said "I will take the butter."'
ileh-key ileh-key cokuma.n bethe
be like that-AD be like that-AD small.MD butter
'A small packet of butter as small as this.'
ileh-key iss.c.an.h.a.yo ileh-key
be like that-AD exist.NOM.not.do.INF.POL be like that-AD
neymonah-kcy
square-AD
'Like this, thc square shaped one.'

DS: al-e
know-INF
'I know.'

In (38) HK is saying that she went the pub with one of her friends and that
person took packets of butter from the pub. Two propositions, such as
(39)a-b, can be recovered from two segments coupled by *-nuntey* in (38).

(39) a. One of HK's friends went to a certain pub with her.

b. The same friend told HK that she would take packets of butter from the
pub.

The propositional relation between (39)a and (39)b is INTRODUCTION because in (39), clause (a) introduces *One of HK's friends* on which the speaker focuses in clause (b). If we apply Blakemore's (2002) approach on *well* to *-nuntey* in (38), a procedure encoded by *-nuntey* in (38) will be the instruction that the segment after *-nuntey* in (38) is relevant in a new contextual assumption about one of HK's Korean friends derived from the segment before *-nuntey* in (38). In a Relevance-Theoretic sense, contextual assumptions about the focused object are highly accessible. However, this approach encounters a drawback. If we attempt to prove the segment after *-nuntey* in (38) to be relevant, we have to suggest that the referent *ku enni* of the segment after *-nuntey* in (38) is assigned to one of HK's Korean friends by a contextual implication derived from the segment before *-nuntey* in (38). This reference assignment is not a specific feature of *-nuntey* in (38) but a common feature of Korean conjunctive verbal suffixes. So, it is difficult see any Relevance-Theoretical basis for relating focusing a certain object to deriving contextual effects.

Let us turn into explaining why late Relevance Theorists rebut early Relevance Theorists. Late Relevance Theorists claim that the procedure of *but* constrains the interpretation of non-conjunctions, i.e., two adjacent utterances, from a Relevance-Theoretic point of view.

What is the relationship between 'constraint' and 'relevance'? Sperber and Wilson (1986/1995: 123-132) define 'relevance' as a function of two factors, i.e. contextual effect and processing effort, and regard the second as a negative factor that is a certain consumption of energy for mental processes. They describe the correlation between these two facts as follows:

> "other things being equal, an assumption with greater contextual efforts is more relevant; and, other things being equal, an assumption requiring a smaller processing effort is more relevant" (Sperber and Wilson: 1986/1995: 124)

Based on Relevance Theory, Blakemore (1992: 137) argues that inserting connectives into non-conjunctions constrains the hearer's selection of contextual assumptions, which identifies the contextualisation of non-conjunctions. She suggests that non-conjunctions can also obtain three types of contextualisation: contextual implication, strengthening, and contradiction, if the hearer gains access to contextual assumptions in his/her encyclopaedic entries, as follows. The hearer identifies the contextualisation of non-conjunctions, such as (40)a-b, as a contextual implication if he/she gets access contextual assumption such as (41) in his/her encyclopaedic entries.

(40) a. David isn't here.

   b. Barbara is in town.

(41) If David isn't here, then Barbara is in town. (Blakemore 1992: 135)

The hearer identifies the contextualisation of non-conjunctions, such as (42)a-b, as a strengthening if he/she has access to a contextual assumption such as (43) in his/her encyclopaedic entries.

(42) a. We shall have to cancel the meeting.

   b. David isn't here.

(43)   If David isn't here, we shall have to cancel the meeting. (Blakemore 1992:
       135)

The hearer identifies the contextualisation of non-conjunctions, such as (44)a-b, as a contradiction if he/she accesses to a contextual assumption such as (45) in his/her encyclopaedic entries.

(44)   a. Barbara is in town.
       b. David isn't here. (Blakemore 1992: 136)
(45)   If Barbara is in town, then David will be here. (Blakemore 1992: 136)

Blakemore (1992: 85) points out the fact the fact that to which contextual assumption the hearer accesses in order to interpret non-conjunctions, such as (46)a-b, is not transparent as a problem in the sense that (46)a-b can involve the above three types of contextualisation.

(46)   a. Barbara isn't in town.
       b. David isn't here. (Blakemore 1992: 136)

She claims that in (47)a-c connectives such as *so, after all* and *however* are used to constrain the interpretation of clause (46)b against clause (46)a.

(47)   a. Barbara isn't in town. So David isn't here.
       b. Barbara isn't in town. After all, David isn't here.
       c. Barbara isn't in town. However, David isn't here. (Blakemore 1992:
           136)

This means that the use of connectives gives a hearer an instruction for interpreting an utterance, i.e. non-conjunctions, at minimal processing effort. That is to say, this tells us that a single procedural meaning of discourse connectives is a prerequisite for their use as constraints on interpreting non-conjunctions.

Here, it is notable that Blakemore is silent about which what causes the hearer to gain access to the contextual assumptions, such as (41), (43) and (45), in his/her encyclopaedic entries when he/she respectively identifies the contextualisation of non-conjunctions (40), (42), and (44) as a contextual implication, a strengthening, and a contradiction. Giora (1996) answers this. Giora (1996: 21) claims that the hearer's choice of "the set of accessible assumptions" for interpreting non-conjunctions "must be constrained by coherence consideration" because non-conjunctions are coherent. In Giora's sense, the hearer considers non-conjunctions as coherent and chooses accessible assumptions for interpreting the non-conjunctions.

So far, we have discussed the notion of procedure. This discussion raises a problem for late Relevance Theorists, who stick to a unitary procedure. This is because our analysis on *-nuntey* proves that Korean conjunctives can encode not only procedures but also concepts. In other words, the unitary procedure view cannot be maintained. In Section 7.2., we will discuss the scale of Default-Semantic meanings.

7.2 Problems with the Scale of Default-Semantic Meanings

The aim of this section is to identify problems with the scale of

Default-Semantic meanings and discuss the nature of the problems.

In applying Default Semantics to Korean conjunctive verbal suffixes *-nikka, -se,* and *-ciman,* H-K. Lee (2001, 2002) argues that meanings of Korean conjunctive verbal suffixes are not clearly divided into concepts and procedures. She treats a propositional relation, which obtains between the two segments coupled by a verbal suffix, as a Default-Semantic meaning of the suffix. She (2001: 10) advocates "the scope of the connective's content meaning". She calls the scope as a single scale. Further, she postulates Default-Semantic meanings of a suffixes are continuously posited on a single scale on the basis of 'the quantity of inductive inference', i.e., the amount of the context, for identifying each meaning. For example, the scales of Default-Semantic meanings of three suffixes *-nikka, -se,* and *-ciman* are as follows.

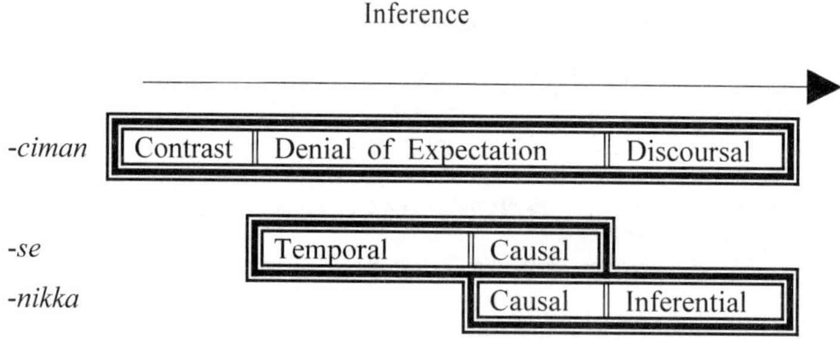

Figure 7.1: The Scale of Default-Semantic Meanings of Suffixes

Adopted from H-K. Lee (2001: 198, 223, 2002: 862)

According to her (2001: 6), the 'context' is divided into two types: "the hearer's background knowledge" and "linguistic context". First, the knowledge is acquired by the hearer's experience and takes the form of a proposition necessary to deriving an implicated conclusion. In this sense, she accepts inductive inference. Second, linguistic contexts are subdivided into two features: 'syntactic' and 'semantic'. On the one hand, a syntactic feature is whether or not the subjects of two segments linked by suffixes are equal, and on the other hand a semantic feature is whether or not the predicate of the segment before a suffix is stative. The issues in this section are linguistic contexts, the arrangement of Default-Semantic meanings, and a single scale.

Let us consider linguistic contexts. H-K. Lee (2001: 180, 2002: 862) says that Default-Semantic meanings of -*se* are continuously posited on a single scale in the order of 'temporal meaning' (in our terms a forward sequential meaning) and 'causal meaning' on the basis of the quantity of inference, i.e., linguistic context, which identifies each meaning, as seen in Figure 7.2 below.

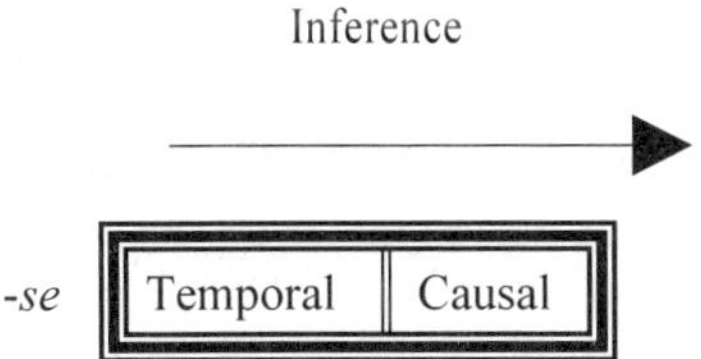

Figure 7.2: The Scale of Default-Semantic Meanings of -*se*
Adopted from H-K. Lee (2001: 198)

According to her, the linguistic context refers to whether or not the subjects of two segments linked by suffixes are equal. That is to say, -*se* has only 'causal meaning' if and only if the subjects of X and Y are not identical to each other. However, these two types of features are not inference because she (2001: 171) calls linguistic contexts "syntactic constraints".

Let us turn into the arrangement of Default-Semantic meanings. H-K. Lee (2001: 218-223) claims that Default-Semantic meanings of *-ciman* are continuously posited on one scale in the order of 'contrast', 'denial of expectation', and 'discoursal meaning' on the basis of the quantity of inference, which identify each meaning, as shown in Figure 7.3 below.

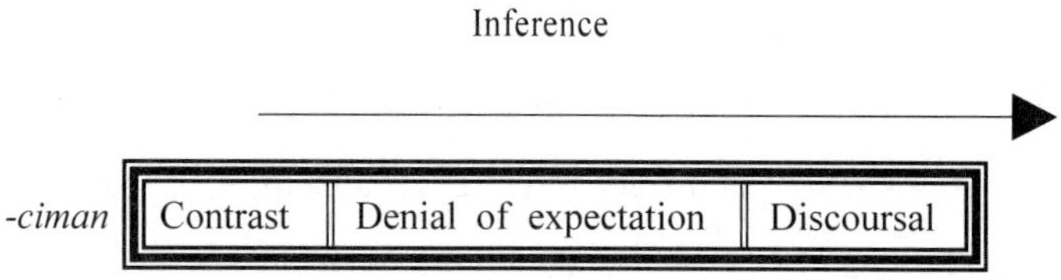

Figure 7.3: The Scale of Default-Semantic Meanings of *-ciman*
Adopted from H-K. Lee (2001: 223)

According to H-K. Lee, three types of Default-Semantic meanings of *-ciman* are composed of two parts. One is an enumeration meaning. The other is the predicates of propositions, which are in CONTRAST to each other: (1) 'contrast' ('P_x and P_y'); (2) 'denial of expectation' ('the expectation, which is derived from P_x, and P_y' or 'the proposition derived from P_x and that derived from P_y'); (3) 'discoursal meaning' ('the expectation derived from P_x and that derived from P_y'). However, the scale in Figure 7.3 above encounters such counterexamples as in (48).

(48) Chelswu-nun khephi-lul masy-ess-**ciman**   Swunhuy-nun

      *-TC coffee-AC drink-PST-**CIMAN***   *-TC*

aisukhulim-ul mek-ess-ta

ice cream-AC eat-PST-DC

'Chelswu drank a cup of coffee, but Swunhuy ate an ice cream.' (Choi

1989: 74)

Choi, whom we have introduced in Chapter 1, claims that *-ciman* in (48)

encodes CONTRAST. In Choi's account, from (48) two propositions, such

as (49)a-b can be recovered.

(49) a. Chelswu drank a coup of coffee.

     b. Swunhuy ate an ice cream.

Further, Choi says that two propositions, such as (50)a-b, can be derived

from (49)a-b respectively.

(50) a. A cup of coffee is hot food.

     b. An ice cream is cold food.

According to Choi, the propositional relation between (50)a and (50)b is

CONTRAST because in (50) taking hot food in clause (a) presents a contrast

to taking cold food in clause (b). In H-K. Lee's sense, *-ciman* in (48) encodes

a 'contrast meaning' and yields a single conjoined truth-conditional

proposition, such as (51).

(51) [A cup of coffee is hot food]$_p$ & [as a contrast to p an ice cream is cold food].

Note that (50)a-b are propositions, which are derived from P_x and P_y (49)a-b respectively. This means that in cases like (48) the quantity of inference for identifying 'contrast' of *-ciman* is the same as the quantity for identifying the 'discoursal meaning' of *-ciman*. Therefore, Default-Semantic meanings of *-ciman* cannot be posited on the scale in Figure 7.3 above before 'denial of expectation' and 'discoursal meaning' according to the quantity of inference.

Finally, let us consider a single scale of Default-Semantic meanings. H-K. Lee (2001: 198, 2002: 864) says that Default-Semantic meanings of *-nikka* are continuously posited on one scale in the order of 'causal meaning' and 'inferential meaning' on the basis of the quantity of inference for identifying each meaning, as follows.

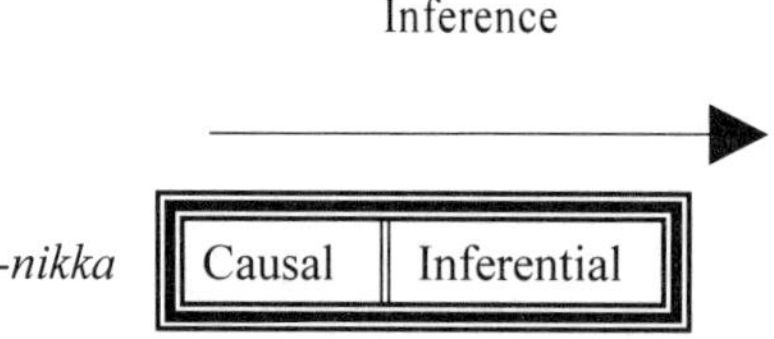

Figure 7.4: The Scale of Default-Semantic Meanings of *-nikka*
Adopted from H-K. Lee (2001: 198)

However, the scale in Figure 7.4 above encounters such a counterexample as (52).

(52) nay-ka ku salam-eykey cenhwa-lul   ha-**nikka**   ku salam-un
      *I-NM   that person-to   telephone-AC do-**NIKKA** that person-TC*
      onul hoyuy-ey mos   o-n-ta.y
      today meeting-to cannot come-IN-DC.QT.say.INF
      'Because I made a phone call to him, (I heard) he cannot come to the
      meeting.' (Lee 2001: 196)

From (52) two propositions, such as (53)a-b, can be recovered.

(53) a. The speaker made a phone call to a certain person.
      b. The speaker heard that the person cannot come to the meeting.

H-K. Lee posits that -*nikka* in (52) has 'inferential meaning' because (53)a
and (53)b do not have a CAUSAL relation. In contrast to H-K. Lee (2001),
Martin et al. (1967) and Martin (1992) claim that -*nikka* has a time meaning
"*when* in the past". This supports strongly our point that -*nikka* in (52) has not
an 'inferential meaning' but a time meaning *when* as follows.

(54) nay-ka ku salam-eykey cenhwa-lul   ha-**nikka**   ku salam-un
      *I-NM   that person-to   telephone-AC do-**NIKKA** that person-TC*
      onul hoyuy-ey mos   o-n-ta.y
      today meeting-to cannot come-IN-DC.QT.say.INF
      'When I made a phone call to him, I heard that he cannot come to the
      meeting.'

Further, our data show that in addition to -*nikka* two suffixes -*nuntey*, and -*to* cannot be posited on a single scale.

Let us take *-nuntey* first. *-Nuntey* encodes five propositional relations TIME, CAUSAL, CONTRAST, DENAIL OF EXPECTATION, and INTRODUCTION (see Section 6.1.2.). From H-K Lee's point of view, CONTRAST, DENIAL OF EXPECTATION, and CAUSAL are identified as 'contrast', 'denial of expectation', and 'causal' respectively, as shown in Figure7.5 below.

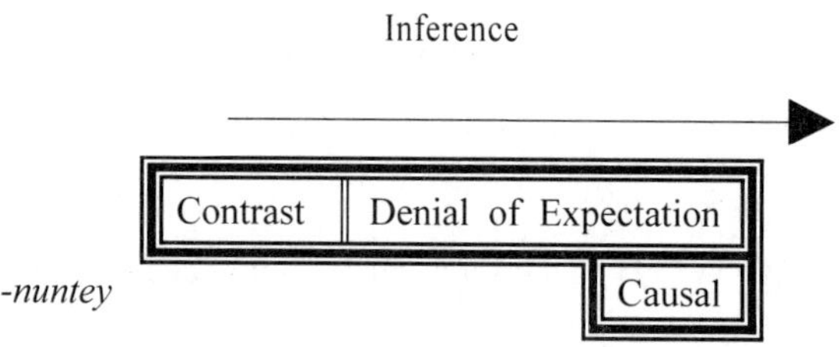

Figure 7.5: The Scale of Encoded Default-Semantic Meanings of *-nuntey*

However, Figure 7.5 above presents two problems for H-K. Lee. One is that Default-Semantic meanings of *-nuntey* are arranged on two scales. Second, two meanings, i.e., the time meaning and the introduction meaning, of *-nuntey* cannot be posited on the scales in Figure 7.5 above. This is because the two meanings cannot belong to the scope of six encoded meanings: 'logical meaning', 'temporal meaning', 'causal meaning', 'contrast', 'denial of expectation', and 'discoursal meaning'. One can say that 'time meaning' belongs to this scope in that in our terms 'time meaning' is identical to in Default-Semantic ones 'temporal meaning'. However, in Default-Semantic terms 'temporal meaning' equals in our ones 'forward sequential meaning', as has been pointed out above.

We now turn into the scale of Default-Semantic meanings of -to. *-To* encodes three propositional relations CONDITION, CONTRAST, and DENIAL OF EXPECTATION (see Section 6.1.6.). From H-K Lee's point of view, two relations CONTRAST and DENIAL OF EXPECTATION are identified as 'contrast', and 'denial of expectation' respectively. So, these two meanings are posited on the following scales.

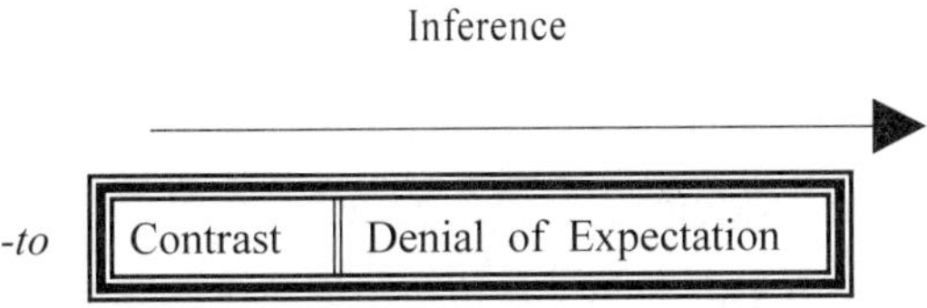

Figure 7.6: The Scale of Encoded Default-Semantic Meanings of *-to*

However, Figure 7.6 above also identifies a problem for H-K. Lee. This is because Default-Semantic meanings of *-to* must be posited on another scale. Consider (55):

(55)　(HY & JS From 'When I was a Primary School Student')
　　　[Context: HY and JS are talking about teachers in their primary schools.]

JS:　　cikum sayngkakha-**y(e)to** cincca ippe-ss-e

　　　*now　think-**TO**　　　really　beautiful-PST-INF*

　　　'If I think of her, she was really beautiful.'

In (55) JS is saying that one of his assistant teachers was beautiful. From (55) two propositions, such as (56)a-b, can be recovered.

(56) a. JS thinks of one of his female assistant teachers in his primary school.

  b. JS is sure of that the assistant teacher was beautiful.

The propositional proposition between (56)a and (56)b is CONDITION because in (56) the thinking of the assistant teacher in clause (a) and the assurance of that she was beautiful are identified as 'antecedent' and 'consequent' respectively.[33] *-To* in (55) has a condition meaning → (Jeon 1989: 92). The condition meaning cannot be posited on the scale in Figure 7.6 above. This is because according to H-K Lee 'contrast' and 'denial of expectation' of a suffix has a meaning *& as a contrast to p*. In this sense, the condition meaning of *-to* (55) must have another scale.

In conclusion, the scale of Default-Semantic meanings is not easily applicable to encoded meanings of Korean conjunctive verbal suffixes because these meanings are not drawn by inference but carried simply by suffixes. In Section 7.3., we propose an area where the notion 'scale' can be applied with more explanatory power: inferred meanings of Korean conjunctive verbal suffixes.

7.3 The Scale of Inferred Meanings

The purpose of this section is to discuss H-K. Lee's (2001) non-truth-conditional inferred meanings of connectives and to develop H-K.

---

[33] One may take this relation as DENIAL OF EXPECTATION without looking closely at the context. However, since the context of (55) does not show the expectation that the assistant teacher was not beautiful, it cannot be DENIAL OF EXPECTATION.

Lee's (2001, 2002) scale of meaning (developed from encoded meanings) to inferred meanings of Korean conjunctive verbal suffixes.

Following H-K. Lee's (2001)'s discussion on 'inferential meaning' , we accept the existence of non-truth-conditional inferred meanings of connectives. However, we make the point that the label 'inferential meaning' itself encounters a problem: the label itself is identified as a procedure. Let us take *because* for example.

(57)   John loves his wife, because he comes home early. (H-K. Lee 2001: 67)

From (57) two propositions, such as (58)a-b, can be recovered.

(58)   a. John comes home early.
       b. John loves his wife.

According to H-K. Lee, *because* in (57) has a non-truth-conditional inferred meaning 'inferential meaning' in that the higher-order proposition, such as (59), is drawn from (57).

(59)   The speaker believes that John loves his wife, because John comes home early. (H-K. Lee 2001: 67)

As has been pointed out in Section 3.2.3., 'a causal relation in a belief world' is related to 'evidence for the speaker's belief' and (58)a is evidence for (58)b, which is the speaker's belief. In a Relevance-Theoretic framework, 'evidence' and 'belief' refer to 'premise' and 'contextual assumption' respectively. From Blakemore's (1992: 36) point of view, (58)b is the implicated conclusion of (58)a if and only if (58)a is relevant as evidence for the claim in (58)b. That is to say, in (57) the hearer adopts both the proposition (58)a and the accessible contextual assumption, such as (60)a, as implicated premises and draws the implicated conclusion, such as (60)b.

> (60)   a. If a husband goes home early, he loves his wife.
>
> b. John loves his wife.

This analysis shows that in (57) *because* encodes a procedure, which instructs the hearer to identify the contextualisation of two segments coupled by *because* as a contextual implication. In terms of Relevance Theory, the label 'inferential meaning' does not designate a non-truth-conditional inferred meaning.

However, the implicated conclusion (60)b is not encoded by *because* in (57) but drawn by inferring two propositions (58)a and (58)b, as H-K. Lee (2001) claims. This means that the non-truth-conditional inferred meaning of *because* in (57) is a certain meaning that occurs when an INFERENTIAL RELATION is inferred from (58)a and (58)b.

We have shown that non-truth-conditional inferred meanings of four suffixes occur when propositional relations are inferred from P_x and P_y (see section 6.2.). Here, it is notable that the inferred relations have a scale. What follows in this section will show the scale, by adopting the assumption of Default Semantics (e.g. H-K. Lee 2001, 2002). However, we do not accept the term "linguistic context". This is because the term is not inference, as has been pointed out above.

Let us take *-ko*. An inferred relation REPETITION that involves a non-truth-conditional inferred meaning of *-ko* is posited on a single scale, as seen in Figure 7.7 below.

Inference

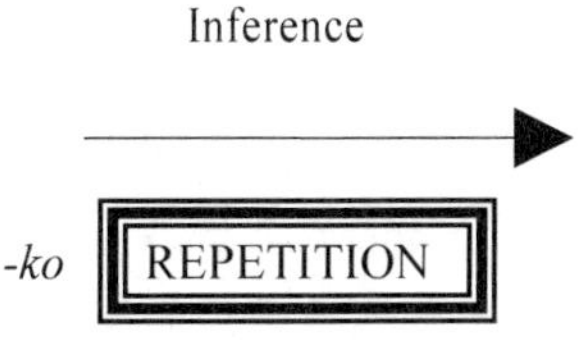

Figure 7.7: The Scale of Propositional Relation that Involves
a Non-Truth-Conditional Inferred Meaning of *-ko*

Let us consider REPETITION that obtains in (61).

(61) (SH & YH From 'My Hobby')
       [Context: SH and YH are talking about kinds of hobbies.]
YH: um nemwu manh-**ko** manh-ci
       *well very   many-**KO** many-SUP*
       'Well, there are many hobbies. There are many hobbies.'

In (61) YH is saying that there are many hobbies in the world. From (61) two propositions, such as (62)a-b, can be recovered.

(62) a. There exist multitudinous hobbies.
       b. There exist multitudinous hobbies.

REPETITION is inferred form from (62)a and (62)b because (62)b equals (62)a. In (61) the inference for identifying REPETITION is to recognise (62)a and (62)b as identical.

Let us take *-se*. As seen in Figure 7.8 below, the inferred propositional relations that involve non-truth-conditional inferred meanings of *-se* are continuously posited on a single scale in the order of REPETITION and REFORMULATION according to the quantity of inference that identifies each relation. Here, inference refers to the hearer's inductive background knowledge, i.e., the proposition necessary to deriving each inferred relation.

Inference

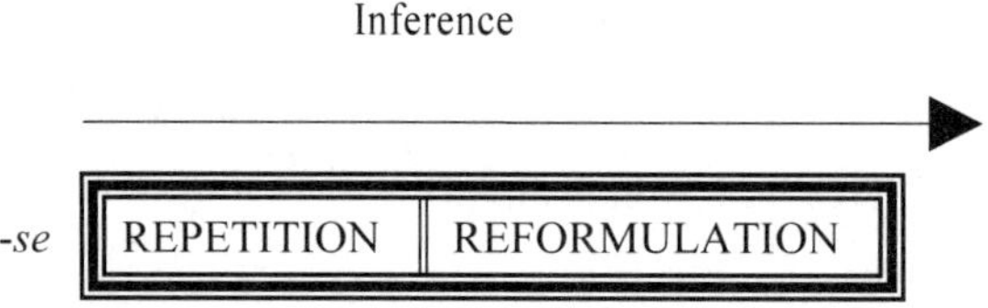

Figure 7.8: The Scale of Propositional Relations that Involve Non-Truth-Conditional Inferred Meanings of *-se*

Let us consider REPETITION that obtains in (63).

(63) (DS & HK From 'When I Was a Primary School Student')
[Context: DS is telling HK of the relationship between his father and him. DS says that he did not apologise to his father for his faults because he did not like his father in his childhood, and that his father and he talked about this after DS grew up.]

DS: nacwungey khe-**se** nacwungey khe-se   twul-i   kule-n
*later grow-up-**SE** later   grow up-SE two-NM be like that-MD*

yeyki-lul hay-ss-ess-nuntey

story-AC do-PST-PST-NUNTEY

'After I grew up, after I grew up, my father and I talked about   it.'

In (63) DS is saying that he and his father talked about his fault after he grew up. From (63) two propositions, such as (64)a-b, can be recovered.

(64)   a. DS grew up.

b. DS grew up.

REPETITION is inferred from (64)a and (64)b. This is because in (64) clauses clause (a) and clause (b) are identical to each other. In (63) inference that identifies REPETITION is to perceive that (64)b is same as (64)a

Let us consider REFORMULATION that obtains in (65).

(65)   (HY & NY From 'My Hobby')

[Context: NY is telling about NY's friend who entered a college of engineering after giving up a teachers' college.]

NY: ipen-ey   hakkyo tasi   tuleka-**se**

*this time-at school again enter-**SE***

kongtay   tuleka-ss-e

a college of engineering enter-PST-INF

'This year, she entered a university again. She entered a college of

engineering.'

In (65) NY is saying that her friend, who had given up a teachers' college, entered a university. Two propositions, such as (66)a-b, can be recovered from (65).

(66)   a. NY's friend entered a university.

b. NY's friend entered a college of engineering.

In (66) *a college of engineering* in clause (b) resembles *a university* in clause (a). In this sense, REFORMULATION is inferred from (66)a and (66)b. In (65) inference for identifying REFORMULATION is to know that a college of engineering refers to a university.

Let us take *-nikka*. The inferred propositional relations for involving non-truth-conditional inferred meanings of *-nikka* are continuously posited on a single scale in the order of REPETITION, REFORMULATION, and INFERENTIAL on the basis of the quantity of inference that identifies each relation. Here, inference refers to the hearer's inductive background knowledge, i.e., the proposition necessary to deriving each inferred relation.

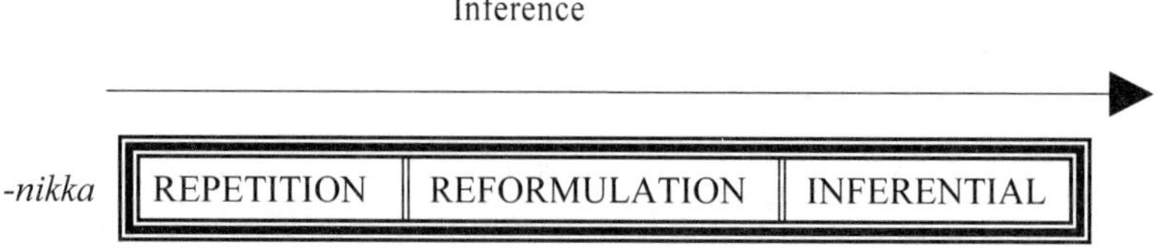

Figure 7.9: The Scale of Propositional Relations that Involve
Non-Truth-Conditional Inferred Meanings of *-nikka*

Let us consider REPETITION that obtains in (67).

(67) (HY & NY From 'When I Was a Primary School Student')

[Context: NY is telling of her experience when her class teacher checked the homework of her classmates and herself in her primary school days. On that day, NY did not do her homework. So, in order not to be penalised, NY completed her homework while her teacher was checking other students'.]

NY: → chotunghakkyo ttay-nun il i   sam sa   pwuntan-kkaci
primary school time-TC one two three four division-up to
iss-**unikka**
*exist-**NIKKA***
'There were four *pwuntan*s 'divisions according to which writing tables were arranged' at each classroom.'

HY: um
'Yeah.'

NY: sa   pwuntan-i-nikka   to-nun   tey
four divisions-be-NIKKA take a walk round-MD case
sikan-i   kelly-ese
time-NM take-SE
'Because there were four *pwuntan*s at in each classroom, it took some time for my teacher to take walk around the classroom for checking our homework.'
kulayse nay-ka ku ttay ta hay-ss-nuntey
so   I-NM   that time all do-PST-NUNTEY
'So, I finished my homework while he was checking other students' homework.'

In (67) NY stresses that she bought time because there were four divisions in each classroom, and that she did her homework before her class teacher had it checked it. From (67) two propositions, such as (68)a-b, can be recovered.

> (68) a. There were four *pwuntan*s in each classroom when NY
>   attended a primary school.
>
>   b. There were four *pwuntan*s in each classroom when NY
>   attended a primary school.

REPETITION is inferred from (68)a and (68)b in that (68)a equals (68)b. In (67) inference that identifies REPETITION is to recognise (68)a and (68)b as one and the same thing.

Let us consider REFORMULATION that obtains in (69).

> (69) (SH & YH From 'My Excursion')
>   [Context: SH and YH are talking about events of the excursions in their school days. YH is explaining how the leader who performed the events was chosen.]

YH:	→	kuntey	olakpwuchang kath-un	ke	ppop-**unikka**
		by the way leader		*same-MD thing appoint-**NIKKA***
		hakkyo-eyse
		school-at
		'By the way, because my class teacher appointed a leader.'
SH:		kule-ci
		do like that-SUP
		'That's right.'
YH:	→	ceyil cal no-nun ay-tul-i-la-tunci mwue.l pwunwiki
		best well play-MD child-PL-be-DC-or what.AC atmosphere

> cal kku-nun   ay-tul   kule-n   ay-tul
> *well draw-MD child-PL do like that-MD child-PL*
> ppop-unikka   kule-n   ay-tul-i   no-nun
> *appoint-NIKKA do like that-MD child-PL-NM play-MD*
> ke.ci
> *fact.be.SUP*
> 'Because the teacher appointed a student who had the best
> talent of entertainment in the class to be a leader, the chosen
> leader performed events of the excursions.'

In (69) YH is explaining that her class teacher appointed a student with the best entertainment talent as a leader of events on the excursions. Two propositions, such as (70)a-b, can be recovered.

(70)　a. The teacher in charge appointed a leader who would perform events on excursions.

　　　b. The teacher in charge appointed a student who had the best entertainment talent in the class as a leader who would perform events on excursions.

REFORMULATION is inferred from (70)a and (70)b because in (70) clause (b) resembles clause (a). In (69) inference for identifying REFORMULATION is to understand that 'a student who had the best talent of entertainment in the class as a leader would perform events' designates 'a leader who would perform events'.

Let us consider INFERENTIAL that obtains in (71).

(71) (NY & HY From 'My Hobby')

[Context: YH and SH are talking about cases of confectionery that they liked in their primary school days. YH says that he liked *Homlenpol*, which was a brand of biscuits produced in Korea, and that ...]

YH: → kuke.n ccikuleci-**nikka** mak kak-i com phocang-i

*that.TC be crushed-**NIKKA** hard case-NM a little packing-NM*

an toy-e iss-c.an.h.[a]

not become-INF is-NOM.not.be.INF

'The box of biscuits was badly packed, because it was crushed.'

SH: [um]

'Yeah.'

mac-e

right-INF

'That's right.'

In (71) YH is saying that the box's being poorly packed is based on the fact that it was crushed. From (71) two propositions, such as (72)a-b, can be recovered.

(72) a. The box of biscuits was crushed.

b. The box of biscuits was badly packed.

INFERENTIAL is inferred from (72)a and (72)b in the sense that (72)b is the implicated conclusion of (72)a. In (71) one more proposition, such as (73), is necessary for identifying INFERENTIAL.

(73) Boxes are crushed easily if they are badly packed.

Let us take *-nuntey* for instance. As shown in Figure 7.10 below, the inferred propositional relations that involve non-truth-conditional inferred meanings of *-nuntey* are continuously posited on a single scale in the order of REPETITION, REFORMULATION, INFERENTIAL, EXEMPLIFICATION, and BACKWARD INFERENTIAL according to the quantity of inference for identifying each relation. Here, inference refers to the hearer's inductive background knowledge, i.e., the proposition necessary to deriving each inferred relation.

Inference

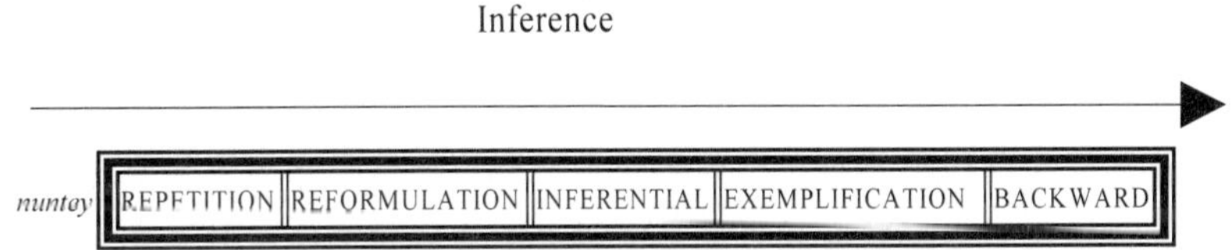

Figure 7.10: The Scale of Propositional Relations that Involve
Non-Truth-Conditional Inferred Meanings of *-nuntey*

Let us consider REPETITION that obtains in (74).

(74) (HY & NY From 'My Excursion')
      [Context: HY is telling an episode related to bugs when she went on an excursion in her school days. HY says that she went to places of nature and amusement parks on excursions rather than places in cities, and that she found it difficult to eat ice cream and soft drink because of bugs.]

HY: e   na pelley toykey silheha-**nuntey**   nemwu silh-un   ke.ya
     *well I bug   very   dislike-**NUNTEY** very   dislike-MD fact.be.INF*
     'Well, I hate bugs very much. Very much.'

In (74) HY stresses that she hates bugs intensely. From (74) two propositions, such as (75)a-b can be recovered.

    (75) a. HY hates bugs intensely.

            b. HY hates bugs intensely.

REPETITION is inferred form from (75)a and (75)b because (75)b is identical to (75)a. In (74) inference for identifying REPETITION is to recognise (75)a and (75)b as one and the same thing.

    Let us consider REFORMULATION that obtains in (76).

    (76) (DS & HK From 'My Excursion)

          [Context: DS is explaining how he writes assignments. HK says that she cannot understand why DS summarises repeatedly the same article given as an assignment. DS explains how he summarises articles. He is saying about articles he summarised recently.]

    DS: pulapepul inpeyicyen-ey kwanlyentoy-n ke.**ntey**

          *probable invasion-to   relate-MD   thing.be.**NUNTEY***

          makheys ilon-uy   olientheyisyen-i ettehkey talu-n   kos-ey

          market theory-GN orientation-NM how   different-NM place-to

          yenghyang-ul michi-na   kiep   sengkong-ey ile-n

          effect-AC   happen-Q enterprise success-to   do like this-MD

          ke.ey   kwanlyentoy-n ke.ta

           thing.to relate-MD   thing.be.DC

          'It relates to 'probable invasion'. It relates to 'how the orientation of market theory affects other parts, that is, the success of enterprises.'

In (76) DS is explaining that the article for his assignment takes up 'probable invasion', i.e., how the orientation of market theory contributes to the success of enterprises. From (76) two propositions, such as (77)a-b, are recovered.

(77)   a. The article that DS summarised as an assignment recently is related to probable invasion.

   b. The article that DS summarised as an assignment recently is related to how the orientation of market theory affects the success of enterprises.

REFORMULATION is inferred from (77)a and (77)b in that in (77) clause (b) resembles clause (a). In (76) inference for identifying REFORMULATION is to recognise that a notion of probable invasion designates how the orientation of market theory affects the success of enterprises.

Let us consider INFERENTIAL that obtains in (78).

(78)   (DS & HK From 'My excursion')
   [Context: DS tells HK about what he is cooking in his dormitory in Australia. DS is expressing the feeling when he eats *kimchi* 'Korean pickled vegetables' made by him.]

HK: a kimchi.**ntey**   eti   ka-na   ku
   *oh Korean pickled vegetables.be.**NUNTEY** where go-although that*
   mas-i   nao-nun   ke.n   tangyenha-ci
   flavour-NM come-MD fact.TC natural-SUP
   '*Kimchi* 'Korean pickled cabbage' is *kimchi*. So, it makes sense that everywhere *kimchi* tastes the same flavour because *kimchi* is *kimchi*.'

In (78) DS is saying that he tastes the same flavour as he did in his home in Korea when he eats *kimchi,* 'Korean pickled vegetables', made by him. From (78) two propositions, such as (79)a-b can be recovered.

(79) a. The thing which DS is making in his dormitory is *kimchi.*

      b. DS tastes the same flavour of *kimchi* wherever he eats it.

INFERENTIAL is inferred from (79)a and (79)b. This is because (79)b is the implicated conclusion of (79)a. In (78) one more proposition, such as (80), is essential for identifying INFERENTIAL.

(80) Anyone tastes the same flavour of *kimchi*, i.e., Korean pickled cabbage, everywhere.

Let us consider EXEMPLIFICATION that obtains in (81).

(81) (HY & NY From 'When I Was a Primary School Student')
      [Context: HY is telling NY about the types of institute she attended in her primary school days.]

HY: → hakwen toykey manhi tany-ess-**nuntey**
      *educational institute very much attend-PST-**NUNTEY***
      'I attended lots of educational institutes.'
      seyey hakwen-twu tani-kwu
      school for calligraphy-also attend-KO
      'I attended private schools for calligraphy. And.'

NY: um

            'Yeah'

HY: sukheyithu-twu tani-kwu   panghak ttay

            skate-also   attend-KO holidays time

            [swuyengcang]-twu tani-kwu

            swimming pool-also attend-KO

            'I attended a private school of ice skating. And, in the holidays

            I attended a swimming pool.'

NY: [a na-twu]

             oh I-also

            'Me also.'

            e

            'Yeah.'

In (81) HY is listing private schools she attended in her primary school days.
Two propositions, such as (82)a-b can be recovered from (81).

(82)   a. HY attended many educational institutes in her primary school days.

        b. [HY attended private schools for calligraphy] & [HY attended a private
            school for ice skating] & [HY attended a swimming pool in the
            holidays].

EXEMPLIFICATION is inferred from (82)a and (82)b in the sense that in
(82) clause (b) gives examples of clause (a). In (81) in order to identify
EXEMPLIFICATION the hearer has to recover a single conjoined
proposition, such as (82)b and has to recognise a swimming pool and private
schools for calligraphy and ice skating as one of educational institutes

respectively.

Finally, let us consider BACKWARD INFERENTIAL that obtains in (83).

(83) (HY & NY From 'My Hobby')

[Context: NY is explaining why she likes being alone at home.]

NY: → wenlay   honca iss-nun   ke   cohaha-ki-n   ha-**ntey**
*originally alone exist-MD fact like-NOM-TC do-**NUNTEY***
'Originally, I like being alone.'
maynnal honcase mak kongsangha-kwu [mak]
every day alone   much daydream-KO   much
'Every day, I daydream very much.'

HY: [um]
'Yeah'

NY: omankaci   sayngkak ta ha-kwu
various kinds of thinking   all do-KO
'And I imagine lots of things. And.'

In (83) NY is saying that she likes being alone at home because she imagines a lot of things and it helps her to forget an insipid life. From (83) two propositions, such as (84)a-b, can be recovered.

(84) a. NY likes being alone at home.

b. [NY daydreams very much at home] & [she imagines a lot of things at home].

BACKWARD INFERENTIAL is inferred from (84)a and (84)b because

(84)a is the implicated conclusion of (84)b. In (83) two more propositions, such as (85)a-b, are necessary for identifying BACKWARD INFERENTIAL.

> (85) a. People, who daydream very much and imagine a lot of things, can forget the tedium of everyday affairs.
>
> b. People like forgetting the tedium of everyday affairs.

The identification of this relation requires the most greatest quantity of inference on the ground the hearer makes an additional effort to derive the two propositions (85)a-b (cf. Carston 1993: 36).

So far, we have shown that propositional relations that involve non-truth-conditional inferred meanings of Korean conjunctive verbal suffixes *-ko*, *-nuntey*, *-nikka*, and *-se* have a single scale as follows.

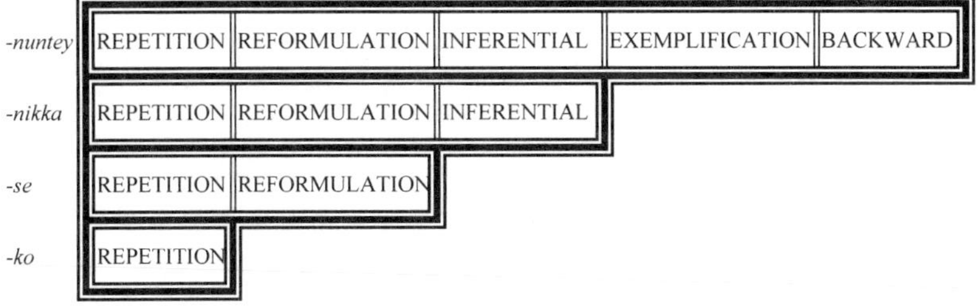

Figure 7.11: The Scale of Propositional Relations that Involve
Non-Truth-Conditional Inferred Meanings of Suffixes

As can be seen in Figure 7.11 above, the inferred propositional relations are continuously posited on a single scale according to the quantity of inference for identifying each relation. This table tells us that the four suffixes involve a different range of inferred relations. The different range casts a question, i.e., what the role is that the four suffixes play in inferred propositional relations that obtain P_x and P_y is. In Chapter 8, we will argue against two answers for this question.

8
Conclusion

This book aimed to gain a deep understanding of their meanings of Korean conjunctive verbal suffixes from the pragmatic angle, using naturally occurring data. It did not use the data to compare them although this study adopted as its reasoning tool four major pragmatic theories, Gricean theory, neo-Gricean theory, Relevance Theory, and Default Semantics. Especially, it emphasised how to elucidate meanings of Korean conjunctive verbal suffixes that modern pragmatic theories cannot neatly explain.

In this book, we have ananalysed in-depth the nature of the meanings of Korean conjunctive verbal suffixes *-ko*, *-nuntey*, *-nikka*, *-se*, *-ciman*, and *-to*, and their use. To do this we have selectively borrowed concepts essential to analysing the meanings of the six suffixes from the four pragmatic theories and developed a theoretical framework. The nature of the given conjunctive verbal suffix has to do with whether the propositional relations that obtain between P_x and P_y are encoded by the six suffixes or drawn by inference. The use refers to whether or not meanings of a given suffix conjoin P_x and P_y truth-functionally.

The specific research questions we posed at the outset were:

(1) With respect to the nature of the meanings communicated by the six

Korean conjunctive verbal suffixes, are they decoded or inferred?

(2) In terms of **the use** of these suffixes, that is, their truth-functionality; do they conjoin or disjoin two propositions truth-conditionally?

In order to answer these questions, we adopted the scope test, taken by Rouchota (1990). This test tells whether or not the meaning of the six conjunctive verbal suffixes are encoded. That is, the meaning of a given suffix falls within the scope of the truth-conditional connective *if... then* if and only it is encoded.

Our findings are: the truth-conditional encoded meanings of six suffixes *-ko, -nuntey, -nikka, -se, -ciman*, and *-to* conjoin P_x and P_y truth-functionally, and the non-truth-conditional inferred meanings of four suffixes *-ko, -nuntey, -nikka*, and *-se* disjoin P_x and P_y truth-functionally.

Our findings are significant in that they bring out complexities involved in the use of conjunctive endings. This book explores the meanings of Korean conjunctive verbal suffixes; in order to understand their meanings, we collected data from natural conversations and characterised fourteen propositional relations that obtain between two segments linked by Korean conjunctive verbal suffixes *-ko, -nuntey, -nikka, -se, -ciman*, and *-to*.

Further, we investigated whether or not the fourteen relations are encoded by suffixes, by using the scope test. This investigation has shown the complexity of meanings of Korean conjunctive verbal suffixes for three reasons. First, contrary to the late Relevance Theorists' assertion, Korean conjunctive verbal suffixes, in particular, *-nuntey, -ciman*, and *-to*, can encode concepts as well as procedures. That is to say, their procedures cannot constrain the hearer's interpretation of two segments coupled by them. Second, contrary to the position of the Default Semanticists, the meanings of suffixes cannot be so easily posited on a single scale according to the quantity of inference. This is because suffixes do have encoded meanings. Third, different non-truth-conditional inferred meanings arise when different suffixes are used between two segments. We cannot, however, distinctly characterise the role played by the suffixes. We will leave that characterisation for some future study.

Let us summarise the main points that we made in each Chapter. Chapter 1 took a bird's-eye view of the previous literature on meanings of Korean conjunctive verbal suffixes *-ko*, *-nuntey*, *-nikka*, *-se*, *-ciman*, and *-to*. The previous studies share the view that propositional relations that obtain between segments coupled by suffixes constitute the meanings of suffixes. It was pointed out that previous studies on the six suffixes failed to notice inferential aspects of meanings of the four suffixes *-ko*, *-nuntey*, *-nikka*, and *-se* that were shown in the data that we collected.

Chapter 2 introduced four pragmatic theories, Gricean theory, neo-Gricean theory, Relevance Theory, and Default Semantics as a preliminary for figuring out how to recover P_x and P_y from segments linked by suffixes. In particular, we have focused on strengths and weaknesses of the four theories. The four theories postulate that there is a gap between the meaning of a word or words, which constitute an utterance, the proposition, which the speaker intends to communicate through the utterance. Furthermore, they claim that the gap is bridged by the following inference.

(1)　　a. Gricean-theoretic inference:

The Cooperative Principle (e.g. Quantity, Quality, Relation, and Manner)

b. Neo-Gricean-theoretic inference:

The default heuristics (e.g. Q, I, and M)

c. Relevance-Theoretic inference:

Relevance inference

d. Default-Semantic inference:

Default-Semantic contexts (e.g. linguistic context and the hearer's background knowledge)

It was pointed out that each inference in (1)a-d, which these four theories adopt as their reasoning tools, encounters a drawback. First, the cooperative principle in (1)a gives rise to the so-called Gricean circle. This circle refers to a circulation where a GCI, i.e., what is implicated, determines what is said and what is said determines a GCI. Second, in some cases the gap is bridged not by the heuristics in (1)b but by contexts. Third, relevance inference in (1)c causes another circle. This circle stands for a circulation where an SW-implicature, what is communicated implicitly, determines an explicature, what is communicated explicitly, and an explicature determines an SW-implicature. Fourth, linguistic context in (1)d is not inference but rather syntactic and semantic constraints.

Chapter 3 explained four notions that are fundamental to our theoretical framework: propositional relations, the scope test, encoded and inferred meanings of suffixes, and the use of suffixes. First, we defined briefly the notion of propositional relation and described inventories of propositional relations, which the [X-target suffix Y] sequence involves. Second, we introduced the scope test and explained why we adopted it as a criterion for deciding whether or not the meaning of a given conjunctive verbal suffix is encoded. Third, we explained that truth-conditional encoded meaning, non-truth-conditional encoded meaning, and non-truth-conditional encoded meaning are identical respectively to conceptual meaning, modified conventional implicature, and improved non-truth-conditional inferential meaning. Here, we clarified theoretical rationales for adopting the three concepts, 'conceptual meaning', 'conventional implicature', and 'inferential meaning' from the four pragmatic theories: Gricean theory, neo-Gricean theory, Relevance Theory, and Default Semantics. Fourth, we described two uses of connectives: truth-functionally conjoining and truth-functionally disjoining.

Chapter 4 was absorbed in the specification on of data. Data were illustrated under the following heads: (1) the methodology for the data acquisition; (2) the data description; (3) frequencies of tokens of Korean conjunctive verbal suffixes *-ko*, *-nuntey*, *-nikka*, *-se*, *-ciman*, and *-to*. Furthermore, it was pointed out that the six suffixes make up two types of forms, i.e., the [X-target suffix Y] sequence and the [X'-target suffix] clause, and that only the former is taken up. This is because the [X'-target suffix] clause has something to do with the recovery of the elliptical segment after the six suffixes. The issue of whether or not the elliptical segment after the six suffixes is recovered causes an entirely different scope of discussion, i.e., divergence between conjunctive verbal suffix and sentence-final verbal suffix.

Chapter 5 has mainly devoted to the characterisation of propositional relations between P_x and P_y, which are recovered from the [X-target suffix Y] sequence. Further, this chapter showed the frequencies of all relations. The propositional relations, which the six sequences involve, and their frequencies are as follows.

(2)   a. The [X-*ko*Y] sequence: five relations (1,156 tokens)
ENUMERATION (409 tokens 35.38%), FORWARD SEQUENTIAL (253 tokens 21.88%), CAUSAL (35 tokens 3.03%), SIMULTANEITY (103 tokens 8.91%), REPETITION (356 tokens 30.80%)

b. The [X-*nuntey* Y] sequence: ten relations (503 tokens)
TIME (63 tokens 12.52%), CAUSAL (27 tokens 5.37%), CONTRAST (88 tokens 17.50%), DENAIL OF EXPECTATION (166 tokens 33.00%), INTRODUCTION (52 tokens 10.34%), INFERENTIAL(8 tokens 1.59%), BACKWARD INFERENTIAL (10 tokens 1.99%), REPETITION (31 tokens 6.16%), REFORMULATION (45 tokens 8.95%), EXEMPLIFICATION (13 tokens 2.58%)

c. The [X-*nikka*Y] sequence: five relations (234 tokens)
TIME (23 tokens 9.83 %), CAUSAL (161 tokens 68.80%), INFERENTIAL (42 tokens 17.95%), REPETITION (3 tokens 1.28%), REFORMULATION (5 tokens 2.14%)

d. The [X-*se* Y] sequence: four relations (230 tokens)
FORWARD SEQUENTIAL (137 tokens 59.57%), CAUSAL (83 tokens 36.09%), REPETITION (3 tokens 1.30%), REFORMULATION (7 tokens 3.04%)

    e. The [X-*ciamn* Y] sequence: two relations (32 tokens)
CONTRAST (9 tokens 28.12%), DENIAL OF
EXPECTATION (23 tokens 71.88%)

    f. The [X-*to* Y] sequence: three relations (27 tokens)
CONDITION (6 tokens 22.22%), CONTRAST (1 token
3.70%), DENIAL OF EXPECTATION (20 tokens 74.07%)

Here, it is notable that the following five relations are propositional relations, which the previous pieces of researches examined in Chapter 1 do not proffer: INFERENTIAL, BACKWARD INFERENTIAL, REPETITION, REFORMULATION, and EXEMPLIFICATION.

Chapter 6 was concerned with the use of Korean conjunctive verbal suffixes *-ko*, *-nuntey*, *-nikka*, *-se*, *-ciman*, and *-to*. We applied the scope test to the meanings of the six suffixes and showed that four suffixes, *-ko*, *-nuntey*, *-nikka*, and *-se,* have inferred meanings as well as encoded meanings but the other two suffixes *-ciman* and *-to* have only encoded meanings. The meanings of the six suffixes are as follows.

(3)   a. *-ko*

        One truth-conditional encoded meaning ($\&$), one
non-truth-conditional inferred meaning (meaning that occurs
when REPETITION is inferred from P_x and P_y)

    b. *-nuntey*

        Three truth-conditional encoded meanings ($\&$, *when*, *as a
result of*), three non-truth-conditional encoded meanings
(contrast meaning, denial of expectation meaning,

introduction meaning), five non-truth-conditional inferred
meanings (meanings that occur when REPETITION,
REFORMULATION, INFERENTIAL,
EXEMPLIFICATION, and BACKWARD INFERENTIAL
are inferred from P_x and P_y)

c. *-nikka*

Two truth-conditional encoded meanings (*when, as a result
of*), three non-truth-conditional inferred meanings (meanings
that occur when REPETITION, REFORMULATION, and
INFERENTIAL are inferred from P_x and P_y)

d. *-se*

Two truth-conditional encoded meanings (*after, as a result of*),
two non-truth-conditional inferred meanings (meanings
that occur when REPETITION and REFORMULATION are
inferred from P_x and P_y)

e. *-ciman*

One truth-conditional encoded meaning ($\&$), two
non-truth-conditional encoded meanings (contrast meaning,
denial of expectation meaning)

f. *-to*

Two truth-conditional encoded meanings ($\rightarrow$, $\&$), two
non-truth-conditional encoded meanings (contrast meaning,
denial of expectation meaning)

Further, it was shown that encoded meanings of suffixes conjoin P_x and P_y
truth-functionally, and that inferred meanings of suffixes disjoin P_x and P_y
truth-functionally. This is because the suffix has a truth-conditional encoded
meaning $\&$ if a given suffix has a non-truth-conditional encoded meaning.

Chapter 7 considered encoded and inferred meanings of *-nuntey*, *-nikka*, *-se*, *-ciman*, and *-to* within frameworks of Relevance Theory and Default Semantics. The issue in this chapter was threefold: a unitary procedure, a single scale, and the label inferential meaning. First, in order to argue against a late Relevance Theorists' hypothesis that a connective that encodes a procedure cannot encode a concept, we proved that conjunctive verbal suffixes encode not only procedures but also concepts. Secondly, in order to claim against H-K. Lee's (2001, 2002) argument that meanings of connectives are posited on a single scale according to the quantity of inference, we proved that the scale does not work well with conjunctive verbal suffixes. Third, it was pointed out that we cannot label the non-truth-conditional inferred meaning of *because* as inferential meaning on the ground that the label 'inferential meaning' itself refers to a procedure. Further, we suggested that the non-truth-conditional inferred meanings of conjunctive verbal suffixes cannot easily be characterised, but we showed that inferred propositional relations, which involve these meanings, are posited on a single scale on the basis of the quantity of the hearer's inductive inference.

Let us conclude by suggesting two remaining questions for further studies. The first is - What is responsible for the discrepancy in grammaticality between examples such as those below?

(4)   a. cip-ey   ka-*se*   pap-ul   mek-ess-ta

       *house-to go-**SE** meal-AC eat-PST-DC*

       'After I went home, I ate a meal.'

> b. * cip-ey ka-*ko* pap-ul mek-ess-ta
>
> *house-to go-**KO** meal-AC eat-PST-DC*

In (4) the propositional relation that obtains between segments coupled by *-se* and *-ko* is FORWARD SEQUENTIAL. This is because going home precedes eating a meal. As has been described in Chapter 1, FORWARD SEQUENTIAL is obtained not only in the [X-*se* Y] sequence but also in the [X-*ko* Y] sequence. However, (4)a is grammatically correct, but (4)b is not. Why is this so? The answer is that the acceptability of *-se* in (4)a and *-ko* in (4)b depends on the meaning of *ka-* 'go' of in the segments before the two suffixes (cf. K-D. Lee 1993: 454-455, 459-460). This means that we can explain why (4)a is grammatically correct but (4)b is not so, if we adopt corpus linguistics as a theoretical framework and survey meanings of verbs of segments linked by suffixes. However, we will leave this for future studies because our study is not the survey of lexical meanings of verbs.

The other question has to do with the role that four conjunctive verbal suffixes *-ko*, *-nuntey*, *-nikka*, and *-se* play in inferred propositional relations that obtain P_x and P_y. As has been point out above, the four suffixes involve the different range of inferred relations. Let us take *-nuntey*, for example. As opposed to the other three suffixes, only *-nuntey* involves EXEMPLIFICATION. Consider (5). (In Chapter 7, we used this example for explaining the scale of propositional relations that involve non-truth-conditional inferred meanings of *-nuntey*. However, we took up it again not for explaining the inferential scale but for discussing the role that four conjunctive verbal suffixes play in inferred propositional relations that obtain P_x and P_y.)

(5)   (HY & NY From 'When I Was a Primary School Student')
      [Context: HY is telling NY about the types of institute she attended in her
      primary school days.]

HY: →   hakwen   toykey manhi tany-ess-**nuntey**
          *educational institute very   much   attend-PST-**NUNTEY**
          'I attended lots of educational institutes.'
          seyey hakwen-twu   tani-kwu
          school for calligraphy-also attend-KO
          'I attended private schools for calligraphy. And.'

NY: um
          'Yeah'

HY: sukheyithu-twu tani-kwu   panghak ttay
          skate-also   attend-KO holidays time
          [swuyengcang]-twu tani-kwu
           swimming pool-also attend-KO
          'I attended a private school of ice skating. And, in the holidays
          I attended a swimming pool.'

NY: [a na-twu]
          oh I-also
          'Me also.'
          e
          'Yeah.'

HY: tto   swuyengcang-ilang
          again swimming pool-and
          yenge hoyhwa hakwen   tani-kwu
          private school for English conversation attend-KO

'And I attended swimming pools and private schools for English conversation.'

From (5) two propositions P_x and P_y, such as (6)a-b, can be recovered.

(6)　a. HY attended many educational institutes in her primary school days.

　　b. [HY attended private schools for calligraphy] & [HY attended a private school for ice skating] & [HY attended a swimming pool in the holidays].

In (6) *a swimming pool and private schools for calligraphy* and *ice skating* in clause (b) are identified as concrete examples of *educational institutes* in clause (a) (6)a and (6)b hold EXEMPLIFICATION. -*Nuntey* in (5) involves EXEMPLIFICATION because a non-truth-conditional inferred meaning of -*nuntey* in (5) occurs when EXEMPLIFICATION is inferred from (6)a and (6)b. If we substitute respectively three suffixes -*ko*, -*nikka*, and -*se* in place of -*nuntey* in (5), this substitution causes irrelevant examples based on our linguistic intuition of as a Korean native speaker. This means that -*nuntey* has a role in EXEMPLIFICATION that obtains between (6)a and (6)b. But, we do not seem to have any answer to the question, i.e., - What role is played in EXEMPLIFICATION by the suffix -*nuntey*? (One can suggest that if we allow the possibility that -*nuntey* encodes a procedure we may find a plausible answer. However, this is not the case because the meaning of -*nuntey* that occurs when EXEMPLIFICATION is obtained from the two segments is not encoded by -*nuntey*. See Section 6.2.2. for more details.)

On the one hand, one is tempted to say that -*nuntey* in (5) encodes a procedure, which instructs the hearer to identify the contextual effect of (6)a and (6)b as a strengthening. This, however, encounters a problem. That is to say, this procedure cannot constrain the interpretation of the [X-*nuntey* Y] sequence. This is because -*nuntey* has more than one meaning.

One could also say in effect that -*nuntey* in (5) is not a conjunctive verbal suffix but a sentence-final suffix, and hence that the [X-*nuntey* Y] sequence in (5) is identified as non-conjunctions. This explains that EXEMPLIFICATION is inferred from (6)a and (6)b. However this is in no better as a position. This is because -*ko* in (7), which involves the inferred propositional relation REPETITION, cannot be identified as a sentence-final suffix.

(7)   (SH & YH From 'My Hobby')

       [Context: SH and YH are talking about kinds of hobbies.]

YH: um nemwu manh-**ko** manh-ci

      *well very   many-**KO** many-SUP*

      'Well, there are many hobbies. There are many hobbies.'

Two propositions P_x and P_y, such as (8)a-b, can be recovered from (7).

(8)   a. There exist multitudinous hobbies.

       b. There exist multitudinous hobbies.

In (8) clause (b) is identical to cluase (a); (8)a and (8)b indicates REPETITION. -*Ko* in (7) involves REPETITION in that a non-truth-conditional inferred meaning of -*ko* in (7) occurs when

REPETITION is inferred from (8)a and (8)b. Here, it is notable that *-ko* in (7) is not a sentence-final suffix but a conjunctive verbal suffix (H-J. Lee and C-H. Lee 1999: 17, 2001: 54-55). In this sense, it is difficult to say that *-nuntey* in (5) is a sentence-final suffix.

We have examined two possible answers to the second question - What is the role that the four suffixes play in inferred propositional relations that obtain P_x and P_y? These two answers encounter a drawback. Consequently, the second question requires an extensive study on its own, which is precisely what this study has been able to identify. That is to say, this is an issue of clarifying what role that the four suffixes play in inferred propositional relations that are obtained from P_x and P_y. However, we leave this for further studies.

References

Blakemore, D. 1987. *Semantic constraints on relevance.* New York: Basil Blackwell.

Blakemore, D. 1989. Denial and contrast: A relevant theoretic analysis of *but. Linguistics and Philosophy*, 12: 15-37.

Blakemore, D. 1992. *Understanding utterances.* Oxford: Blackwell.

Blakemore, D. 2002. *Relevance and linguistics meanings: The semantic and pragmatic of discourse markers.* Cambridge: Cambridge University Press.

Blakemore, D. & Carston, R. 1999. The pragmatics of *and*-conjunctions: The non-narrative cases. *UCL Working Papers in Linguistics*, 11: 1-20.

Blakemore, D. & Carston, R. 2005. The pragmatics of sentential coordination with *and. Lingua*, 115: 569-589.

Carston, R. 1988. Implicature, explicature, and truth-theoretic semantics. In R. Kempson (ed.), *Mental representations: The interface between language and reality.* New York: Cambridge University Press: 155-181.

Carston, R. 1990. Quantity maxims and generalized implicature. *UCL Working Papers in Linguistics*, 2: 1-31.

Carston, R. 1992. Conjunction, explanation and relevance. *UCL Working Papers in Linguistics*, 4: 151-165.

Carston, R. 1993. Conjunction, explanation and relevance. *Lingua*, 90: 27-48.

Carston, R. 1996. Enrichment and loosening: Complementary processes in deriving the proposition expressed. *UCL Working Papers in Linguistics*, 8: 61-88.

Carston, R. 1998. Implicature, explicature and truth-conditional semantics. In A. Kasher (ed.), *Pragmatics: Critical concepts (Vol 4).* London: Routledge: 464-79.

Carston, R. 1999. The semantics/pragmatics distinction: A view from relevance theory. In K. Turner (ed.), *The semantics/pragmatics interface from different points of view (CRiSPI1).* Oxford: Elsevier Science: 85-125.

Carston, R. 2002. *Thoughts and utterances: The pragmatics of explicit communication*. Oxford: Blackwell.

Chang, K-K. 1999. *hankwuke yenkyelemiuy phyohyenlon (A theory of Korean conjunctive verbal suffixes)*. Seoul: Welin.

Choi, J-H. 1989. kwuke cepsokmwunuy kwusengey kwanhan yenkwu (A study on the construction of conjoined sentence in Korean). Unpublished Ph.D. thesis. Sungkyunkwan University, Seoul.

Choi, J-H. 1991. *kukeuy cepsokmwun yenkwu (Studies on Korean Connectives)*. Seoul: Thapchwulpansa.

Cohen, L. J. 1971. Some remarks on Grice's views about the logical particles of natural language. In Y. Bar-Hillel (ed.), *Pragmatics of natural languages*. Dordrecht: D. Reidel: 50-68.

Foolen, A. 1991. Polyfunctionality and the semantics of adversative conjunctions. *Multilingua*, 10: 79-92.

Gazdar, G. 1979. *Pragmatics: Implicature, presupposition, and logical form*. New York: Academic Press.

Giora, R. 1996. Discourse coherence and theory of relevance: Stumbling blocks in search of a unified theory. Journal of Pragmatics 27: 17-34.

Grice, H. P. 1961. The causal theory of perception. *Proceedings of the Aristotelian Society, Supplementary*, 35: 121-152.

Grice, H. P. 1968. Utterer's meaning, sentence-meaning, and word-meaning. *Foundations of Language*, 4: 225-242.

Grice, H. P. 1975. Logic and conversation. In P. Cole & J. Morgan (eds.), *Syntax and semantics 3: Speech acts*. New York: Academic Press: 41-58.

Grice, H. P. 1981. Presupposition and conversational implicature. In P. Cole (ed.), *Radical pragmatics*. New York: Academic Press: 183-98.

Grice, H. P. 1989. *Studies in the way of Words*. Cambridge, MA: Harvard University Press.

Hall, A. 2004. The meaning of *but*: A procedural reanalysis. *UCL Working Papers in Linguistics*, 16: 199-236.

Han, K. 1986. hyentaykwuke panmaley kwanhan yenkwu: panmal congkyelcepmisalul cwungsimulo (A Study on the plain speech in Korean: With special reference to the closing suffixes of plain speech). Unpublished Ph.D. thesis. Yonsei University, Seoul.

Han, K. 1991. *kwukecongkyelemiyenkwu (A study on the Korean sentence-final suffixes)*. Chuncheon: Kangwon University Press.

Han, K. 2004. *hyentay wulimaluy machimssikkuth yenkwu (A study of modern Korean sentence-final suffixes)*. Seoul: Yeklak.

Hobbs, J. R. 1979. Coherence and coreference. *Cognitive Science*, 3: 67-90.

Hobbs, J. R. 1985. *On the coherence and structure of discourse*. Stanford, CA: CSLI Publications.

Hurford, J. R. & Heasley, B. 1983. *Semantics: A coursebook*. Cambridge: Cambridge University Press.

Itani, R. 1996. *Semantics and pragmatics of hedges in English and Japanese*. Tokyo: Hituzi Syobo.

Iten, C. 2000. 'Non-truth-conditional'meaning, relevance and concessives. Unpublished Ph.D. thesis, University College London, London.

Iten, C. 2005. *Linguistic meaning, truth conditions and relevance: The case of concessives*. Hampshire: Palgrave Macmillan.

Jaszczolt, K. M. 1999. Default semantics, pragmatics, and intentions. In K. Turner (ed.), *The semantics/pragmatics interface from different points of views*. Amsterdam: Elsevier Science: 199-232.

Jeon, H-Y. 1989. hyentay hankwuke cepsokemiuy hwayongloncek yenkwu (A pragmatic study on connective endings of modern Korean). Unpublished Ph.D. thesis. Ehwa Womans University, Seoul.

Jeong, J-D. 1986. kwuke cepsokemiuy uymi thongsaloncek yenkwu: Congsok cepsokemilul cwungsimulo (A syntactic and semantic study on connective endings on Korean: Centered on subordinate connective endings). Unpublished Ph.D. thesis. Hanyang University, Seoul.

Jung, Y-H. 2001. hankwuke yenkyelemiuy mwunpephwa (Grammaticalization of Korean clause connectives). Unpublished Ph.D. these. Hankook University of Foreign Studies, Seoul.

Katz, J. J. 1972. *Semantic theory.* New York: Harper and Row.

Kempson, R. 1975. *Presupposition and the delimitation of semantics.* Cambridge: Cambridge University Press.

Kim, T-Y. 1998. kwuke picongkyelemihwaey tayhaye (The functional shift of endings from nonfinal to final). *enehag* (Journal of The Linguistic Society of Korea), 22. 171-189.

Kim, T-Y. 2001. *Kwuke congkyelemiuy mwunpep* (Grammar of Korean final ending). Seoul: Kookhak Community.

Ko, Y-K. 1974. hyentaykwukeuy congkyelemiey tayhan kwucocek yenkwu (A structural conclusive-endings in Modern Korean). *Language Research*, 10. 118-157.

Kwon, J-l. 1984. hyentaykwukeuy pokhapmwun kwusengey kwanhan yenkwu (A study on complex sentence constructions in Korean). Unpublished Ph. D. thesis. Seoul National University, Seoul.

Kwon, J-I. 1992. *hankwue thongsalon (A theory of Korean Syntax).* Seoul: Minumsa.

Kwon, J-I. 1994. *hankwuke mwunpepuy yenkwu (A study of Korean grammar).* Seoul: Pagijong Press.

Lakoff, R.1971. If's, and's, and but's about conjunction. In C.J. Fillmore & D.T. Langendoen (eds.). *Studies in linguistic semantics.* (114-149). New York: Holt, Rhinehart and Winston, Inc.: 114-149.

Lacey, A. R. 1986. Second Edition. *A dictionary of philosophy.* London: Routledge & Kegan Paul Ltd.

Lee, H-J. & Lee, C-H. 1999. *sacensik theyksuthu pwunsekcek kwuke uymiuy yenkwu (A study of Korean suffixes according to the analysis of texts).* Seoul: Hankookmunhwasa.

Lee, H-J. & Lee, C-H. 2001. *emi cosa sacen (A dictionary of suffixes and particles)*. Seoul: Hankookmunhwasa.

Lee, H-K. 2001. The semantics and pragmatics of connectives with reference to English and Korean. Unpublished Ph.D. thesis. University of Cambridge, London.

Lee, H-K. 2002. Towards a new typology of connectives with special reference to conjunction in English and Korean. *Journal of Pragmatics*, 34: 851-66.

Lee, K-D. 1979. yenkyelemi nunteyuy hwayongsanguy kinung (The pragmatic function of the connective *nuntey*). *inmun kwahak (Cultural Sciences)*, 40 & 41: 117-142.

Lee, K-D. 1980. The pragmatic function of the connective *nuntey. ene (Language)*, 5: 119-135.

Lee, K-D. 1993. *A Korean grammar on semantic pragmatic principles*. Seoul: Hankookmunhwasa.

Lee, H-S.1991. Tense, aspect, and modality: A discourse-pragmatic analysis of verbal suffix in Korean from a typological perspective. Unpublished Ph.D. thesis. University of California, Los Angeles.

Lee, H-S. 2000. mwunpephwa ilonuy ihay(Grammatic(al)ization and a panchronic view of grammar). In K-D. Lee (ed.), *incienehak (Cognitive linguistics)*. Seoul: Hankukmunhwasa: 255-298.

Levinson, S. 1983. *Pragmatics*. Cambridge: Cambridge University Press.

Levinson, S. 1995. Three levels of meaning. In F. Palmer (ed.), *Grammar and meaning*. Cambridge: Cambridge University Press: 90-115.

Levinson, S. 2000. *Presumptive meanings: The theory of generalized conversational implicature*. Cambridge: MIT Press.

Lyons, J. 1977. *Semantics*. Cambridge: Cambridge University Press.

Mann, W. C. & Thompson, S. A. 1985. Assertions from discourse structure. *Proceedings of the Eleventh Annual Meeting of the Berkeley Linguistic Society*: 245-258.

Mann, W. C. & Thompson, S. A. 1986. Relational propositions in discourse. *Discourse Processes*, 9: 57-90.

Mann, W. C. & Thompson, S. A.1988. Rhetorical structure theory: Towards a functional theory of text organization. *Text*, 8: 243-281.

Martin, S. E.1992. *A reference grammar of Korean*. Vermont: Charles E. Tuttle.

Martin, S. E., Lee, Y-H. & Chang, S-U. (eds.) 1967. *A Korean-English Dictionary*. London: Yale University Press.

Moon, S-P. 1994. palhwauy enehyengsikkwa cekhapseng: yenkyel, naypho mich uymwunul cwungsimulo (Linguistic forms in uttreances and relevance: Connectives, complements and interrogatives). Unpublished Ph.D. thesis. Seoul National University, Seoul.

Park, K-Y. 2001. hankwuke cisi tayyongeuy mwunpephwa (Grammaticalization of Korean Substitutes). Unpublished Ph.D. thesis. Hankuk University of Foreign Studies, Seoul.

Park, Y-Y. 1996. The Korean connective *nuntey* in conversational discourse. *Japanese/Korean Linguistics*, 5: 131-147.

Park, Y-Y. 1997. A cross-linguistic study on the use of contrastive connectives in English, Korean, and Japanese conversation. Unpublished Ph.D. thesis. University of California, Los Angeles.

Park, Y-Y. 1998. Interactive Grammar: The turn-final use of *nuntey* in Korean and *kedo* in Japanese. *Japanese/Korean Linguistics*, 8: 45-59.

Park, Y-Y. 1999. The Korean connective *nuntey* in conversational discourse. *Journal of Pragmatics*, 31: 191-218.

Posner, R. 1980. Semantics and pragmatics of sentence connectives in natural language. In J. Searle, F. Kiefer & M. Bierwisch (eds.), *Speech act theory and pragmatics*. Dordrecht: Reidel: 168-203.

Rouchota, V. 1990. *But*: Contradiction and relevance. *UCL Working Papers in Linguistics*, 2: 65-81.

Schiffrin, D. 1987. *Discourse markers*. Cambridge: Cambridge University Press.

Searle, J. R. 1976. The classification of illocutionary acts. *Language in Society*, 5: 1-24.

Sohn, H-M. 1994. *Korean: Descriptive grammar.* London: Routledge.

Sperber, D. & Wilson, D. 1986/95. *Relevance: Communication and cognition.* Oxford: Blackwell.

Strawson, P. F. 1952. *Introduction to logical theory.* London: Methuen.

Suh, C-S. 2006. Third Edition. *kwukemwunpep (Korean Grammar)*. Seoul: Hansebon.

Suh, C-S., Rowan, B., Cho, Y-J., Park, S K. & Suh, Y-W.(eds.). 2005. Korean-English Dictionary. Seoul: Hansebon.

Tsai, L-K. 1985. hyentayhankwuke yenkyelemiey tayhan yenkwu: uymikinungul cwungsimulo (A semantic functional study on conjunction endings in modern Korean). Unpublished Ph.D. thesis. Sungkyunkwan University, Seoul.

Wilson, D. 1998. Discourse, coherence and relevance: A reply to Rachel Giora. *Journal of Pragmatics*, 29: 57-74.

Wilson, D. 2004. Pragmatic theory online course lecture notes. UCL dept. file.

Wilson, D. & Sperber, D. 1990. Linguistic form and relevance. *UCL Working Papers in Linguistics*, 2: 95-112.

Wilson, D. & Sperber, D. 1993a. Linguistic form and relevance. *Lingua*, 90: 1-25.

Wilson, D. & Sperber, D. 1993b. Relevance and time. *UCL Working Papers in Linguistics*, 5: 277-298.

Wilson, D. & Sperber, D. 1998. Pragmatics and time. In R. Carston & S. Uchida (eds.), *Relevance theory: Applications and implications*: Amsterdam: John Benjamins: 1-22.

Yang, I-S. 1971. hankwukeuy cepsokhwa (Clausal conjunction in Korean). *Language Research*, 8: 1-25.

Yi, E-K.1996. kwukeuy yenkyel emi yenkwu (A study on connective endings in Korean). Unpublished Ph.D. thesis. Seoul National University, Seoul.

Yi, E-K. 2000. kwukeuy yenkyel emi yenkwu (A study on Korean connective endings). Seoul: Thayhaksa.

Yoon, P-H. 1989. kwukeuy cepsokemidy tayhan yenkwu: Uymiloncek kinungul cwungsimulo (A study on the conjunctive endings of Korean). Unpublished Ph.D. thesis. Chonnam National University, Kwangju.

Yoon, P-H. 2005. *hyentaykwuke cepsokemi yenkwu (A study of modern Korean conjunctive endings).* Seoul: Pagijong Press.

Index

INDEX OF NAMES

〈A Korean Translation of Thesis Abstract〉

한국어 연결어미의 형태-화용론 이론을 향하여

본 논문은 인위적인 예문이 아닌 실제 담화를 연구 데이터로 채택하여 화용론의 관점에서 한국어 연결어미를 깊게 이해하는 것을 주목적으로 한다. 이러한 목적을 달성하기 위하여, 본 논문은 한국어 연결어미 "-고, -는데, -니까, -서, -지만, -도"의 의미의 본질(nature)과 그 용법(use)을 심도 있게 분석한다. "용법(use)"은 연결어미의 진리 함수성(truth-functionality), 즉 다시 말해서 연결어미가 두 세그먼트(segment)에서 복구한 두 명제를 진리 함수적으로 (truth-functionally) 연결(conjoin)하는가 혹은 비연결(disjoin)하는가를 뜻한다. 본 논문의 데이터는 360분 동안 녹음된 한국어 자연담화이다. 본 논문은 현대 화용론의 대표적인 4가지 이론인 그라이스 이론(Gricean theory), 신그라이스 이론 (neo-Gricean theory), 관련성 이론(Relevance Theory), 디폴트 의미론(Default Semantics)을 그 논증 도구(reasoning tool)로 채택한다. 단, 본 논문은 데이터를 사용하여 단순히 이들 4가지 이론을 대조하는 것이 아니며, 현대 화용론에서 대두되는 이론들이 명확하게 설명해 주지 못하는 한국어 연결어미의 의미를 해명하는 데 중점을 둔다.

1장은 위의 여섯 연결어미의 선행 연구를 고찰한다. 이 장에서는 이들 선행 연구가 연결어미의 의미를 두 세그먼트(segment) 사이에서 이루어지는 명제 관계(propositional relation)로 보고 있지만, 그 연결어미의 용법(use)의 중요성을 간과하고 있다는 점을 지적한다. 2장은 위의 4가지 화용론 이론을 개괄하며, 각 이론의 장점과 단점을 제시하는 데 초점을 둔다. 3장은 명제 관계(propositional relation)와 암호화(encoding), 추론(inference)의 개념을 소개한다. 더불어, 진리 함수적(truth-functional) 연결(conjoining)과 비연결(disjoining)을 설명한다. 4장은 본 논문의 데이터를 상술한다. 5장에서는 두 세그먼트(segment)에서 복구되는 두 명제 사이의 명제 관계(propositional relation)를 기술한다. 6장은 범위 테스트(scope test)가 연결어미의 의미가 암호화된(encoded) 것인가 혹은 추론된(inferred) 것인가를 판별해 주는 척도가 된다는 것을 입증한다. 특히, 이 장에서는 위의 여섯 연결어미의 암호화된 의미(encoded meaning)가 두 명제를 진리 함수적으로(truth-functionally) 연결(conjoining)하고 추론된 의미 (inferred meaning)가 두 명제를 진리 함수적으로(truth-functionally) 비연결 (disjoining)한다는 점을 논한다. 7장은 관련성 이론(Relevance Theory)과 디폴트 의미론(Default Semantics)의 두 가지 시각에서 위의 여섯 연결어미의 성질 (nature)을 논한다. 특히, 이 장에서는 단일 절차 가설(unitary procedure hypothesis)의 문제점을 논의한다. 8장은 이후 연구 과제와 더불어 본 논문의 결론을 제시한다.